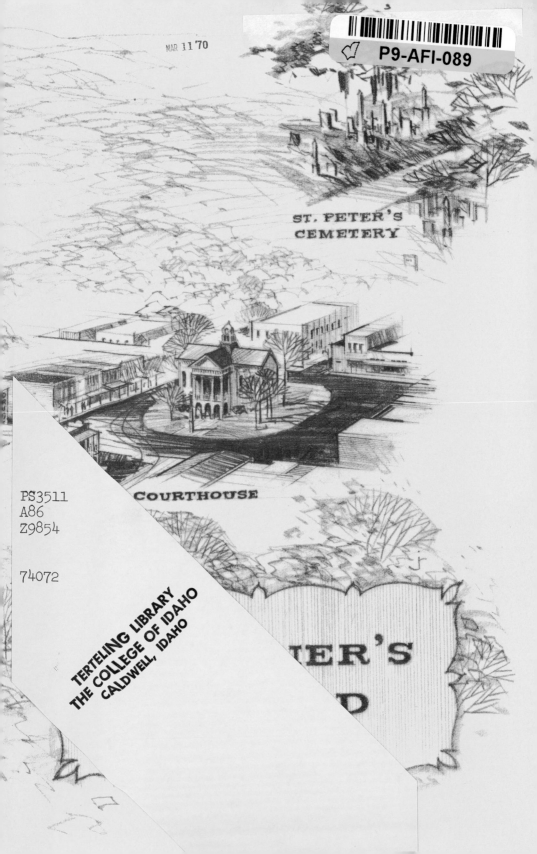

MAR 11 '70

P9-AFI-089

ST. PETER'S
CEMETERY

COURTHOUSE

ER'S
D

WILLIAM FAULKNER
OF OXFORD

WILLIAM FAULKNER
OF OXFORD

edited by JAMES W. WEBB and A. WIGFALL GREEN

LOUISIANA STATE UNIVERSITY PRESS

PREFACE

*W*illiam Faulkner of Oxford was not a native of Oxford; nor was he born with the name *Faulkner*. He was born in New Albany, Mississippi, on September 25, 1897, and the family spelled the name *Falkner*. He published his first book when he was twenty-seven. He was awarded the Nobel Prize for Literature when he was fifty-three. He was generally acknowledged as the major American writer of his time when he died on July 6, 1962, at the age of sixty-four. *Faulkner* or *Falkner*, he spent almost the whole of his life in the Mississippi town which millions who read his works know not as Oxford but as Jefferson.

Even to the people of Oxford, Faulkner was a kind of legend in his own lifetime. There was, for example, the mystery of who put the u in William's last name. For many years the commonly ac-

v

cepted story was that it was a careless printer, in setting type for *The Marble Faun* (1924). Faulkner biographer Carvel Collins demonstrates that the writer himself added it, and, at least occasionally, as early as 1918. Thirty years later Faulkner drafted and printed by hand two amusing documents commissioning a boat owned by him and several other persons in Oxford. In one he signed his name "William C. Falkner II"—perhaps because in this document he pays tribute to his great-grandfather, Colonel William C. Falkner; but in the other, in which he calls himself the First Sea Lord of Lafayette County, Mississippi, "William Faulkner."

Mythmaking was a part of the cultural tradition of Faulkner's country. Asked by one early interviewer where he was born, the writer replied, "Born? Yes. I was born male and single at an early age in Mississippi. I am still alive but not single. I was born of a Negro slave and an alligator . . ." The interviewer (Marshall J. Smith, whose story was published in *The Bookman* for December, 1931) added to the confusion by reporting that he had to turn elsewhere for his facts (apparently to *Living Authors*, published earlier that year) and that Faulkner was born in Ripley, Mississippi, rather than in New Albany and that the month of his birth was October and not September.

Even had Faulkner given him the "facts" there is no certainty that they would have been the correct ones. Six years before his death the writer told another interviewer (Jean Stein, for *Paris Review*) that when he was asked questions about himself, "I may answer or I may not, but even if I do, if the same question is asked tomorrow, the answer may be different."

And so, with the help of Faulkner himself, the myth grew. Faulkner was shy. Faulkner was arrogant. Faulkner went barefooted on the streets of Oxford. Faulkner tore up his driveway to discourage visitors. Faulkner served in the British Royal Air Force in World War I and was wounded in France. Faulkner served in the Canadian Flying Corps and had two planes shot down under him. (Actually, it was the Royal Air Force Canada, and he got no closer to the fighting than Canada.)

But to sift all the myth from the reality is not the purpose of this book. That is the job of Mr. Faulkner's biographers. This collection attempts to catch the composite image of the man in a more informal way: by probing the memory of some of those who knew him—but, more important, who knew him on his home ground.

The editors, like many other fellow townsmen of the writer, have long had in mind such a book. The Faulkneriana brought together by Miss Dorothy Oldham, curator of the Mississippi Collection in the University of Mississippi Library and sister-in-law of Mr. Faulkner, and by her predecessor Mrs. Louise Kimbrell Thompson (now Mrs. Logan A. Hunter) inspired the editors to enlarge that collection by asking friends and acquaintances of the writer to write or talk about him as they knew him. They recognized, of course, that in a small town like Oxford, in which formality is essential to the preservation of dignity, there might be reluctance to speak ill or well of an acquaintance. Yet everyone who has contributed has written or spoken with frankness and understanding and high appreciation of Mr. Faulkner.

No requirements were established, or suggestions made, to guide those who wrote. No prior notice was given to those interviewed, but they graciously agreed to talk: an attorney left his clients and a physician left untouched his steak to talk spontaneously into the tape recorder about Mr. Faulkner. Those interviewed were sometimes asked leading questions, but no attempt was made to direct the course of the speaker. Once the person interviewed began to talk, he followed his own train of thought. In transcribing the recordings, the questions were omitted, but where they existed they are implicit in the answers. Occasionally, in both the written and the spoken contributions, some slight alteration of order of thoughts has been made to create better unity. But, in general, the words of the contributors have been reproduced faithfully and their order remains unaltered. Thus the contributors emerge as distinct individuals, sometimes with personalities as engaging as that of Mr. Faulkner.

The editors set out to throw light on Faulkner the boy and man and Faulkner the author. There are some forty sketches, and likewise there are forty pictures: it is as though Faulkner, surrounded by forty mirrors, slowly turned and gave off forty reflections, all of which have been photographed. Like all other writers—and to a lesser degree like all other men—he had to act out the part played by each of the characters whom he was creating, and thus he became many men, not one.

There was inevitably some slight carry-over of multiple personalities from his professional life to his personal life. In the sketches in this collection we see Faulkner as a boy ecstatically watching the berry trains roll through the railroad cut, as a young man writing verse, and as a man growing old but retaining the stamina to jump spirited horses.

Always present is the small world which surrounded him and which he converted into the great world because he had the sympathy to create, as it exists everywhere, the hardship and cruelty and humor and love of all humankind. In the center of the small world, called Oxford or Jefferson, is the courthouse square, where even now everyone stops and chats with friends. On the northeast corner of the square is the Federal Building, forbidding and domineering but commanding respect; and nearly on the southwest corner is the Gathright-Reed Drug Store. To the north is the road that Faulkner took for a mile before he turned east to go to his farm; to the south and then west is his home. And all about is the countryside and the distant baying of the hunting hound, "mournful and valiant and a little sad," and the smell of the fragrant buds as spring comes on in Bailey's Woods.

With three exceptions all of the pieces which follow were written or taped especially for this volume. The sketch by Phil Stone, originally published in a somewhat longer version in the *Oxford Magazine* more than thirty years ago, was selected not only because any collection such as this must of necessity include Stone but also because it wonderfully sets the stage for the rest. An excerpt from John Faulkner's *My Brother Bill* seemed an appropriate closing for the book. And a reminiscence of Faulkner by John E.

Fontaine, who had known the author in their early years, seemed deserving of a wider audience than that first given it.

The editors are grateful to the people of Oxford and the University of Mississippi who have given generously of their time and knowledge with the sole reward of having honored a man not greater or lesser but one of them. They are no less grateful to those outside Oxford who have shared their memories.

Special thanks must be given to Murry C. (Jack) Falkner of Mobile, who has contributed perceptive glimpses of his brother William as well as a number of family photographs. Mrs. Phil Stone has kindly permitted the editors to use materials in her valuable collection. Louis Cochran has not only contributed his memories of Faulkner but also given his entire file of Faulkner materials to the library of the University of Mississippi.

J. R. Cofield, who opened his splendid gallery of Faulkner photographs and his storehouse of Faulkner stories, said, "Take what you will in memory of my little friend." His son Jack, of the Office of Public Information of the University of Mississippi, has given photographs and professional advice concerning the illustrations to be included in this collection. Edwin Meek, also of the Office of Public Information, and Patrick D. Smith, Director of Public Information, have graciously permitted the use of their photographs.

With the encouragement of Charles East, assistant director of the Louisiana State University Press, William Faulkner of Oxford became a reality. He launched the work and shared with enthusiasm the recording of interviews with contributors. Mrs. Charles East and Mrs. James W. Webb helped with the transcription of recordings.

Mrs. Nina Goolsby, through her columns in the Oxford Eagle, has repeatedly encouraged contributions. And many of those who persuaded others to contribute have been of great help.

To all those named, and to the numerous others who have made possible William Faulkner of Oxford, the editors express their gratitude.

J.W.W. AND A.W.G

CONTENTS

xi

WILLIAM FAULKNER
OF OXFORD

PHIL STONE

The Man and the Land

P hil Stone, more than any other single person, influenced the early development of William Faulkner as a writer. Member of an aristocratic North Mississippi family, Stone earned two degrees (including a bachelor of laws) from the University of Mississippi and then was awarded identical degrees by Yale. He returned home to practice law and to promote the literary career of the young man to whom he was close friend, severe critic, and publicity agent.

In an article in the New Republic in 1938 the writer Stark Young recalled: "I used every summer to go for a short visit to my father in Oxford, Mississippi. I used also to see there always a friend of mine, Phil Stone, something younger than I was and older than William Faulkner, about whom he often spoke, and whom he soon brought to our house. That was about 1914. Later on I used to see Bill Faulkner and read the manuscripts that his friend had praised and pushed so."

3

It was Phil Stone who in 1924 paid for the publication of Faulkner's first book, The Marble Faun, *a collection of poems. And it was to Stone that Faulkner dedicated the three volumes which comprise the Snopes trilogy.*

In 1934 Stone took time out from a busy law practice to write a series of three articles on William Faulkner for the Oxford Magazine, a local literary magazine which folded after three issues. The following sketch has been drawn from those articles.

❧ Perhaps it may be important in some ways to know that William Faulkner carries his handkerchief in his coat sleeve, that he strikes matches with unnecessary force, that he is far above the average as an amateur golfer, that he is a very capable carpenter and house-painter, that he enjoys most the company of simple unliterary people—and why. Certainly most of the people, if any, who read this will be most interested in such things. And I'm not sure that they are wrong.

Contrary to the ideas of those who deduce a man's life and character from his work—God only knows why!—this will not be the portrait of a man of mystery or romance, nor that of a withdrawn and sardonic cynic. It is the likeness of a man who loves his native soil and prefers its people to all others. It is the likeness of a simple-hearted country boy leading the life of a country squire except for the vice of spoiling good white paper with little black marks. It is the likeness of the sanest and most wholesome person I have ever known. It is also the likeness, in the main, of a person most deserving of admiration and respect and friendship in all the walks of everyday life and of a person who, at times and in some small ways, is the most aggravating damned human being the Lord ever put on this earth. Still, and all in all, the true likeness is of a person far and away superior to the great mass of human beings with whom we are all constantly tried—and with whom we try others.

.   .   .   .   .   .

It is impossible to understand a tree without knowing its source, the soil in which it grows, and the nature of the country which surrounds it.

In the blood of William Faulkner—even as you and I—runs, whether he will or no, the blood of those who came before him. In his thoughts, his emotions, the very gestures of his body, whether he will or no, move millions of unconscious reflections of the land which gave him birth and which has surrounded him all but a few of his years.

In considering William Faulkner, it is important to consider this land.

It is a country of not a great deal of riches and of almost no poverty. Situated in the northern part of Mississippi, not far from the Tennessee line, it is a country broken, to some extent, with many little creek bottoms and some small river bottoms, both of which have a soil of fair fertility, a country of hills with no mountains, a country with many lovely trees and countless birds, with a climate variable but mostly temperate as to both cold and heat and with few days of the year that cannot be spent comfortably out-of-doors. It is a country of abundant rainfall and of a general plenty without that luxuriousness of the Delta counties which lie to the west of it.

.   .   .   .   .   .

Except for his first five years William Faulkner has spent most of his life in Oxford. So in considering his background, Oxford becomes important. As for himself, as I have already said, he loves Oxford and its surrounding country dearly, prefers them above all others in the world.

Oxford is a fairly old town, almost one hundred years old. Since 1848 it has been the location of the State University, the University of Mississippi, colloquially known as "Ole Miss." It has its heritage of Civil War romance, though no important battle was fought near Oxford. There were several companies raised in the county for the Confederate States Army, the most well known probably being the University Greys, raised mainly from students at the University. In the latter part of the war it was frequently visited by troops of the opposing armies. Grant stopped here once on one of his early attempts to reach Vicksburg and on one of the window panes in the house in which I live is scratched with a diamond "U. S. Grant 1862." On South Lamar Street there still stands a house where the girl who later married General Nathan Bedford Forrest lived and her name is scratched on the pane of the front door.* Legend has it that one time when Confederate troops were retreating before the Yankees this girl came to her front steps and attempted to persuade them not to go. The old residence of L. Q. C. Lamar and the residence of Jacob Thompson, who was a member of the Cabinet of Jefferson Davis, still stand in Oxford. So Oxford has the usual quota of Civil War memories.

A stranger would say sincerely that Oxford was just like all Southern county-seat country towns. Yet to the initiated there is a subtle flavor of difference, to be distinguished and savored only by patience and time. The usual course for the new and unacquainted resident in Oxford is to hate the place for the first six months and then, when he has grown into the place, to love it devotedly the rest of his life. I know that in all my memory there has never been a time when I have left it without sadness or returned to it without joy.

It is significant of Oxford that I sit writing this in the room next to the room where I was born more than forty-one years ago. It is also typical of Oxford that Bill Faulkner should write me on his last extended trip to New York when *Sanctuary* was being ballyhooed several years ago that he "felt sorry for all these millions of people here because they don't live in Oxford."

The business section of Oxford is principally located as usual around the courthouse square. There is the usual monument to the Confederate soldier with his figure atop of it and the usual white courthouse with the four-sided clock in the cupola at the

---

* The incident of the girl scratching her name in a pane of glass appears in the "Ambuscade" section of *The Unvanquished* (1938). Faulkner identifies her as Celia Cook, but does not say she married General Forrest, which she did not.

top. In this cupola pigeons coo on warm summer days and in the yard below loafers sit under the shade of the trees. It is true that the courthouse clock frequently keeps separate time on all four of its faces but it is of no importance. We set our watches daily by Western Union time and we in Oxford have long ago learned that the importance of time has been greatly exaggerated.

In many ways Oxford has been a most favorable field for the development of the talent of William Faulkner. Nothing is more fatal to the creation of a living and growing art than the dead hand of culture. This is even more true in later years since contemporary art has become fashionable. Of course, nothing can stifle genius. Otherwise it would not be genius. But, alas. So few of us have genius. The dead hand of culture can certainly stifle talent, especially talent in literature.

So Oxford was about as ideal for the creation of literature as are most Southern country towns. There was no one to lionize the budding author, no one to make a martyr of him, no crowd with whom to be different and clever and with whom to talk of the great things one was going to write some day—when one got through talking and being clever and different, if ever. There was no one but me with whom William Faulkner could discuss his literary plans and hopes and his technical trials and aspirations and you may be sure I kept his feet upon the ground. Nay, I stood upon his feet to keep them on the ground. Day after day for years —and his most formative years at that—he had drilled into him the obvious truths that the world owed no man anything; that true greatness was in creating great things and not in pretending them; that the only road to literary success was by sure, patient, hard, intelligent work; that you reached the throne if you deserved it and not otherwise. Most of all was drilled into him through that great weapon ridicule the idea of avoiding the contemporary literary cliques with their febrile, twittering barrenness, the idea of literature growing from its own natural soil, and the dread of the easy but bottomless pit of surface technical cleverness. Such surroundings were most important in the formative development of a writer who has almost no conceit but very little humility—possibly not enough humility to ever become truly great.

In this situation Oxford fitted ideally. For the most part the people care very little about any literature that smacks of art. They talk about the crops and the weather and politics, go to church, to the movies, to the college occasionally—quite wisely living life instead of talking about life or writing about life or reading much about it.

For years Bill Faulkner and my claims as to his literary talents were regarded by most of the people of Oxford with a tolerant, good-natured amusement. Now Bill is regarded with a great deal of respect, some municipal pride, and a little awe. This is partly due to the fact that a number of people a long way off have said that he was a great writer but mainly because in the past few years he has made a good deal of money, the amount of which has been fabulously exaggerated by popular rumor.

In justice to Bill and me it should be said that we have never believed that Oxford should support him because he might possibly be a genius. We have always realized that people should buy with their money what they wish, that if Bill Faulkner got some money for a piece of writing and bought whiskey with it the average citizen of Oxford should, if he wished, buy whiskey with the money for which he had worked instead of spending his money to buy something which Bill Faulkner had written.

We both feel that Oxford and the country around it have done enough for a man when they permit him to live here. From any part of Oxford it is only a little walk to numerous places where one can find the unspoiled golden peace of legendary days and where the sound of mankind's so-called progress comes only dreamlike and from afar. There are dim and shadowy groves of silver-white beeches where springs gurgle out from the foot of the hill and sunlight spills dimly through the trees and there is no company but the birds. There are soft carpeted pine hills white with dogwood in the spring. There are rows on serried rows of far hills, blue and purple and lavender and lilac in the sun, hills upon which you can look day after day and year after year and never find light and shadow and color exactly the same.

No matter how much a man may eat he can only digest so much. No matter how much a man may read or learn or think he can only digest so much, can only make of it a certain small part of his own individual personal wisdom. Here, out of the contemporary mad rush, we have time and quiet to think and savor the taste of things without having to gulp them down. Here we can see the stars. Here on frosty nights of fall we have only to listen to hear, faint and afar, the bay of the hunting hound, as in *Sartoris* —"mournful and valiant and a little sad." Here, as I sit writing this, it is quiet enough to hear the cool rustle of the leaves of the ancient oaks and the mellow liquid call of the whippoorwill from the front yard.

MURRY C. FALKNER

The Wonderful Mornings of Our Youth

*W*illiam *Faulkner, the oldest of the four "Falkner boys," as Oxford knew them, was born September 25, 1897, at New Albany, Mississippi. His brother Murry was born less than two years later in the nearby town of Ripley.*

Murry C. Falkner (named for his father, but called Jack) grew up in Oxford and now lives in Mobile. Mr. Falkner served overseas in two world wars, and in the first was wounded in France. He joined the Federal Bureau of Investigation in 1925, resigned in 1928, rejoined in

1934, and, with the exception of extended leave for military service during World War II, has been with the bureau ever since.

Murry Falkner has traveled far and seen much, but he has, like the other Falkners, retained a fondness for the simple things of home. He is the only surviving brother of the four. Dean Swift Falkner, the youngest, was killed in a plane crash near Pontotoc, Mississippi, in 1935. William died in 1962, and John (who followed William's lead in adding the u to his last name) the year afterward.

The sketches which follow show several sides of William: his love for a devoted nursemaid and friend; his fondness for railroads; his enthusiasm for flying after wartime training in Canada; and his joy—that of a small boy in a sandbox—on the golf course.

Our family moved from Ripley, Mississippi, to Oxford in 1902, Bill being almost five years of age at the time. Our father came by road with the wagons bringing the furniture. Mother brought Bill and John and me by train and opened a wide, new, exciting world to us. Trains in themselves, though fascinating beyond belief, were not new to us, seeing that our people had owned a railroad and we had each been born within hearing of the fine whistles of the little steam locomotives of that day. The time and length of the trip was something else, covering the better part of two days and more than a hundred miles—an enormous distance for us.* Oppressed by the heat, restrained by our mother, and pelted by cinders, three grimy little boys finally arrived at Oxford, where at least a thousand people were said to live; the town we left had 497, including the three little Falkner boys.

Mother and the nurse herded us off the train, and (I remember it as though it were yesterday) Bill was the first to see them—arc lights! Even as a child nothing escaped his discerning eye; but unless it interested him, he was done with it immediately. The

---

* Ripley is only about fifty miles from Oxford. However, to make the trip by rail the Falkners had to travel a roundabout route. The rail line which they started out on had been built by William and Murry's great-grandfather, Colonel William C. Falkner.

strange new arc lights were a case in point, it being many years before he would see need or desire by man or beast to be abroad after sundown; therefore, why light up the place?

Sometime after moving to Oxford we acquired a new "Mammy," she being Mammy Callie Barr, born into slavery and soon to become a beloved and honored member of our household. Her inability to pronounce "William" left her addressing him as "Memmie" during the rest of her life. She had a formidable imagination, a good memory of the "old days," and kept Bill, John, Dean, and me spellbound with her tales of the War Between the States. Surely from her came many of Bill's writings about events in Lafayette County, especially those dealing with whites and blacks. She was, like our mother, small in size, and, also like our mother, big in will power and a sense of right and wrong. It was understood that while Mother always had the last say, we were never to disobey Mammy Callie, and we never did, at least not for long. Her seat to the left of the fireplace in the living room was for her alone. I can close my eyes and see her now: small, neat, completely unself-conscious, a kerchief wrapped just so about her little gray head and her lower lip filled with snuff. To her we were always "dem boys" and she would take turns holding us in her lap and gently stroking our heads with her aged hands while she told us wonderful stories of birds and little animals. I say "little" because she always talked of such as rabbits, small dogs, squirrels, and the like, apparently having no truck with big animals about which she knew and cared little, probably feeling that she could not have coped with them in any event.

We loved the woods and Mammy loved to take us there, which was not hard to do in the early part of the century in Oxford: one needed only to step out of the back door. Until Dean was old enough to walk, Mammy had to carry him; the rest of us shifted for ourselves. We went "bird nesting" in the spring, and Mammy taught us to recognize the different birds on sight. We would spot a nest, then shinny up the tree to get eggs for our collection. Most of that work fell to Bill, who was the most agile and the strongest. Those halfway up a tree I would get, while those on the lower branches were left for John. In the fall we would return to the woods and gather hickory nuts and walnuts which we would take to Mammy's cabin in our back yard. Mother would furnish us with some big peppermint sticks; Mammy would build a big fire; and we would eat and talk the rest of the day. Here, as I recall it, Bill began telling tales on his own, and they were good ones too. Some of them even stopped Mammy, and she was a past master in the field if ever there was one.

Changes came with the passing of the years and in the early 1940's Bill was the only one of us still living in Oxford. Mammy, of course, had her cabin in the yard behind Bill's home. She had passed away by the time I returned from the war.* Bill told me about her last days. They ended as she had lived them—in peace and quiet and close to one whom she loved and who loved her in return. One day she closed her eyes and her heart just stopped beating. She had already told Bill how she wanted to be buried, in her newest kerchief, her prettiest dress, and her "Sunday-go-to-meeting" shoes—and, above all, some member of the family to pray over her. Bill saw to it that these things were accorded her. Her coffin was then brought into Bill's living room where, amid her friends and loved ones, white and black, Bill "rared back" and preached her funeral sermon. I was not there to hear it, but I'm sure that Mammy did in heaven, and very likely looked down at my brother, a gentle smile on her face, and said, "Memmie, you is a *good* man." And indeed he was.

In one of the early years of this century the great day had finally come, the one on which a man was going aloft in a real balloon. Oxford had been on edge with this exciting news for weeks, and surely none was more keyed up with anticipation and wonder than Bill and John and myself. We were determined not to miss this momentous event. We knew that our father would either be at work or watching the balloon himself, that Mammy Callie would

---

* Mammy Callie died in 1940 and was buried in the colored section of St. Peter's Cemetery, not far from the Falkner family lot. William was buried in a new section of the cemetery.

be helping Mother about the house, and that Mother had paid no more attention to stories about a balloon than she would have to rumors about a visitor from Mars; so all we had to do was to ease out the back door and hurry up South Street the short distance to the town square.

On reaching the square we beheld a sight never to be forgotten: an enormous grayish, black bag was attached by ropes to stakes set in a circle on the ground, in the center of which a hole had been dug for the fire which was to produce the smoke to inflate the balloon. The fire was already burning briskly, and, though an almost overwhelming amount of smoke was blowing into the eyes of the onlookers, it seemed that at least some of it must be causing the gentle billows within the bag itself. All of this was being administered by the crew—an incredibly dirty and surly white man and a very tall gangling Negro, whose job, so far as we could see, was to furnish fuel for the fire and drinking whiskey for the white man.

By noon all the horses and mules had been removed from the square, partially to save them from blindness and partially to provide more room for the ever-increasing number of townspeople who were happy to risk it in order to see what was going on. By this time the fire was a roaring one, but still the balloon was not more than half inflated. The spectators were covered with soot and John, happy though he was, had some misgivings. "Just wait 'til Mother sees us," he said. Bill reassured him, "Don't worry, she won't recognize us." Now the greasy smoke was pouring out from under the bag and we could barely make out the white man sitting on a keg beside the raging fire. When the wind blew the smoke away for a moment we could see him take another swig from the crock and dash another bucket of coal oil on the crackling flames. We wondered how he could live in such a place. Bill said that the man had probably spent so much time enveloped in smoke that good fresh air would likely kill him.

Although a tremendous amount of heavy smoke was swirling about the square, some of it was manifestly rising within the balloon, which had begun to sway back and forth and tug at the restraining ropes. We could see some smoke spewing out of several breaks in the fabric and, because the Negro was so tall, we could see him towering above the smoke clouds as he went languidly about closing the ruptures with clothespins. By this time Bill and John and I were covered with black, greasy soot, tears were streaming down our faces, and we had never been so excited and happy. We had to be careful though, for Mother had sent Mammy Callie to get us. We could easily hear her as she pushed through the crowd calling out, "Where at dem Falkner boys?" Then louder, using her name for Bill, "Memmie, Memmie. Yo' Mammy says where at is us all and git home." We stayed put and did not reply; nothing could have dragged us away.

By now the motley crew had attached four ropes to the basket which was to hang beneath the balloon and carry the pilot, or whatever it was that individual called himself. It took considerable threshing about to get the white man and his crock aboard. During the process the basket was dragged too close to the flames and one rope was promptly burnt through, leaving the basket canted over on one side with the pilot lying on his back and taking a good swig from the crock the while. Thick black smoke was pouring from the fire, and the balloon was straining at the ropes. We were beside ourselves with excitement. The pilot took the crock away from his mouth long enough to yell at the Negro, "Cut, damn it, cut." In a second the Negro became a flying dervish. With axe in hand he charged the restraining ropes one after the other—swish pam, swish pam, swish pam. His transformation was amazing. We could see his head and shoulders above the billows of dense black smoke as he slashed a rope, then darted to the next one, slashed it, and so on until the last one had been severed. Smoke seethed; we were rigid with attention and anticipation. The balloon slowly began to rise and we could easily hear the pilot cursing the canting basket, the smoke spewing balloon, and, very likely, the general laws of physics as well. Anyway, he was airborne and as soon as the craft rose above the buildings on the square, a gentle north breeze set its course a little east of due south, toward our home. Bill sensed it at once, caught John by the arm and called out, "It's going directly over home—let's go." Lots of other folks had the same notion, but they rushed headlong down South Street. We took a short cut, every foot of which was known to us.

We squirmed through the crowd and scurried down the wooden steps and into the lot below Brown's Store. Now we were on our own—alone and streaking across the lots and gullies between the square and our back lot. We realized quickly that it was tough to run headlong over the rough countryside and look up in the sky at the same time. It took us weeks to get over our collective skinned knees, hands, and faces, but we had to follow the flight of the wonderful balloon, not having any idea as to its cruising range, altitude, or speed. One astounding thing we learned pretty quickly was that the thing had very little forward speed. Indeed we were outrunning it. And, more than that, it was already beginning to lose altitude. In fact it was moving so slow and so low that we were suddenly shocked in realizing that the pilot, still stretched out full length on the low-hanging side of the basket, was talking right at us between swigs at the crock. We could not make out what he was saying, but he was certainly addressing us as we were the only ones in sight. Now we had arrived at Mrs. Powell's fenced-in backyard, where that good lady had chased us out of her apple trees often enough. This time she was waiting for us on her back steps, but she hadn't yet seen the balloon and we didn't propose to lose it, fence or no fence. Bill never hesitated, knowing that where he went we would follow. We shinnied over the fence and pulled John along with us, then charged across the yard to the fence on the other side. The lady must have seen us a split second before the balloon came into view. She gathered her apron about her, waved her duster at us and called out, "William Falkner—you boys stop right—" then, "Oh My Lord," as she suddenly noticed the low-flying, slow-drifting balloon with the cursing pilot on his back in the canted basket drifting silently across her yard. It was truly fantastic. As we scrambled over the fence on the far side of her yard, Bill said that if we could have had a balloon overhead every time we had been in Mrs. Powell's orchard she never would have caught us taking green apples.

By this time the marvelous craft was barely floating over the tree tops and our back lot was just beyond. As we climbed up and out of the last gulley we saw that there were two people near our barn, Mother and Mammy Callie. The latter, not having to contend with the balloon every step of the way, had beat us home and was doubtless explaining to Mother that she couldn't find "dem boys" on the town square. Mother was not often in the back lot, but was there this time seeing about some flower stands that one of the handymen had built for her and left near the barn for the paint to dry. Our three ponies were standing happily in a row behind Mother and Mammy, being the most docile of beasts and given to following any member of the family like the pets they were.

Now we had climbed over the last fence and were in our own back lot, and we could see that the balloon was certainly going to land there. We hesitated but a second in reflecting that if we continued on we would find ourselves face to face with Mother and Mammy in our collective states of being covered with soot, clothes ripped and torn and gashes all over us. But it couldn't be helped: we had lived with this splendid aircraft too long to give it up before the end—which was fast approaching. There was a quick and heavy swish just above the chicken house and the ponies instantly looked upward. Surely these were the first horses in the whole South to see a machine coming down from above. They backed off, stamped their feet, and shook their heads in disbelief. Mother followed their gaze and saw it too, just as the collapsed bag enveloped the barn and the basket plunked down on the roof of the chicken house. It dumped the pilot out onto the roof on the back of his neck; his hand holding the crock made a big arc, smashing into the shingles and breaking the crock, from which whiskey poured down on the unsuspecting chickens calmly at roost below. Instantly they set up a cackling that could be heard a mile away. The pilot slid gently off the roof and onto a pile of hay beside the chicken house. Mother and Mammy were transfixed, but not for long. Both were small in stature but ten feet tall in determination and will power. Mother said, "This man may be hurt." But Mammy was all action in a very respectable endeavor; she was setting out to protect her folks. She grabbed a scantling, longer than she was tall, and muttered, "Effen he ain't hurt, ah garntee he gwine ter be." She charged toward the pilot stretched out on the hay and drew back the scantling. As she did so she saw Bill and John and me standing beside the chicken house, clothes torn, covered with soot, and scratched all over.

For once in their lives Mother was shocked into speechlessness and Mammy into frozen immobility. Mammy's feet were set far apart; she was stretched to her full five feet in height with the scantling held by both hands high above her head, and she literally seethed with anger and astonishment. Even the fringes of her perpetual kerchief on her fine little head seemed to stand out and quiver in rage. This was a sight to sober even the pilot who, seeing his chance, quickly rolled away from the chicken house, jumped to his feet and bolted with speed and precision that put his wonderful balloon to shame. Mother recovered her speech and, seeing that Mammy was set to haul off in hot pursuit of the pilot, touched her on the arm and said, "Mammy, let him go." Then they turned and looked at the three ragged, dirty little Falkner boys. Mammy dropped the scantling, turned to Mother, and said, "Miss Maud, what we gwine do wid dem boys?" We knew the answer to that one, yes indeed we knew.

Steam locomotives had an everlasting attraction for Bill, in common with every other male Falkner. Production of fruits and vegetables began early in South Mississippi and Louisiana, sometimes as early as February. For almost two months they were moved to the northern markets in refrigerated cars by the most direct route, which meant via the Illinois Central cut-off through Oxford.

Bill, our brother John, and I would get up early and trot through the dusty streets to the high bank overlooking the railroad at a point which would now be at or near the rear of the Ole Miss Alumni House. There the three of us would sit and wait, soon to hear the fine sound of the whistle of the first of the "berry trains," as we called them. How exciting it was! Sometimes there would be twelve or even fifteen of them spaced about twenty or thirty minutes apart. And as they whistled, long before coming into view, Bill would call out not only the number of the locomotive but the name of the engineer whose hand was on the whistle cord: "That's number 1102 with Mr. McLeod," or "That's number 961 with Mr. Markette." Of course, he didn't have to tell us; we knew them all, but since he was in charge of our group we looked to him to keep us informed in this as we did in pretty nearly everything else.

When the runs were especially heavy the railroad had to make use of all sorts of locomotives. The first few trains would be pulled by beautiful 1,000 and 1,100-class passenger locomotives; then would come the heavy freight engines; and finally even some stubby switch engines, with drive wheels no larger than the truck wheels on the big fellows. I can hear Bill now explaining to us about their classification by wheel arrangements, such as 2-6-4 or 4-8-2, etc. Our father knew a number of the enginemen and, through him, Bill and John and I were allowed to ride in the cab on a number of occasions when engines were switching on the Oxford tracks. We were even allowed to shovel some coal and to pull the whistle cord. Then home again to the quick, thorough, and inevitable bath to wash the grime away. As may well be imagined, our mother was not kindly disposed toward steam locomotives. On the other hand, Bill's love for them never waned, for even in much later years our conversations nearly always got back to the wonderful mornings of our youth when we would sit on the University bank and watch the beautiful locomotives pass in review as though all this was being done just so three little boys could be as engrossed as much as anything would ever cause them to be.

In the early twenties Bill was, incredibly enough, appointed postmaster at the University. It was a very small office, located in a small red brick building down the hill from what was then the Premedical School. Business became a little hectic while school was in session, but eased off considerably during the summer months. One season or another, though, Bill was no more concerned about mail for others than for himself, which was just as near zero in interest as a literate man could get. Of course, mail piled up, as did the indignation of some of the good boxholders. The less patient and most outraged would come to the single window and demand to know how come their various boxes were always empty. Depending on the hour, these calls would interrupt our daily tea or card game. In either event, Bill would have to go to his side of the window (one is inclined to say "working side," but I'm afraid the adjective would require some strict qualification) and patiently listen out his complaints. As with all male members of our clan, gray came into our hair before we reached thirty years of age. In the early twenties Bill's hair was still light brown and of a fine wavy texture. I can see him now standing patiently at the window, moving air from the electric fan running faint ripples through his fine, light hair, shoulders erect as always, saying little and listening to some indignant and perplexed customer complaining at length about Bill, his employees, the University, the South, and finally the whole United States postal system. Sometimes mail could actually be found, after sifting through countless seed catalogues, old bills, and sheets of instruction on how to run a post office.

During the calm and quiet months of summer, we had the University nine-hole golf course to ourselves. The "greens" were of sand. Dragging a sturdy putter blade from the ball to the hole meant a one-putt "green" anywhere on the course. Our friends of the faculty even called them "fighting-chance" putts, though we all knew that the only way for the ball to be kept out of the hole was either not to stroke it at all or to belt it in the opposite direction. Bill, having more conscience and ability than some of the rest of us, disdained these gentle ditches from ball to hole and generally beat the socks off us in the process. As a matter of fact, he was an excellent golfer. I have seen him shoot the course in under thirty many times. His droll humor gave another name to the course. He called it "the golfing yard." The high tees used by our little

brother Dean, Bill called "stobs." He beat me so consistently that
I went to a cross-handed grip on the clubs. Bill used to say that I
was surely the only golfer on earth who could slice every shot right-
handed, left-handed, or cross-handed.

When Bill was twenty years of age, in the early part of 1918, he
went to New York City, I believe to visit with Stark Young. The
next news we had was that he had joined the Royal Canadian Air
Force, as it was known in those distant days. Since we were already
in World War I he had to claim, and somehow prove, Canadian
citizenship for acceptance in that air force. What guile he used to
convince the Canadian authorities that he was one of their coun-
trymen I do not know, but he succeeded and entered training in
that country and eventually, just before the termination of the
war, obtained his pilot's rating and was commissioned a second
lieutenant. He never got any farther toward the war, which quit on
him before he could do anything about it; but he must have enjoyed himself a lot doing what time, effort, and some entirely
honorable falsehoods permitted him to do. I can almost hear him
now as he chuckled in recounting how, to celebrate the Armistice,
he fortified himself with some good drinking whiskey, took up a
rotary motored Spad and spun it through the roof of a hangar.*

After his return home, while still in his RCAF uniform, he took
Mother to Memphis. She used to tell us about what a commotion
he caused. His was a fine figure in uniform, as indeed it was in anything he ever wore. But this uniform stopped traffic. No one had
ever seen the likes of it, nor was Bill, with his natural reticence
and built-in sense of remarkable humor, prone to properly identify

---

* In the spring of 1918 Faulkner spent some two months in New Haven, Con-
necticut, where his friend Phil Stone was then enrolled at Yale. He roomed with
Stone and worked for an armament company. The trip he made to New York to
visit Stark Young came later, after he withdrew from Ole Miss late in 1920 and
before he became acting postmaster at the University in December of the following
year. While Faulkner was away from Oxford the first time, he joined the Royal Air
Force Canada. He was still in training in Canada when the war ended, and, as his
brother says, never got into the action.

himself. So they decided, practically without exception, that he was a "Rooshian" general.

His Canadian experiences were the beginning of a lifelong love for airplanes and, I'm sure, a feeling of close kinship for all who flew them. One of the first things he did after his writings began to sell was to buy a plane. It was a Waco biplane, four passenger and equipped with a 210 HP Continental motor. He took flying lessons for his civilian pilot's license under Captain Vernon Omlie at the old Memphis airport. Omlie was later to die in the crackup of a passenger plane, and the Waco was to take the life of our little brother Dean.

We were back and forth to the Memphis airport a great deal in those days. I remember Bill flying me up there once in an old open cockpit plane. He flew it from the front seat and I rode tandem behind him. Goggles were essential and from my position I could see only the back of his head in any event. He was all pilot; his head never moved an inch until we approached the Memphis airport and he turned and shouted to me above the roar of the moter to be sure that my seat belt was fastened. By this time Bill, John, and Dean had obtained their licenses and I had begun to take flying lessons. What everlasting pleasure we had flying or just sitting about the airport, looking at airplanes and talking about them. When World War II came along I was called to active duty from Alaska. I flew my plane to Oxford and checked out Bill and John on it so they would have the use of it during my absence. I think one of the greatest disappointments of Bill's life was that he was not accepted for service, though he made every conceivable effort to get into uniform. But he did have my plane which he flew throughout the war years.

He had some close calls, but was able to walk away from them all. He came in from New Orleans once and landed upside down, leaving him with nothing more than a few scratches on the head and arms. His emotions were ever under control, even when the biggest hurt of all came to us—when Dean was killed in the Waco, and he was the best pilot of us all. I'm sure that Bill always felt a sense of guilt, since he had financed Dean's flying lessons and given

him the airplane. John and I tried to make him realize that what
he had done for Dean was what the latter wanted above all else.
Bill said little in reply, but when Dean's only child was born several months after his death, Bill began looking after her. This continued to the end of his life, and I'm certain that her own father,
had he lived, could not have done more. My brother Bill had a
great heart and few people realized, or perhaps cared, how easily
he could be hurt.

ROBBIE EADES

A Love of Drawing

*The following sketch by Miss Robbie Eades provides a rare glimpse
of the boy William, and it additionally attests the kindness of the man
William to children. Miss Eades is a resident of Oxford. For many
years she taught in the Oxford Elementary School, where she delighted
and awed her students with tales of the Civil War passed down to her
by her father.*

*William Faulkner's mother, referred to in a number of the sketches
which follow as "Miss Maud," was Maud Butler. His Grandmother
Butler, introduced in this sketch, was born Lelia Dean Swift. To the
Falkner children she was "Damuddy," the name which William later
gave to the grandmother of the Compson children in The Sound and
the Fury.*

*Many of the older residents of Oxford attribute William's artistic
talent to his grandmother. His brothers Dean and John also painted,
as did their mother.*

❦ Very few people remember when William Faulkner was a small child. He went with his mother and Grandmother Butler to the Baptist Sunday school and church. Mrs. Butler worked in the primary department of the Sunday school, and she would illustrate her stories with what would now be chalk talks on the blackboard. Thus William early cultivated a love of drawing.

One Sunday when he sat near my mother he got a song book and drew a picture of a train in it. His grandmother was so much engrossed in the sermon that she did not see him drawing.

After Mrs. Butler moved away from town, William no longer went to Sunday school even though his mother's name was on the church roll as long as she lived.

When he was a small boy and some of the Falkner relatives came from Ripley, Mississippi, to visit, he was dressed in a little tweed suit with a Buster Brown collar and tie. He wore tweed most of his life, especially in his golf clothes.

When William was shoveling coal at the University power plant, he worked on the night shift. When he got home very early in the morning, dead tired, Estelle would get up and play soft music for him on the piano. He also painted signs around town. He was not ashamed to do manual labor.*

When Victoria (ChoCho) and Malcolm Franklin, the children of Mrs. Faulkner by her first marriage, were quite young, William wrote stories for them. ChoCho brought one of them to school to be read to the children. The beautiful story, typewritten, dealt with the adventures and pleasures of children as they roamed through a meadow in quest of a silver leaf tree. In later years when Malcolm brought the story back to school for the children to read —and they enjoyed it very much—it had been made into a fine little book. Mr. Faulkner was gifted in entertaining children.

When the children at the Faulkner house gave a dance, all the girls in ChoCho's class were invited. One little girl, a newcomer

---

* During the late twenties, a productive period for Faulkner the novelist, he took odd jobs to help earn a living. In 1929, the year he married Estelle Oldham Franklin, he wrote *As I Lay Dying* while working on the night shift at the power plant.

to Oxford, did not have a party dress. When she got there and found all the other children so much dressed up, she was very much embarrassed. Mrs. Faulkner took her upstairs and fixed her up with a party dress, either hers or ChoCho's. When she came downstairs, William, who was standing at the foot of the stairs, said, "May I have this dance, please?" Wherever Lois is now, I know she remembers that.

ROSE ROWLAND

William and His Grandmother

*R*ose Rowland (Mrs. Herron Rowland) is the curator of Oxford's Mary Buie Museum, in which have been placed the Nobel Prize medal which William Faulkner brought home from Stockholm in 1950 and the other awards that he received over the years.

A lifelong resident of Oxford, Mrs. Rowland knew the writer when they were children, and their friendship continued to the end of his life. She was, to him, "Miss Rose."

At the time she first knew William, the family had only recently come to Oxford, though William's Falkner grandparents were already living there. Murry C. Falkner, William's father, had worked for the family's railroad at New Albany and later at Ripley. When he came to Oxford he operated a cottonseed oil mill and ice house, and later a livery stable and a hardware store. Still later, as Mrs. Rowland recalls, he held an administrative post with the University of Mississippi and the Falkners moved to the campus.

"William and His Grandmother" was taken from the tape recording of an interview with Mrs. Rowland on November 11, 1964.

When I was a child, I lived down on South Eleventh Street, the same street that the Falkners lived on. Mr. and Mrs. Murry Falkner, Mrs. Butler ("Damuddy," Mrs. Falkner's mother) and the three little boys made up the family.* William was the oldest of the three. I was a little older than William but that made no difference in our playing about the yard and on the street. The Falkner house was located on an incline some distance off the street near the intersection of South Eleventh and Buchanan. You know that most of the east-west streets in Oxford are named for the Presidents—even Lincoln. There naturally was a large front yard where all the children of the neighborhood came to play.

"Damuddy" was a wonderful person and she spent much time in the yard—even playing with us and showing us how to build little villages of sticks, rocks, and other odds and ends. I think she was there chiefly to keep an eye on the small ones. We even built stockades by driving sticks in the ground around the little huts, which had roofs made of grass. We hunted for pretty pieces of broken glass, pebbles, and stones. We built walks, streets, churches, and stores. Both William and his grandmother were good at improvising and using materials at hand. At the time I didn't fully realize that this is what they were doing. It all seemed so realistic to us. William was the leader in these little projects. He had his grandmother's artistic talents for making things, and his imagination was obvious even then.

In 1906 I went away to school and was away for three years. In the meantime, the Falkners had moved up on Front Street, now South Lamar, at the intersection of South Lamar and University Avenue. There is the big house that William's grandfather built and that has since been turned and moved west on University Avenue far enough to make room for a filling station.

When William was a young boy he often served my father-in-law, Dr. Peter Whitman Rowland, who was dean of the School of Medicine, as caddy on the University golf course. It was there that he learned the fundamentals of golf. In later years, he spent a good

* Dean, the fourth of the Falkner boys, did not come along until 1907.

many hours on the golf course with Dean R. J. Farley of the Law
School and others.

William's father Murry was at one time financial secretary for
the University and he moved with his family out to the old Delta
Psi house on the edge of the campus. William was in his late
teens about that time. It was also about that time that he went off
to Canada to join the R.A.F.

I remember when he and Estelle were married out at the College Hill Presbyterian Church. That was in the late twenties. They
went to the Gulf Coast on their honeymoon and then moved into
an apartment in Miss Elma Meek's house. Later they moved down
to Rowan Oak.*

The Faulkners loved to entertain their children and they had
parties for them. Halloween was a favorite time. They would build
a fire. Estelle and William brought sofa pillows for the ladies. It
was just typical of him; he was a gracious host. We usually phoned
before we came. The children would sit around the fire, and soon
William would begin to spin ghost stories. The fire and the shadows would begin to look eerie and we could just see goblins down
at the edge of the darkness. The children had the feeling of being
down in the woods. Sometimes, someone would come out dressed
as a witch. The children were spellbound. William always seemed
to enjoy being down there. He was relaxed and showed no sign of
being aloof or of desiring to be aloof—that came later, that is his
reserve after he became famous. I don't remember any of the
stories now, but I do remember that I was just fascinated by them.
Some of the mothers would be along with the children and they
seemed to enjoy the ghost stories as much as the children did.

While in conversation with William one day, I asked him why
he didn't make a collection of all those stories and write a book
for children. He laughed and said, "Miss Rose, I never tell them
the same way twice." I remember now that he didn't. He let the

* The two-story antebellum home which Faulkner bought in 1930 (and paid for
over the next eight years) had been built by Robert Shegog but had passed into
the Bailey family and was referred to by Oxford citizens as the Bailey Place. Faulkner named it Rowan Oak.

location, the time, the children and others who were present help make the story. He always referred to them as tales and they were simply told to amuse the children on a given occasion.

The Faulkners' first child died because there was no incubator here; so William bought an incubator and gave it to the hospital. (That was before Jill came along.) There was no preparation of this kind for the premature child in Oxford in those days, and he felt deeply grieved over the fact that they could not care for the little thing. They named her Alabama. I think this name is sometimes misunderstood. Of course, Bama was for his Aunt Bama McLean in Memphis. She grew up in Ripley.*

I remember when William's brother Dean was killed. Somebody said it was near Water Valley, but it was near Pontotoc. Someone was in here not long ago saying he remembered the afternoon it happened. He was barnstorming. Is that what they call it when they take people up for rides? I also heard that he was giving someone instructions and the man being instructed froze to the stick, causing the plane to crash. Anyway, William took much of the responsibility for seeing that Dean's daughter, little Dean, was educated and given the opportunity to travel abroad. He was certainly good to that little girl and she is such a nice young lady.

* Faulkner dedicated his 1931 collection of stories These 13 to "Estelle and Alabama." The great-aunt for whom the baby was named was a daughter of Colonel William C. Falkner by his second marriage.

JOHN RALPH MARKETTE

Railroad Days

*The grandfather of Dr. John Ralph Markette settled on a plantation
south of Oxford, and the boyhood friendship the doctor describes in
the following sketch grew out of the friendship between families. At
the time that Dr. Markette recalls, his father was an engineer for the
Illinois Central Railroad (we get a brief glimpse of him in the sketch
by Murry Falkner) and the family lived in the nearby town of Water
Valley.*

*When Dr. Markette entered the University of Mississippi in 1920,
his friend Bill Faulkner was also a student; he had enrolled the previous
September. But Faulkner withdrew from the University late in 1920
and not long afterward left Oxford for New York City. It was following his return from New York, late in 1921, that he accepted the tem-
porary postmastership on the campus—a post which became permanent
the following year.*

*Dr. Markette earned his undergraduate degree at Ole Miss and went
on to earn the M.D. degree. He is now a practicing physician in Brook-
haven, Mississippi.*

The Falkners and Markettes have been close friends for many
years. Through this family relationship I became associated with
Bill Faulkner and his brothers and we exchanged weekend visits.
That was between 1912 and 1915, when we were in our teens.

My father was a locomotive engineer and he would stop at several stations, including Oxford, on his local runs. Quite often Bill would make his trip to visit me on my dad's locomotive. Likewise I would make a trip to Oxford on the locomotive to visit Bill. The two of us would ride with Dad while switching cars at Oxford. Bill seemed to love railroading and would often shovel coal in the fire box of the engine. When he visited me he loved to ramble through the shops, observing the locomotive making preparation to go on a trip. He also enjoyed watching engines being made from bottom to top.

Bill was a quiet boy and never had too much to say. He didn't seem to enter into many activities in which the other boys participated. He would roam through the woods with us looking for plums, chestnuts, and blackberries. When we piled up leaves to jump in, or made sand houses, he would stand by and observe. Maybe he would say, "Here is a tornado," and tear everything to pieces.

After I entered the University of Mississippi in 1920, I had many occasions to see him, especially while he was postmaster at the University. Often when I opened my box he would be looking through at me. We would talk to one another and reminisce about past events. He seemed to be interested in my studies and questioned me about my professors. He would often stroll through the campus alone and stop to gaze into the trees. Maybe he would stop occasionally, look into the skies, make a few quick turns and then pursue his course—possibly in a state of oblivion or deep thought. Some of the students felt his actions very queer or possibly believed he just had had a few too many drinks. I was fond of Bill and he seemed to think as much of me.

On another occasion, while my son was a medical student at Ole Miss he was in an oak tree gathering mistletoe for Christmas decoration. Bill walked up to the tree and asked, "What are you doing on my property?" My son replied, "I'm Dr. John Ralph Markette's son and I'm gathering mistletoe." Bill said, "I don't give a damn whose son you are. Get to hell out of that tree and off my property." I was amused because I knew Bill's disposition.

I told my son that probably Bill was a bit moody at the time, but that he was a very good friend of mine and would do anything for me if I requested it.

JOHN E. FONTAINE

Never the Ordinary Genius

*J*ohn E. Fontaine was one of several student editors who knew William Faulkner during the period when his work (mainly drawings and poetry, but some prose) was appearing in one or another of three University of Mississippi publications: Ole Miss, the annual; the student newspaper, The Mississippian; and later a humor magazine, The Scream.

Faulkner's first published work was probably the signed drawing which he did for the 1916–17 Ole Miss; this was followed by two signed drawings reproduced in the 1917–18 annual. His first piece of published writing was the poem "L'Apres-Midi d'un Faune," which appeared in the August 6, 1919, issue of the New Republic. Later that year The Mississippian began to publish more of his poetry.

After his graduation from the University, John Fontaine became a sales and advertising executive. An artist and a patron of the arts, he established an art center at Allison's Wells, near Canton, Mississippi, where he was the proprietor of a resort hotel. Mr. Fontaine died August 30, 1962, less than two months after the death of his friend William Faulkner.

The sketch which follows was prompted by Faulkner's death and appeared in the Jackson (Mississippi) Clarion-Ledger and Daily News on July 15, 1962.

❦ Long before William Faulkner began to write the words which millions yearn to read, the writer of these few faltering paragraphs knew him in his native habitat and in what he must have looked back upon always as among his happiest days. For those were his courting days, when he gave every indication, at least, of being head over heels in love with the perfectly beautiful and exceedingly gracious girl whom he was to lose a couple of years later . . . only to regain her on the rebound.*

From this vantage point in time and space, it appears that Bill's agonizing during that period was due partly to love and partly to genius: for while it was as plain as the nose on your face that this boy of eighteen had a lot to communicate, it was equally evident that a decision was long overdue as to which of the several channels open to him would be the one of his choice.

Now, in those years when Faulkner was toying with his troubling problem, we were privileged to pass an abundance of hours together in the Oxford home of the beguiling young woman whom he always loved and who, in due time, became his wife. There was always music there, for Estelle Oldham was a talented pianist and her younger sister Victoria was better with a harp than the disheveled one of the Brothers Marx. Nevertheless, the high spot of many an evening for this fascinated friend was the moment when Bill was at last persuaded to break out the latest product of his brush or pen.

If it hasn't yet been made clear, Faulkner was never the ordinary sort of genius: he was a triple-threat one—with ability to spare in any one of three directions. In fact, it is this bemused writer's opinion that his work as an illustrator would not have fallen far short of his literary gems; and though his brief expeditions into the art of stagecraft did not catch on, the consensus of the experts is that experience rather than genius was at fault there.

At the time his prevailing choice was art, and with the gifts of boundless energy and complete concentration which were to serve

---

* Estelle Oldham, who grew up in the same block with the Falkner boys and who was William's boyhood sweetheart, married Cornell Franklin in 1918; they were divorced in the late twenties.

him through the years, he was turning out scads of combination ink and watercolor sketches, in a style bordering on that of the then popular John Held, Jr., and yet bearing the unmistakable marks of his flair for originality.

In those years, and although he had a lot to show then as later, Bill was never the type who would perform or produce at the drop of a hat. Indeed, had it been left to him, we might never have seen such stray bits of his original and uninhibited art as the two examples at which we are gazing through eyes which have seen a world of fine work across the intervening years—gazing, that is, with the same admiration which enabled us to secure his consent to their publication in the Ole Miss annual of 1918.

And lest we forget it, let us say here that the girls in these pictures—indeed, those in all of his pictures—looked for all the world like Estelle!

One of the treasures which Faulkner brought out on one of those occasions—or that Estelle brought out for him, since at that time, as to his dying day, praise seemed to embarrass him as much as criticism does less gifted ones—was a short play, a satire, if memory serves us. We persuaded him to read it to us and later beguiled him into permitting us to print it in The Mississippian, a paper which this writer, as editor, and many others succeeded in getting out once a week for what we hoped was an eagerly waiting world of readers.

And though it is of far from world-shaking consequence, it is just possible that this little gem of wit and satire which found its way into our University newspaper sometime during the year of 1917 was the first thing of Faulkner's ever to be committed by type to paper.*

It is not our intention, by telling of these two encounters with Faulkner's emerging genius, to take out anything resembling a

---

* Search through the files of The Mississippian has failed to retrieve this play. Carvel Collins, in his William Faulkner: Early Prose and Poetry (1962), gives October, 1919, as the time of Faulkner's first appearance in The Mississippian. The first of his published fiction appeared in the student newspaper the following month. During this period Faulkner wrote a one-act play called Marionettes, but apparently it was never published.

Faulkner drawing (signed Falkner) reproduced from the 1920-21 Ole Miss

claim to the Kohinoor mine of astonishing literature which Bill eventually proved to be. What we had in mind to set out here is simply this: no such sign as "Genius at Work" was ever required to impress anyone who knew Bill at all with the fact that here was a rumbling volcano of talent from which there would someday erupt some astonishing and interesting things.

"Count No-count," indeed! We never heard of such a title even in those days, when it might have been applied to Faulkner by neighbors like the ones who wagged their heads and poked fun at Old Noah while he sat and planned the ark. He was nicknamed "The Count" with something far from laziness or slovenliness in mind: we liked his clipped mustache and his distinguished appearance in a dress suit.

Bill was extremely fond of dancing and seldom missed one of the University proms, although he invariably came alone and without any previous commitment, due, we presumed at the time and still do, to that certain uncertainty having to do with John Barleycorn which later on was to upset many a well-laid plan of host or hostess to present him as the *pièce de résistance* at some dull soiree.

As we were saying, Bill generally came alone to the dances at Gordon Hall as a tribute to that same John Barleycorn which was responsible as well for the somewhat canted position in which he danced from the first intermission forward. . . .

But tower-of-Pisa lean and all, he was always a good dancer and a gentleman: one who carried his liquor as well inside as on the hip—which, as the saying goes, "is something."

Even in the after years, when the genuflections to genius were a source of so much concern to some, Bill remained always the gentleman, and such headknocking as it took to keep him free from time-killing and temper-raising interruptions fell to the lot of his most gracious and charming lady.

Those were the days when Faulkner's family and friends were doing their level best to press him into some orthodox pattern of life—as a clerk perhaps in his grandfather's bank. . . . Bill simply wouldn't be forced into orthodoxy, they found; and one day so the story goes, his father—or as my version has it, his banker grandfather—was heard to remark, in disgust, "People keep wondering what William is going to be; and all I can say is: 'He'll either turn out to be a genius, or just a plain damned fool.' "

One thing is certain: in those days preceding America's entry into the First World War, when Bill was to be seen at any hour holding up the posts in front of Rowland's Drug Store or the Bank of Oxford, any bets on the genius side of that statement would have found few takers among the run-of-mine citizens.

Many's the time I've stopped in front of Bill as he leaned against a post, smiling dreamily while looking off into space, and passed my hand up and down in front of his eyes, with never a sign of recognition or anger, or anything else.

I didn't know then what I learned a few years later: Bill wasn't really there: he was away off in Yoknapatawpha County, spinning yarns with the boys on the courthouse square, peopling the town with the Sartoris clan and other creatures pictured in his mind with a Saturday afternoon crowd of models to choose from.

The bootleggers, the moonshiners, the half-beaten-to-death wives and the half-starved children born without benefit of clergy or resulting from incestuous passion were all around the square. There, Bill would stand from early morning until dark, looking them over, so as to file them away in his mind against the day when they would be needed to fill a vacant spot in *Intruder in the Dust* or some other yarn; whereupon they would be retrieved from memory and converted by some mysterious alchemy to the fictional form which his tale required.

At that moment in history when the *Lusitania* was torpedoed, Faulkner was dreaming away his life in the small town of Oxford; and, though it seems incredible, he might have continued to do so. Then came the April day in 1917 when we entered the war and Faulkner became a citizen of the world. At that instant his horizon began a widening process which never ceased until he was turned to the soil of his native Lafayette County.

Aiding in Bill's rise to greater things was his failure for some reason or other to make the grade for our own eager but insufficient air arm and his acceptance subsequently by the Royal Canadian Air Force, in which he served out the war, partly in Great Britain and France, all the while broadening his knowledge of people and places.*

During the struggling years, as always, Bill's reticence seemed to attract rather than repel people: thus there was always an ample supply from which to select his friends by some love-me, love-me-not process which will forever remain a mystery to me: for his friends were of all sorts and conditions of men.

There were the greats, like Charles MacArthur of *Front Page* fame, who joined him in producing a meritorious movie with a World War I theme, and Somerset Maugham, and that other talented son of our soil Stark Young, all of whom gave him capable and friendly hands-up at crucial moments; or the others of lesser fame, but no less feeling for him whose encouraging words supplied starch for the backbone at just the right moments in his career. There were, for instance, the two Phils—Phil Stone and Phil Mullen—and Jim Stone, who, when fraternities were forbidden at Ole Miss, nursed SAE and many of its members, like Bill, at his big lodge in the woods.

And lest we forget, there were the friends of forest and stream, with whom the great fellow spent so much carefree time over the years. Those were the sporting friends who joined our hero—then above caring what the neighbors said and now beyond it—in one of his many escapades, designed as much as an exercise in showmanship as a test of ability to shock the natives.

If shocking were his purpose, he chose the perfect time to stage his performance: It was a quarter of eleven o'clock on Sunday morning when he led his motley crew of huntsmen, emerging from the woods south of the University campus astride of horses, mules and even an ox or so. There were approximately twenty in the raiding party, each one wearing several portions of the more than ample and exceedingly handsome set of uniforms for every occa-

* Mr. Fontaine, like *Twentieth Century Authors* (1942) and other sources, errs. Faulkner ended his wartime career where he had started it some five months earlier: in Canada.

sion which belonged to Colonel Hugh Evans, who had stopped off to visit with the Faulkners before reporting to Washington for another assignment.

Armed with weapons of every conceivable kind from swords to shotguns, and paced by several tin pans in place of drums, the riders made two complete circuits of the campus, after which, flushed with success, they rode off up town, where they were disbanded by the town marshal who thought he was stretching mercy to the limit of elasticity by not locking all of them up.*

MAUD MORROW BROWN

An Old Friend Remembers Fondly

*W*illiam Faulkner never finished high school; in the words of his brother John, "he simply quit going." William once added a footnote of his own: "Now about education," he said, "a man cannot be educated into happiness."

In the piece which follows, Maud Morrow Brown tells how a young man without a high school diploma came to be admitted to the University of Mississippi. Mrs. Brown is the widow of Dr. Calvin S. Brown, Sr., who took over the German Department at the University in 1901 and later served with distinction as head of German and French.

Mrs. Brown received the degree of bachelor of arts at the University

* Such a procession did move through the streets of Oxford one Sunday morning in 1938. But in the telling and retelling the story has been enlarged upon. No one rode oxback, and the riders were not disbanded by the town marshal; had he seen them he probably would have joined them. For the account of a participant, see pages 120–21.

of Mississippi in 1897 and was salutatorian of her class; in 1902 she was
awarded the degree of master of arts. She is the author of The University Greys, *the tragic story of the young men who left Ole Miss to fight*
in the Civil War, never to return.

❦ I have always felt close to Bill Faulkner because I knew his
family background. I was named Ida Maud Morrow: Ida for my
mother's sister and Maud for Bill's mother. She was Maud Butler.
My aunt and Bill's mother grew up together and were close friends.

When William wanted to enter the University but did not have
the entrance credits, Stark Young, who earlier had been a member
of the faculty, presented a letter to the administration stating that
William had gifts that would prove to be of value to the University and asked, as a personal favor, that he be allowed to enter and
take such courses as he desired. He was admitted.

William attended a class in French and, at first, appeared regularly; then he missed a class but returned once more; then he
missed two meetings of the class but again returned; finally he
failed to attend. When he was in the class he did very well. That
was in 1919.

On Tuesday, June 20, 1920, my husband, Dr. Brown, made the
following notation in his diary: "The little prize which I offered
for the best poem went to William Falkner."

About 1952, after the poet Peter Viereck had spoken at the
University of Mississippi, I attended the Southern Literary Festival
at Blue Mountain College at which Mr. Viereck was the guest of
honor. One of the speakers, introduced as an authority on Faulkner, said that William could not get along with his professors at
the University. He also stated that he had told William that he
had better write prose because he would not write poetry.

In a seminar held later by Mr. Viereck, I said I thought that
William had the gifts of the poet; that he did not write with
rhyme and meter, and that, for the most part, he wrote prose; but

that sometimes he wrote a paragraph of prose that is rhythmic. Mr. Viereck agreed with me that the prose of William is poetic, even though a popular magazine had referred to him as a frustrated poet.*

Later I told Billy what Peter Viereck had said and what I had told him. "Thank you, Miss Maud," he replied, "for telling him that."

Of course, during the time that Billy's father was an official of the University, the Falkners lived on the campus. Later, after he and Estelle were married, they lived down at the old Shegog place.

While Billy's daughter Jill was still a small girl she went to him and said that she had been told that the spirits of the dead come back on Halloween. She had written a letter to the little Shegog girl who had been buried in the front yard of Rowan Oak, in which the Shegogs had once lived, and she wanted to put the letter in her grave.

Billy planned a procession after dark on Halloween. When night came, he got a lantern and lit it; Malcolm, Jill's half brother, carried an old, rusty sword; and, after Estelle had draped a table cloth around herself, all the others threw sheets around themselves.

Reverently they formed a procession and slowly marched down the double lane of singing cedars to the little girl's grave. With the old, rusty sword Malcolm dug a hole in the grave and Jill solemnly put the letter into the hole. Malcolm filled the hole in the grave, and somberly the procession returned to the house.

Some wanted to return to the grave, dig up the letter, and read what Jill had written to the little spirit. But Billy stoutly said, "No!"

---

* "I'm a failed poet," Faulkner told Jean Stein in a 1956 interview. Somewhat earlier (in 1925, in the *Double Dealer*) he wrote that he "read and employed verse, firstly, for the purpose of furthering various philanderings in which I was engaged, secondly, to complete a youthful gesture I was then making of being different in a small town."

CALVIN S. BROWN, JR.

Billy Faulkner, My Boyhood Friend

Calvin S. Brown, Jr., son of Mrs. Maud Morrow Brown, is a professor of English at the University of Georgia. During the period that he re-calls, between William Faulkner's return from wartime training in Canada and his none too successful career as postmaster, William was in his early twenties.

In "Billy Faulkner, My Boyhood Friend," Professor Brown reveals Faulkner's love of the woods and his fondness for games. To the end of his life, there were glimpses of Faulkner the boy in Faulkner the man.

Professor Brown holds degrees from the University of Mississippi, the University of Cincinnati, and Oxford University, which he attended as a Rhodes Scholar; the University of Wisconsin awarded him the de-gree of doctor of philosophy. He is the author of several books and many articles.

When William Faulkner died, his death struck me as the loss of two separate people. One was a distinguished novelist whom I had read with pleasure and admiration but had seldom seen per-sonally. The other was an older friend of my boyhood days whom I had known intimately for a year or two. The loss of William Faulkner was a shock, of course, but in a sense it was a loss only of unknown works that he would have written if he had lived longer: he and his completed work will survive. The loss of Billy was more disturbing, for it brought with it the threat of total oblivion for one of the kindest and finest men I have ever known.

There were four of us boys together—my older brother Robert, William (Rip) Van Santen, Billy's youngest brother Dean, and myself. Robert is now a government administrator of biological research, and Rip is a banker, I believe, in New Orleans. Dean was killed in a plane crash nearly thirty years ago. Neither Robert nor Rip is likely to record our hours in the woods with Billy, and they must not be utterly lost. So the job falls to me.

First of all, let me say that I am going to write what I remember, not what I can dig up. This is a reminiscence, not a work of scholarship. I cannot give dates, for my early friendship with Billy falls during that time of childhood when everything flows together unless there is a death or a move or some other disaster to plot it by. We had no disasters; hence the best I can do is to say that the period of our close-knit group and its Sunday afternoons with Billy was at some time in the very early twenties and lasted a couple of years or so. Everything else I shall have to say will be, like this statement, essentially true though some of it may not be absolutely accurate.

Dean and I were the youngest of the four boys and were close to the same age. Robert was two years older, and Rip fell about halfway between. My father was head of the Modern Language Department of the University of Mississippi. Rip was an orphaned cousin of Mrs. Bondurant (the wife of the Latin professor next door), taken in by the Bondurants at about ten or eleven years old and, I believe, adopted. When Murry Falkner, the father of Billy and Dean, moved to the campus as business manager of the University, Dean became the fourth member of our neighborhood group.

Billy belonged to an older generation. A dozen years older than I and ten years older than Robert, he was a man while we were still young boys. I don't know when or under what circumstances he first took to the woods with us, but it was only natural that he should do so sooner or later, since he liked hunting and fishing and general prowling around (I don't say "hiking" because that implies something too organized and goal-directed, as the sociologists now say), and was not much given to the conventional social rituals. At any rate, it soon came to be the usual thing for the five of us to head for the woods together on Sunday afternoons.

These afternoons were strenuous. More often than not, we had a paper-chase. This game, known also as hare and hounds, is seldom played now, and it has many variations. Here is how we played it. First we would tear up newspapers into small bits until we had a big bag full of pieces averaging about an inch square. Then we would draw straws to select two of the group to be *it*. Those who were selected would then announce a place where the trail was to begin, as well as a final goal. Then they would leave. When they got to the designated starting point, they would begin to leave a trail of dropped bits of paper, and this trail usually had its loops and even its dead-end spurs. When the paper was all used up, they would drop the empty bag at the end of the trail and cut straight across country for the announced goal. The rest of the group would give the trail-layers a five-minute start. Then they would go to the starting point, pick up the trail, follow it, get the empty bag, and cut for the final goal. The bag was the proof that they had actually followed the trail.

The object, of course, was for the "hounds" to overtake the pair constituting the "hare" before they got to the goal. The start and finish were usually a mile or so apart, but the total course was likely to be about four miles, what with getting to the starting point and following all the windings of the trail. The five-minute start compensated for the time the hares lost laying the trail and gave them a chance—if they were fast and crafty enough—to keep out of sight. Craft was as important as speed and stamina. If the hounds caught a glimpse of the hares laying the trail, they would head straight for the spot and pick up the trail there, usually cutting off some loops and always saving some trailing. If the hares were too unimaginative in their course—if they stayed on a field road too long, for example—the hounds might guess where they were heading and gamble on taking a short cut and picking the trail up again without having to follow it all the way. The game had many such tricks, and we used them all, because it was a real game rather than what most of our over-organized "games" have now become, a mere winning-match. Both sides liked to take chances and show their virtuosity, and I don't suppose there was ever a time when any one of us had the remotest idea whether he had been on the winning side oftener than on the losing.

In all this Billy asked no quarter, and it is no mean feat for a man in his twenties who makes no fetish of training and fitness to keep up with boys in their early teens. Most of the running was done at a jog-trot, but if the hounds picked up the bag close behind the hares, three miles of trotting might be capped by a half-mile cross-country sprint. Billy once talked his contemporary and early literary mentor Phil Stone into coming on a paper-chase, and it nearly killed him. It was probably the first time Phil had been off a sidewalk in ten years. After that, Phil confined his association with the youth of Oxford to something more in his line—taking a group of girls considerably younger than he (including my sister Edith) to the drugstore for sodas and milk shakes.

(In later years, I have often been struck by the parallel of Billy with his group of boys and Phil with his similar group of girls. I don't know which began first, and I don't believe either was an imitation of the other. Phil's group was, of course, the starting point for Gavin Stevens' interest in Linda Snopes in Faulkner's Snopes trilogy.)

When the paper-chase reached its goal, we spent the rest of the afternoon in the vicinity. Sometimes we played games like running-through, which is to football what nip-strike is to baseball. In this sport a goal line is established and one man, with every other man's hand against him, has one chance to back off and run through to it. If he does, he gets to try again; if he doesn't, the one who tackled him gets to try. For the most part, though, after the paper-chase we looked for something less taxing than running-through. Occasionally we took wieners and buns, and cooked the wieners on sticks over a fire. More often, it would be just a few marshmallows to toast. We had to carry a canteen of water unless the chase was to finish near a spring, and elaborate picnics are not very appealing when you have to run several miles with the groceries.

Most often we played stalking games. These, with their minimum of physical activity, were a perfect counterpoise to the paperchase, but still called for craft and woodsmanship. There was one elaborate game whose details I can't recall, in which there were two camps a couple of hundred yards apart in good cover, and each side tried to slip up and steal the other side's flag (a handkerchief, or anything like that), while keeping its own flag from being stolen. Simpler and better was the game in which one person was *it* and the rest tried to stalk him. The one who was *it* had to stay in one place, usually a commanding one like the top of a stump. He shut his eyes while the others scattered. Then they began to stalk him. The object was to touch his stump before being challenged by name. If one could get in fairly close, he might achieve this by a sudden rush when the stalkee's back was turned. Anyone challenged by name and accurately located had to show himself. If the name was right, he lost, but if it was wrong, he won just as much as if had got to the stump unchallenged. Thus the man who was *it* would spot a stalker, see what he could of him, weigh the probabilities, and call, "All right, Rip, come out from behind that hickory ten yards to my left." Whoever was there had to come out. If it was Rip, he was a loser; but if it was anyone else, he was a winner.

One of the most triumphant moments of my life happened in this game. Somehow or other, we had gone out on a moonlit night —this was not usual—and were playing in the Chancellor's pasture. In those days, all the faculty kept cows, and a large private pasture was one of the status-symbols of the Chancellor of the University. Billy was *it* and was on a slight knoll on an open hillside. Knowing the territory well, I went off some distance and got into the lower part of a ditch that started from the base of the knoll. I could then walk, bent double, to within about thirty feet of Billy, and could crawl to within fifteen feet. But beyond that there was no cover, and a rush was out of the question because one can't start a rush from an absolutely flat prone position. I decided to try an old *Leatherstocking Tales* expedient. After crawling backward down the ditch until it was deep enough, I turned around, went off far enough away not to be heard, and cut a small, scraggly, inconspicuous bush. With it I went back, and when I got to the open space I continued across it with infinite care, advancing the bush a few inches and creeping along behind it when I was sure Billy was looking elsewhere. It was a glorious moment when I finally seized him by the ankle.

To this day I am not sure how the trick succeeded. Billy was far too good a woodsman to be taken in by it, and I was not a good enough stalker to get by with it. But I am certain that Billy did not deliberately ignore me and *let* me do it. This would have been a violation of our unspoken code, and he was utterly incapable of such a betrayal of our relationship. Most probably he became engrossed in his own thoughts, as not infrequently happened, and was oblivious of his surroundings. His astonishment was certainly not put on, but it was probably not because I had outwitted him. It was more likely because he had forgotten that he was being stalked.

This ability to lose himself in his own private world was one of the unheeded signs of things to come. A clearer one, but still unheeded, was his ability to improvise fascinating ghost and horror tales by a campfire. I can't recall any of the plots, but the general impression is clear enough. The tone was one of supernatural horror, but always relieved by enough humor, fantasy, or irony to give the tale some aesthetic distance. A sadistic adult, or one who merely felt himself superior to his audience, might have amused himself by terrifying us. Billy set out to amuse *us* by terrifying us, and as hard as this self-imposed assignment was, he never failed to pull it off.

He could be caustic and superior enough on occasion, but about institutions and organized idiocies rather than persons. Two instances come to mind. There was a church league that fielded

baseball teams in the summer, and one day I was sitting with
Billy watching a game between the Baptists and some other sect.
After some particularly virulent demonstration of Baptistism,
Billy remarked reflectively, "I don't know what church God be-
longs to, but I know he isn't a Baptist because he permits the other
sects to exist." Another time I ran into him in the crowd watching
the Lyric Theater (the local picture show owned by Billy's cousin-
by-marriage Bob Williams) burn up. It was a really splendid fire,
with vast billows of black smoke rolling up from the tarred roof,
and the volunteer fire department was making futile efforts to put
it out. After watching them for a bit, Billy said, "This is the only
good show they've ever had in that place, and there are a lot of
damned fools out there trying to ruin it."

It is hard to give any real notion of Billy's relationship to us
boys. Like everything that he ever said, did, or wrote, it was built
on a foundation of genuineness. I have never known a man less
capable of sham. Billy never pretended to be "one of us"—the difference in ages was too great to be overlooked. He accepted the
leadership and authority that naturally fell to him, but he exercised
them with a wisdom which was deeper than mere tact. If he never
condescended or talked down to us, neither did he boss or domi-
nate us. He did not have to restrain himself from doing these
things. They were simply foreign to his nature. He accepted the
difference in ages for exactly what it was worth (which was intrin-
sically not much), not playing it either up or down. This balance
was all the easier for him because he was never effusive or demon-
strative; he was always somewhat aloof, even with close friends of
his own age. Billy's attitude toward us boys was simply that of a
close friend who keeps his distance because of a basic respect for
the individual; and this attitude was almost the direct opposite of
the regimented, supervised-play, group-leader sort of thing that
Billy's play with us superficially resembles. I am sure that he never
thought of us as a "group"; we were simply four quite different
persons that met with him to do things that all five of us enjoyed.
I am equally sure—and it is to Billy's eternal credit—that he did
not set out to work with youth, to lead us in the way that we

should go, to do us good. And I am convinced that because of this he did us a great deal of good, largely in ways beyond all demonstration or explanation. I suppose the most tangible thing was to teach us by example some of his own independence and respect for the independence of others.

Our group never broke up, any more than it was formed. It simply drifted apart as it had drifted together. We boys began to make our own individual friends farther afield than the immediate neighborhood. (We had always taken other boys on the paper-chases occasionally, just as Billy took Phil Stone, but though these guests ran better than Phil, they didn't really fit much better. By mutual tacit agreement, they didn't come back.) We began to plan other things with individual friends, and I believe that about this time we also began to discover girls. Billy doubtless developed other interests just as we did. It may well be that he began to prefer to spend Sunday afternoons in literary talk with Phil. At any rate, we had never gone out every Sunday or had any sort of club or organization, and so, just as we had drifted together casually, we could drift apart painlessly.

My next recollections, from a few years later, are not of my friend Billy but of "Count Faulkner." (This was the regular title; "Count No-Count" was only an occasional witticism.) I don't like to linger over these memories. Billy was now postmaster at the University post office (which was an independent one, not a branch office), and I was well along in high school. We used to chat a bit at the stamp window from time to time, but our relationship was gone. I'm afraid that, with the cocksure intolerance of the adolescent, I shared the general contempt for the ineffectual Count Faulkner. He must have known this, but with his own invincible independence of public opinion, he was probably neither surprised nor hurt. I am sure that he never held it against me.

It was several years more before I met William Faulkner in print. By this time I was a student of literature at the other Oxford. During a vacation trip to Florence in 1932 I bought and read Sanctuary—with excitement, amazement, and plenty of reservations. Soon afterwards I reviewed the British edition of Light in

August for one of the Oxford undergraduate magazines. This was probably one of the earliest reviews of Faulkner in England, and for me it marked the beginning of a lifetime of literary admiration, punctuated by an occasional personal visit, a joint family picnic to St. John's or Bay Springs Church, or something of that sort when I was back home for a visit. By this time I had managed to put Count Faulkner out of my mind, but whenever we met I had the strange feeling of being in the presence of two different people who were incommensurable and yet somehow one and the same person—the great novelist William Faulkner and my old boyhood friend Billy.

EDITH BROWN DOUDS

Recollections of William Faulkner and the Bunch

E dith Brown Douds, daughter of Mrs. Maud Morrow Brown and sister of Calvin S. Brown, Jr., was brought up on the campus of the University of Mississippi within a stone's throw of the Falkner home. Mrs. Douds is chairman of the Department of French at Albright College, Reading, Pennsylvania, where her husband, Professor John B. Douds, heads the Department of English.

Identification of some of the places and people may enhance appreciation of "Recollections of William Faulkner and the Bunch." The Shack was a two-story frame building opposite the Oxford railroad station; in the twenties it was a popular gathering-place. The Bunch was a group of young people of Oxford and the University who gathered around Phil Stone's law office, a one-story red brick building with a turret, about fifteen strides from the town square. Puggy is now Mrs. P. C. Whitehead of Oxford; her wit made her a natural leader. Sonny Bell was the son of the dean of the School of Commerce, and Branham Hume the son of the Chancellor of the University. General Stone was the father of Phil Stone. Sallie (now Mrs. Baxter Elliott), who acted as secretary for Phil Stone and typed and helped to edit William's manuscripts, was and is a close friend of Mrs. Douds.

❧ "It is a writer's duty," said Faulkner in the Nobel Prize speech, "to write about these things." These things which I have let my mind run upon are not important things, but I write them down because the Bill Faulkner whom I knew was a dear person and is now a precious friend hid in death's dateless night. Perhaps the smiles which these recollections will evoke are smiles he would have been glad of.

I am remembering the time when I was getting ready to go to the Delta to be in a friend's wedding. All the Bunch—this was before there were gangs, or even sets; we were a Bunch—all the Bunch at Phil Stone's office were taking a genuine interest. Martha, and Puggy, and Rosalie, and Dot, and Sallie were chattering about what I would wear, and who would be the other bridesmaids, and other such matters of vital concern. Bill and Phil, who were "older men," had adopted our Bunch and the boys who were our contemporaries. Branham Hume and Earnest Jarrett Beanland and Sonny Bell were there that day, I recall, and maybe others. Bill and Phil were taking my plans and my trip very seriously and were working on the buildup which they always arranged for any one of us who was going out of town on a visit. "We've got to boost Sister Edith's stock with those Delta boys," they decided, and got down to the detailed planning. There were to be telegrams, spaced throughout the visit; there were to be long-distance calls, planned to be put through at the moment when some out-of-town date in the other town would be calling in person; there

were to be flowers. The whole plan, whenever put into operation
for any one of us, was designed to give the impression that we
were *femmes fatales* who had left desolation behind in Oxford's
male population by even brief absence. This was kindness and per-
ception such as I have seldom seen equalled since I left Phil and
Bill. Both worked with absorbed and painstaking detail on the plan
for me. They wrote down addresses, worked out a time-table, and
took my pleasure and excitement as much to heart as if it had
been their own. Soon the other boys were bored. "Sister Edith
don't need all that help," said one of them crossly. "Everybody
needs all the help he can get," replied Bill.

The year 1921, and especially the spring of 1922, was the beginning of the close association of Bill and the Bunch. He was almost ten years older than I, but I was younger than the rest of
the crowd. Bill was thinking about writing then, and Phil was
constantly urging him to get at it. Bill had already had a poem
published in the *New Republic*, and during 1919–20, when he
was taking some French and Spanish courses at Ole Miss, he was
writing a lot of poetry. Some of it was published in *The Mississippian* and won the Brown Poetry Prize for 1920. Bill and Ben
Wasson formed the Marionettes, the Ole Miss dramatic club, that
year, with some others, and Ben did a lot for Bill, because he read
poetry beautifully, with meaning and without self-consciousness, as
I came to know several years later in Greenville, where he introduced me to much of modern poetry.* Phil, however, was interested in seeing Bill write down the stories which he could tell
aloud so well. To say that Phil "encouraged" Bill, as so many
biographers do, is gross understatement. He cajoled, browbeat, and
swore at him; he threatened and pleaded; encouragement came
later.

Phil had a car named Drusilla, and all of us were free to drive
her. She sat, habitually, in front of General Stone's office, where
Uncle Mulberry could keep an eye on her as well as on the Gen-

* Wasson, now book editor of the Greenville *Delta Democrat-Times*, knew Faulkner over a period of many years, first in Oxford and later in New York and Hollywood. At one time he was Faulkner's literary agent.

eral's horse. We checked Drusilla in and out with Uncle Mul, and used her whenever the need arose to go to The Shack for a bacon-and-tomato sandwich and a forbidden cigarette. Bill's father had been appointed secretary of the University a few years before, and Bill and I often needed Drusilla for transportation back and forth to the campus. We would park her on the slope between Bill's house and mine. She took off on her own from there one day and crashed slowly from tree to tree, until she finally came to rest down by the bridge that led over to the railroad track. I was much surprised, nearly twenty years later, to find Drusilla in *The Unvanquished*, in the story "Skirmish at Sartoris," metamorphosed into a southern Joan of Arc. And so it is, when you read Faulkner. Moving in and out of a Bergsonian or Proustian time, the past of Oxford appears and changes and flows, now recognizable, now transmuted in form, but living on in essence.

From 1921 to 1929 Bill was in and out of Oxford. The chronology of those years is so well known that there is no need to, say here that he went to New York in 1921 and stayed with Mr. Stark Young, and in 1925 went to New Orleans and spent a lot of time with the Sherwood Andersons. When he was in Oxford or on the campus we saw a lot of him at Phil's office, or at Miss May Carter's place, or at Ella Somerville's Tea Hound, or at the post office, or at The Shack. He wrote *Soldiers' Pay* mostly in New Orleans, and then brought the manuscript to Phil's office.* My chief reaction at the time was to be shocked at how badly it was punctuated. I offered to repunctuate it, and Bill said he didn't care, so I did. As I remember it, Bill didn't seem to care a bit about that novel, or about *Mosquitoes*, which followed hard on it. And yet, as I reread *Soldiers' Pay* now, it seems that something wonderful took place midway in the writing of it. I do not mean that some important external event took place, although perhaps it did. I am more inclined to think that as Faulkner was writing that novel,

* Out of Faulkner's six-month stay in New Orleans, from January to early July of 1925, came *Soldiers' Pay* and a number of prose pieces which appeared in the *Times-Picayune* and a literary magazine, the *Double Dealer*. During this period Faulkner made several trips home to Oxford.

the power of his craft took hold on him, and his characters took over from him and became living beings who dominated their author. The novel begins haltingly; in fact, the first part of it seems to me to be so bad that I am puzzled that any publisher's reader, no matter how pushed he was by Sherwood Anderson, could possibly have persevered to the place where the book comes alive, and then have recommended its publication. I am puzzled, too, that Bill seemed to care so little about it. Later, the second miracle took place, in the conception and writing of *Sartoris*, where the author learned to ride herd on his characters and keep them vital but under his will. And William Faulkner cared deeply about *Sartoris*.

Several other things puzzled me about *Soldiers' Pay*. How could I have punctuated it so badly? And how does it come about that on page 57 one word is omitted and one case wrong in "Integer Vitae," and we didn't catch it, for all of the Bunch had studied with Miss Stacy Furr, and we knew our Latin poets. And why didn't Liveright catch it, and why does the Signet Paperback preserve the errors? I mention these details only because they rise up to substantiate my memory that we talked avidly about Bill's writing as he wrote. Sallie Simpson had left the University by that time to become secretary to Phil and General Stone, and she did a lot of work for Bill, taking infinite pains with typing and proofreading and making sensitive suggestions.

I say that we all took enormous interest in Bill's writing. That is true, but *Sanctuary* was in the writing at this time, and we girls were firmly excluded from details about it.* We knew that Bill was doing a "bad" book and that he and Phil had to go to Memphis to do a lot of research on it, but we were not allowed to know the theme, or what the "research" consisted of, and I've no idea who typed it. I am sure Sallie didn't. All of us felt that Bill would have to write something to get his name known, before people would take him seriously, and that the surest way to get his name

---

* Apparently it was not until the latter part of the period Mrs. Douds writes about, early 1929, that Faulkner began work on *Sanctuary*, which was published two years later. The "research," however, may have been done somewhat earlier.

known was to write a shocker. Though Bill had not seemed to care about *Soldiers' Pay* or *Mosquitoes,* he did care deeply about writing, and we all knew that. We cared, too. Faulkner dates the time of his dedication to writing from 1923, and he wrote in the Foreword to the Modern Library Giant *Faulkner Reader:* "I wrote a book, and discovered that my doom, fate, was to keep on writing books."

During much of this period Bill habitually went barefooted, and Phil wore a hat all the time, indoors and out. He would not go anywhere where it was not possible for him to keep his hat on, except to court. All of us understood that if we should go to court and see Phil without his hat, and so break down his right to privacy in that matter which was of consummate importance to him, we would immediately forfeit his friendship. I recall that we did not question at all Bill's right to bare feet, and Phil's to a covered head, and I recall, too, that we reacted with fury to criticism from "outsiders" of Phil and Bill's right to do as they pleased. Much that is written about Faulkner nowadays assumes that Oxford was hostile to him and heaped ridicule on him. My recollection, on the other hand, is that he enjoyed, as did we all, a degree of individual freedom which would be difficult to duplicate in most places in the more regimented present-day society.

Between 1918 and 1928 the apprenticeship of a writer became the flowering of a creative genius. Perhaps there was a sudden change; more probably what happened was gradual and internal. I do not know. I left Oxford in June of 1929 for Paris, and within the year came to know both Hemingway and Fitzgerald. I wonder whether anyone else knew all three of them at that time. Sherwood Anderson, perhaps? Gift books with typical inscriptions from all three of them stand side by side on my bookshelves. I was greatly privileged.

BEN GRAY LUMPKIN

The Awesome Postmaster

*W*illiam Faulkner's career as a public servant, and specifically as postmaster at the University of Mississippi, lasted almost three years—from late 1921, after his return from a sojourn in New York, to October of 1924. The wonder is that it lasted so long: the postmastership was not a job for a man given to thoughtful reflection and even then more concerned with writing poetry than with seeing that mail got into the right boxes.

What did the Ole Miss students think of their postmaster? One of them, Ben Gray Lumpkin, provides an answer in the sketch which follows. Dr. Lumpkin is a native of Holly Springs, Mississippi. A specialist in folklore (for which Faulknerland provided rich background), he is now a member of the English faculty at the University of Colorado.

The Gathright-Reed Drug Store, referred to in this piece and in others which follow, is located just off Oxford's courthouse square. It was a favorite stopping place for William Faulkner on his frequent walks to town.

❧ While I was a graduate student at Ole Miss in the mid-thirties I happened to go into the Gathright-Reed Drug Store one afternoon, and walked up to the counter where either Mr. Mac Reed or Mr. Gathright was talking with a gentleman who was wearing a gray felt hat and who had both elbows propped on the showcase near the cash register. While Mr. Reed (I think) handed me a package of razor blades, he glanced at the man leaning on the showcase and said, "Mr. Lumpkin, have you met Bill Faulkner?" I said, "Yes, sir, but I'm glad to see him again."

Mr. Faulkner turned from the counter, extended his hand, and in a half-reserved and half-shy manner bowed courteously and shook my hand firmly. Then he leaned one elbow on the showcase and waited to resume his conversation with Mr. Reed. Though he did not say a word, I got the impression that he wanted to be courteous without getting encumbered. As I was leaving, he nodded and smiled ever so slightly.

When Mr. Reed introduced us, he did not know—and Mr. Faulkner almost certainly did not remember—the circumstances of our only other meeting, a dozen years earlier.

While I was a sophomore, during the fall or spring of 1922–23, some of my fellow students (probably Girault Jones or Wilson Lyons) spoke of Mr. Faulkner as a writer and said that he was contributing stories to "big" magazines. That rumor put me somewhat in awe of our postmaster. I wanted to talk with him, but I suspected that he didn't like students. While he put letters in the boxes at the post office after the arrival of the morning mail train, a few students good-naturedly yelled comments about his being slow. On several occasions, one or two boys chunked marble-size pieces of clay and pebbles through the grating over the mailboxes. Actually, Mr. Faulkner distributed the letters to the boxes with great speed after he began to put them into the boxes. But usually ten or fifteen minutes elapsed between the arrival of the mail on the old one-horse spring wagon and the time that Mr. Faulkner began to put the letters into our boxes. He was probably arranging the mail for efficient distribution; and he seemed oblivious to the noisy students, who were packed into the tiny space between the wall and the boxes, and who kept up a steady commentary in the third person on "that slow poke postmaster." Every once in a while some of the girls would tell the big mouths to shut up and let the man work; but nothing could repress the high spirits of such fellows as Lonnie Moseley and Johnnie Stovall!

Finally I got the opportunity that I had been hoping for. Dr. Jim Bell gave us a test that I could write up in a few minutes. So, being out of Lyceum on a bright morning between eleven and twelve, I headed past the Confederate monument for the post office to get my mail. After I looked into my box and started out, I realized that Mr. Faulkner and I were the only persons in the building. I decided to buy a book of stamps to get in a word with the awesome postmaster.

I walked up to the stamp window; but Mr. Faulkner, who was seated in some kind of a high-backed chair, seemed completely absorbed in a magazine. As I stood waiting, I could look directly down and see some of the garish pictures of the magazine. I recognized the bold compositions of reds and dark blues, for I had been reading the same issue of *Liberty* magazine, which was running a serial about aces and air battles over France during World War I.

After waiting at least half a minute, I gently tapped with a quarter on the shelf of the stamp window. Mr. Faulkner stood up with his magazine in his left hand and looked at me with a poker face. I pushed the quarter across the window shelf and said, "A book of two-cent stamps, Mr. Faulkner, please sir."

Without a word and with one continuous motion, he slid the book of stamps over toward me, swept the quarter into the open till, sat down, and resumed his reading. Having invested a quarter in the venture, I tried again to get a word out of him. "Mr. Faulkner," I said, as politely as I could, "I hear that you have contributed some very interesting stories to national magazines."

He looked up from his magazine and in a matter-of-fact tone, completely without color, said, "I haven't met you, yet."

That squelched me. But I felt no resentment. All of us knew that Mr. Faulkner would not talk with students.

GEORGE W. HEALY, JR.

No Beck and Call for Bill

There are several versions of Faulkner's departure from the postal service. All involve, in one way or another, the surprise visit of a U.S. Post Office inspector.

In "No Beck and Call for Bill," George W. Healy, Jr., gives his account of the incident. The visit which he describes was preceded, or perhaps followed, by a letter in which the inspector detailed a number of complaints against Faulkner, among them that he was in the process of publishing a book (The Marble Faun) which some patrons said was written in the post office. Whatever the exact chronology, the badly miscast postmaster submitted his resignation on October 31, 1924.

Mr. Healy, who was a student at Ole Miss in 1924, is now editor of the New Orleans Times-Picayune and vice-president of the Times-Picayune Publishing Corporation. He was a close friend of William Faulkner and has been, and is, a friend of many other literary people.

❦ I remember Bill Faulkner well and pleasantly from meetings both at the University of Mississippi and on the streets and in the newsroom of the *Times-Picayune* in New Orleans.

When I enrolled at the University in 1922 Bill was postmaster at the campus station. One of his assistants was the late James

Warsaw Bell, Jr., whom I met soon after I took a room in West
Gordon Hall. It was Sonny Bell (so named because his father,
dean of the School of Commerce, had the same name) who introduced me to Bill, and it was also Sonny who occasionally participated with a small group, of which I was a member, in bridge
games in the post office.

The interruption of one of these games by a post office inspector
marked Bill's departure from the federal service. As he was leaving
the post office he was asked by the late Holden Van (Skeet)
Kincannon how he felt about leaving that clubby building for the
last time as lord and master. Bill thought a few minutes as the
retreating bridge players walked toward the Delta Psi house, which
was then the Falkners' home, and finally replied, very slowly,
"You know, all my life I probably will be at the beck and call of
somebody who's got money. Never again will I be at the beck
and call of every son-of-a-bitch who's got two cents to buy a
stamp." *

Through Bill I got to know his whole family. His mother and
his youngest brother Dean, who then was in high school, were
particular favorites of mine. Dean used to come out to my
dormitory room when I was a freshman to listen in on our bull
sessions.

Bill was quite a golf player, and he once pulled me out of a
tight spot. I had arranged for the then professional at Milwaukee's
Tuckaway Country Club—an old friend who spent the winters
in Natchez—to play an exhibition in a foursome of pros on the
campus links. Bill Eidt from Milwaukee and a professional from
Muncie, Indiana, named Byrd showed up, but we were short two
players for our match—for which I had sold quite a few tickets.
When I told Bill my predicament, he said, "Don't worry about
that, George; I'm willing to give up my amateur standing to help
you out." He did and, if my memory hasn't faltered, he was the
low scorer in the match.

About the time that Bill left the post office, Phil Stone per-

* Nothing Faulkner said, or wrote, has been so frequently quoted as this. There
are several slightly different versions.

suaded him to publish *The Marble Faun*, a book of verse. Phil paid a vanity publisher to publish the book; he hoped to recoup his money by selling copies to Bill's friends. At one time I had four copies, all of which I gave away. I wish I had them back because the last copy of *The Marble Faun* whose sale was reported brought $1,700. Incidentally, I'm sure Phil Stone never got back the money he put into publication of Bill's poetry.

When a group of us on the campus started a publication that was alleged to be humorous, Bill came by my room one night and suggested that he had time on his hands and would like to write some things for us. Fearing that his verse or prose wouldn't appeal to the audience we were trying to reach and knowing that he drew, I talked him into becoming our cartoonist. I believe I had the only bound volumes of copies of that magazine, *The Scream*, extant. A New Orleans friend who is a Faulkner collector persuaded me to part with them for art's sake. The collector, however, did send a sizeable check to one of my favorite charities.

Bill preceded me to New Orleans and, through the good judgment of the late Roark Bradford, got an assignment writing pieces for the Sunday *Times-Picayune*. We didn't copyright those columns, and they've been reprinted in practically every language from Japanese to Hindi. The pay for those columns, Phil Stone told me, was five dollars each—which was eating money for Bill while he was living in the Vieux Carré and writing his first novel.

In addition to writing for money, Bill also did some writing for fun while he was in New Orleans. Sherwood Anderson then was living in the Vieux Carré, and Bill and an artist-architect named William Spratling did a book called *Sherwood Anderson and Other Famous Creoles*. It was circulated about the time I joined the *Times-Picayune* staff as a reporter and caused quite a stir in the French Quarter. Anderson, a mutual friend told me, was infuriated. Bill wrote the introduction and mimicked Anderson's style.

Although Bill never was, strictly speaking, a member of the *Times-Picayune* staff, he made many a visit to our newsroom to talk with Bradford, Lyle Saxon, and others on the staff who, like himself, were turning out books.

I had two later-year meetings with Bill in New Orleans. The first I probably shouldn't discuss and the second was when he came here with his mother to receive a decoration from the French Consul General.* At the second meeting Bill's mother thanked me profusely for having got Bill back to Oxford all in one piece after the first.

THOMAS ALTON BICKERSTAFF

Mr. Burleson, The Bold Mouse

*N*ot long after Faulkner left the postal service, Thomas Alton Bickerstaff, then a student, was employed as a helper in the University post office. Faulkner's departure was, of course, still a favorite topic of conversation.

But the retired postmaster left more than a legend behind. In "Mr. Burleson, The Bold Mouse," Dr. Bickerstaff adds a charming footnote to the story.

A mathematician and an authority on the law of probability, Bickerstaff is chairman of the Department of Mathematics at the University of Mississippi. He has been a member of the faculty since 1928—longer than any other person.

* In 1951, the year after Faulkner traveled to Stockholm to receive the Nobel Prize for Literature, he was made an officer of the Legion of Honor.

⚓ After William Faulkner left the Ole Miss post office, James W. Bell, Jr. acted as postmaster for a period of several months. He was succeeded by Taylor Dunn, a citizen of Oxford with whom I worked from the beginning of his period as postmaster in 1925. I was then a student at the University, and I went into the post office as a helper—at a salary, incidentally, of twenty dollars a month.

One of the carryovers from the Faulkner "administration," I remember, was a mouse which had the distinction of being named by the famous writer when he was postmaster. "Mr. Burleson" was named for Albert S. Burleson, the Postmaster General in President Woodrow Wilson's Cabinet. It may have been another student, H. V. Kincannon, who passed the story along, since he had worked in the post office before Dunn or I—under Bell, and possibly under Faulkner. At any rate, Mr. Burleson, Faulkner's mouse, had a very fine personality thrust upon him by the people who had heard his name. How he survived a barren post office with no nourishment falling from magazines and letters is a good question for others to explore. It is true, anyway, that, arrogant in his cabinet privileges and immunities, he was sufficiently bold to come into the back of the privileged area of the post office without any fear of danger or harm from the workers.

Another thing which carried over from the Faulkner administration was our great respect for the postal inspector. The inspector at that time was a Mr. Duncan, from Corinth, Mississippi. He had a key to the back door of the post office, and he was the typical detective. To say that we respected him would be making a mild statement. It might be better to say that we were fearful (and especially after what had happened to Faulkner) of his sudden appearances. This was a part of the system, and is no reflection on Mr. Duncan, who was a very fine inspector.

I regret that, in later years, I never mentioned Mr. Burleson to Faulkner. I think he would have welcomed a full discussion. But I recall an amusing incident a few years ago when I mentioned the post office mouse to a Faulkner scholar from Italy. One Sunday morning a group of old friends met at the popular Gathright-Reed

Drug Store here in Oxford. There we saw Signora Barbarossa, who was in search of information about Mr. Faulkner. Her special interest stemmed from the fact that she had translated several of his books into Italian. Apparently she had already met Mr. Mac Reed and knew what genuine welcome and assistance would be forthcoming at the drug store. It seems that Mr. Reed already knew her mission, and when she entered he proceeded to introduce her to each of the group. Mr. Reed suggested that each one might give a report or tell an anecdote relating to Mr. Faulkner.

Remembering my days as a postal employee, I put "Mr. Burleson" into the report. Mr. Jeff Hamm, business manager of intercollegiate athletics at Ole Miss, then told the story of Mr. Faulkner's resignation from the office of postmaster. Mr. Hamm is well known for his gentlemanly conduct and dignified language; therefore, after the manner of the spicy President Harry S. Truman, he used the initials to quote Faulkner. He said that Faulkner had reported that he became "damned tired of finding himself at the *beck and call* of every s.o.b. that had two cents and wanted to buy a postage stamp." At this point Signora Barbarossa interrupted to say, "*Beck and call!* What is that? Sohn-of-a-beesh I understand!"

CLAUDE MAXWELL SMITH

He Just Wanted To Be Old Bill

*E*arly in January, 1925, Faulkner headed for New Orleans, apparently with the thought in mind of taking a freighter for Europe. But he did not sail until July of that year. With the exception of occasional trips home to Oxford, he spent those six months in New Orleans, where he wrote his first novel, Soldiers' Pay.

Late in 1925 Faulkner returned from Europe, and it was during this period that Claude Maxwell (Tad) Smith first knew him. Smith was then an Ole Miss freshman, and Faulkner, fresh from his tramp abroad, with a book of poetry behind him and a novel ahead, was something of a campus character.

Tad Smith became freshman football coach following his graduation from the University, and later he coached the Ole Miss varsity. He returned from service as an officer in the Navy during World War II to become director of intercollegiate athletics.

The following piece was drawn from a tape recording made by the editors on September 11, 1964.

❧ When I first knew Bill Faulkner (that was in the twenties) I was a freshman at Ole Miss. Bill was not a student; he was just up in the dormitory quite often. In Bob Terry's room. Bob and Bat Mustin would call me in there. I was their freshman. Back in those days you had to wait on them, and rather than take those paddles I was all for it—and still am. They'd take me out of Gordon Hall, the Ole Miss dining hall, and take me up there and make me wait on them. That's all it amounted to.

As I say, I was a freshman. I didn't even know what liquor was! What I knew was moonshine. I remember that Bob Terry was the son of a well-to-do mule trader from Terry, Mississippi, out of Jackson, and they had plenty of money. Bob was several years older than me, and they had alcohol that they got from New Orleans. That's what I'd mix with sugar in glasses that we stole from Gordon Hall. We didn't really steal them; we just borrowed them. Sugar and water and alcohol—and in the morning! My last job before hurrying to class was to give Bill a little drink with sugar and water. He'd lie down and sleep until Bob and Bat got back from class, and then they'd start him all over again. They'd get him to tell them about the trip he had made to Europe. He had gone to Italy or France, or somewhere, on a freighter. I remember Bill did quite a lot of reading. He had something in his hand all the time.

Some mornings on my way to class I'd go through the Lyceum where Bill's father worked, and he'd want to know, "Tad, have you seen Bill?" I was always hard of hearing, especially regarding things of that kind, and I'd tell him no. Bill stayed in the dormitory two or three days at a time. That was the latter part of 1925 or maybe the first part of 1926.* I was about eighteen. I was a little older than Bill's brother Dean, and Bill was about nine years older than me.

George Healy, now of the New Orleans *Times-Picayune*, and I were in school together. George was about a junior my freshman year. He and Branham Hume, the son of the chancellor, were editors of *The Scream*. It was a student publication—sexy little jokes and such. My job for George Healy and Hardy Lott, now a lawyer—both George and Hardy were from Natchez—was to help get material. Old George would make me go out and get some jokes, and he'd take a joke and put it in his language—he was a good writer—and he'd put it in *The Scream*. I had to come up with something that he hadn't heard about; just give him a good idea and he'd go ahead on with the rest of it.

About that time, or a little later, Dean was in school—he was in school with me and he played baseball with me. Bill and their father—Mr. Murry Falkner—were big baseball fans; they'd come out lots of afternoons and watch the Ole Miss baseball team practice. I was on the team at that time. I used to kid Dean and tell him that when he died I'd be the ugliest man in the world. Dean had talent—all those Falkners had talent. None of them would work much. Dean was hedgehopping in one of those old square airplanes, and he'd charge so much on Sunday afternoons to take people for rides. That's how he got killed; it was near Pontotoc. I

---

* Carvel Collins, in his *William Faulkner: New Orleans Sketches* (1958), says that Faulkner returned from Europe at the end of 1925, "reaching Mississippi in time for the Christmas holidays with his family."

think somebody got up in the air and got scared and grabbed the stick or something, and they were killed. What I was leading up to: Dean could draw—he was drawing, or was going to draw, things for Bill's books. They were kind of clannish together.

The Falkner clan, as we called them while I was going to school, were out there on the golf course, arguing and fighting and having fun with those wooden shafts. They were all pretty good golfers. There were four of them: Dean and Bill and John and Jack. Bill, I think, was the oldest. Later on I got to know him more. I hunted and fished with him a little. He was always quiet, as we know. He was the type of person who would be around a campfire sitting back in the shadows, maybe listening; he always looked to me like he was dreaming.

I remember very distinctly that Bill and John had a farm out here in the country. That was sometime in the thirties. Every Fourth of July they'd have a sort of barbecue and singing, and they'd have lots of Negro singers, and they'd start early and go late. They had the old commissary store there. Bill liked to live that type of life, it seemed to me. He'd have eight or ten or twelve colored singers and they'd have some good music and he'd just stand there and listen and dream some more.

There were funny things about Bill. I was very fond of Bill. I knew him and respected him. I've seen many times when he'd pass you right on the street and not see you. I could always tell when he was busy writing a book. His mind was on but one thing, and that was the writing of that book. Lots of other people are that way. I'm that way myself! I could always tell when he was writing a book.

Whether Bill's mother ever read some of his books or not, I don't know. Bill told me he wasn't going to let her read Sanctuary when it came out, but I know she read it later. After Sanctuary came out, I asked him this one night when we were together: "Bill, how come you to write such a nasty book?" To me it was a nasty book. He said, "I had to make a living; I had to make some money, Tad." I always liked to hear Bill talk; I've never heard him ruffled up. He talked in what I called "mealy-mouth" talk—that

soft voice of his never did get ruffled up. You'd be telling jokes that
were nasty—how he got his ideas of a lot of the stuff he wrote, I
don't know—but he'd turn and walk off whenever anybody told a
nasty joke.

Bob Farley, a law professor, and Bill were about the same age,
and Bob liked the same things that Bill liked. They'd go out and
camp together. That was the big thing in those days. Up until
his death Bill had a bunch of cronies around here, including the
sheriff. There were three or four of those people who would go
every year and stay a week or two. Jim Stone, Phil's brother, you
know died on one of them over there. Deer hunting. Old Bill
could tell you about bear hunting. I don't know whether he ever
killed a bear or not, but he'd make you think he had—in that
"mealy-mouth" voice of his.

We went camping up there before the Sardis Reservoir was
made at the mouth of the Tippah. I was with Dr. Bell, the dean
of the School of Commerce. I was kind of Dr. Bell's boy. Bill and
C. D. Bennett and Dink Kelly, some of the characters around
here, and another who was pharmacist in that old drugstore—
he went to Jackson—went along. I don't know whatever happened
to them. They were people about town; and the circuit clerk that
died, and the postmaster that died, they were in that group. Anyway, I'll never forget that night the mosquitoes were so bad that
everybody took his own mosquito bar. We'd get a mattress from
the campus here and put it right on the ground, then fish and then
start cooking the food. We would always take a Negro, Ed Means
from the University dining hall, out there. Bill always had one or
two with him to do the cooking and clean up the camp. Sometimes they'd play poker. I remember one night I was camping
and sleeping under the same mosquito net with Dr. Bell and I
just lay there and listened to them. They didn't have any money
in it, but they were playing for matches and the matches were a
million dollars apiece. They had a gallon of corn whiskey, and
about four or five of them sat there and played poker all night
long: "I bet two million." I can hear them right now. It was the
funniest thing in the world. Bill would sit there, and he'd call.

You'd have to know his voice: he'd just sit there and say, "I call." I never was much of a poker player, and I don't know whether he was a good player or not, but he liked to play.

He wasn't much of a fisherman. He just liked to be out in the open. He'd go out by himself. You see, we'd go out there and they'd say, "We're going to have a stew. Tad, you're supposed to kill three squirrels, and you're supposed to get a bird or two." That was my job for the morning. And they'd throw all of them in that old pot. Bill would just walk off by himself. He never did talk too much. He'd always just stand around in the shadows and watch.

There could be a lot said about Bill and Ross Brown and Dr. Ashford Little and Colonel Hugh Evans, and about that boat they all built.* Bill would go out on the boat and stay by himself. He didn't want anyone to stay with him. He'd just lie around on the boat out on Sardis Reservoir and dream. They named the houseboat the Minmagary, a combination of the names of some of the wives. One Fourth of July—I don't know what year it was—they were having a big party and they had the boat to come in at Cole's Camp on Sardis Lake. They had it so that when you got there in your car they'd be there to take you across to some point and all the old natives were out there. Bill was the captain, and Bill had been up, I think, for two or three nights, but never out of line. He was the captain of that boat. He had on a funny suit of some kind—I don't know what kind of suit it was—with one of those English admiral's hats with a feather on it. He had Coca-Cola tops sticking all around and he was standing at attention all the time to welcome folks aboard. I can still see him! That boat! He used to have a lot of pleasure out of that boat. He'd go out there by himself. Remember that the road was pretty bad: he had a Jeep, and he'd get in that old Jeep. He was liable to try to climb a tree in it; it didn't make much difference with Bill. When he got back didn't make any difference. The boat just disappeared, and they don't know what happened to it. And on a little body of water like that!

* Faulkner and his friends built this boat in the latter part of 1947 and the early part of the following year. See Appendix.

It just disappeared like a ghost. I can still see Bill at the gangplank welcoming the people aboard—and never out of line—just like a statue—and with those Coca-Cola buttons and Orange Crush buttons stuck all over his coat, and this hat stuck out like that with a feather in it!

Along about that time he got his own little sailboat, and he might get in that boat and get way out and if the wind quit blowing, it didn't bother Bill. He'd just stay out there until the wind came up again. You never did know where Bill would be or how Bill would be.

I like to think of Bill. I enjoy talking about Bill. He was a part of the community. He didn't always pay his bills on time—not that he wanted to beat you out of anything—he didn't want to be bothered. He knew what he wanted, and money didn't mean anything to him. He didn't want people to think of him as a writer. He just wanted to be Old Bill. His wanting to be buried in a pine box—that was just Bill. The glory and all that didn't mean a thing to Bill Faulkner. He would have been just as contented in a forest.

THOMAS D. CLARK

The Greenskeeper

*T*homas D. Clark, born in Louisville, Mississippi, and graduated bachelor of arts by the University of Mississippi, is now one of the country's leading historians. He is the author of a number of important books, among them Frontier America and The Emerging South.

Since 1931 Professor Clark has been a member of the University of Kentucky faculty. He is a former president of the Southern Historical Association, and he was for several years managing editor of the Journal of Southern History.

In "The Greenskeeper" he returns in memory to his early days in advanced education and to a minor writer who became a distinguished novelist.

❧ My association with William Faulkner was that of a greenskeeper on a country golf course where people had no knowledge of grass greens and only a limited knowledge of golf. In the fall of 1925 I entered the University of Mississippi as a freshman. Earlier in the year I had written to Dr. Peter Rowland, professor of materia medica in the little two-year medical school, asking if I might have the job as greenskeeper. I did not know what a golf course was, but one of my teachers in the high school said he thought I might be able to get this job to help pay my expenses. My second afternoon at Ole Miss I went out to the golf course to see if there was any possibility of my having the job. A tall, stately man literally thrust a grass-lined drag into my hand and told me I was greenskeeper. It was "Uncle Peter" Rowland.

Sometime later during my freshman year a short little man dressed in baggy, worn golfknickers showed up on the golf course with Dr. Rowland. He was only a few years older than me (I was then in my early twenties), but his hair was graying and he had a funny mustache. I learned that the little man's name was Faulkner, and that he was the son of Mr. Murry Falkner, the business manager of the University.

The golf course at the University of Mississippi in those days was like none other in the country—not even in Scotland could such a course be found. It lay out back of the frowning pile of brick called Gordon Hall, and behind the baseball field. It was up beyond the steep bank which lined the muddy Sardis road. No doubt the poor scrawny fairways had once been a cottonfield, but the ground was so badly eroded and so poor that it scarcely grew bitter-weeds and bermuda grass. There were nine holes which wound around clumps of trees and across three little branches. Some of the fairways ranged down sidling slopes, and others went over steep hogbacks. It was hard to tell at times where fairways ended and roughs began—it was all rough. The greens were stomped out clay hardpans which had small mud embankments around to keep the sand from being washed away every time it rained. Periodically we placed a new coat of sand on the hardpans and dampened it down with spent motor oil.

As greenskeeper I had four jobs: to cut the "fairways," to keep the "greens" raked, to take in membership dues, and to keep poachers off the course. I shoveled sand, rescued it from the low corners, sprinkled oil, and cut grass and raked leaves. Often I had as helpers Bill Faulkner and a little Negro boy we called "Willie"; I never knew what his name actually was. Bill worked on the course partly for exercise, partly because he tried to help improve it, and maybe because he liked to be off with a couple of lads who asked no questions. There might have been another reason—there were three big water holes on the course, and we learned from Willie that these were good places to find lost balls knocked there by the sporty duffers, and Bill was not averse to picking up a few stray balls to replenish his own slender stock.

For almost three years Bill, Willie, and I fought sand, oil, grass and leaves, and trampled the water holes barefooted. Sometimes Bill would be talkative and we discussed such weighty subjects as how scrubby the grass was, how cantankerous oiled sand was once it got packed down into a corner, or how thick leaves were around a green, or how many balls Willie had found in the big water hole down the hill below the monument where the Confederate and other Civil War dead were buried. This monument was over the fence on top of the hill behind the third tee. We were more interested, however, in the fact that the medical students sometimes buried the finely whittled remains of their cadavers there. When he was in a good humor Bill was a talkative man. He seemed to enjoy our company. At other times he was as silent as the Confederate monument. He seemed to be in what Mississippians called "a deep brown study."

We knew that Bill Faulkner had written a couple of little books and that he was a literary man, but that was all we knew. He would come out and play golf and go around the course ignoring Willie and me. It was truly marvelous to see him play by us as though we were complete strangers. There were times when he would play with the Oxford lawyer Phil Stone, and at times he would play with Miss Ella Somerville and Dorothy Oldham. Sometimes, not often, he might fill in for the old duffer foursome of old university deans who pawed their way around the course, improving their lie both on the ground and score card by fudging on strokes. They, however, felt above playing with their colleague's trifling son.

Bill was a good golf player when he tightened up his game and got down to brass tacks. He knew every gully, stump hole, and clump of weeds on the course. As time went on I began to hear all sorts of funny stories about my friend of the golf course. The old post-office stories were told and retold. He had been into other scrapes around the community. I knew that many evenings he could be found down in the University power plant. He perhaps had a job firing the boilers there at one time. I am not sure. Anyway he had a tenuous sort of friendship with two brothers named Furr. One of them was a big, harried-looking man who constituted almost the entire technical staff of the buildings and grounds department. He actually had more degrees than many members of the faculty. His brother carried far fewer responsibilities on his shoulders. In fact, the only responsibility any student ever saw him bearing was a bulbous rubber cup mounted on the end of a long stick with which he administered to the aged plumbing in the ramshackled old dormitories. Everybody on the campus, in any way connected with the staff of the University, service or otherwise, was called "Dr."; so no doubt Bill Faulkner enjoyed this distinction along with his companions of the heating plant, the "Drs." Furr.

Sometimes we would go to town in Oxford to look around on Saturday nights. We would go by a little old "greasy spoon" restaurant near the depot to splurge on fried oyster sandwiches, and then we would climb the winding path up through the Negro houses between the railroad and town. Occasionally I would see Faulkner along that path. He seemed to have the same love of getting around on Saturday night as did all other rural Mississippians. In fact, the Falkners lived "right up in town."

Occasionally Bill Faulkner would go off for several weeks, or even months, at a time. I remember on one or two of these extended absences he would say that he had been down in New Orleans visiting. I had no way of knowing that it was perhaps on some of these visits that he himself was first becoming aware of the renascence of Southern writing. He never said whom he visited, what he learned, if anything, or what he did. He had just been, so far as I was concerned, off down in New Orleans looking around. Never do I remember Faulkner saying one thing about writing, or showing any curiosity about what was going on in the University, or what I was studying. Our world was strictly the nether side of golf, keeping up the fairways, greens, and finding lost balls.

By my third year at the University I had come to know Faulkner fairly well so far as his golfing was concerned. I long ago had become adjusted to his eccentricities, and his coming and going on the course. I enjoyed being with him, even when he lapsed into one of his deep silent moods. It did not take a whole lot of conversation to get along in lifting sand and running lawn mowers. There was one thing I did know, and this much showed through clearly: Bill Faulkner was a man who had certain qualities about him which did not seem present in any of my other customers. He had a certain kind of sophistication about him which belied the general regard with which most people seemed to hold him. I thought it was all due to the careless, irresponsible existence which he seemed to lead. He might come out to the golf course early in the morning and play all morning long by himself, or he might come along late in the afternoon. Time seemed not to mean anything to him. He appeared to live independent of the tyranny of the clock.

One afternoon I was startled when he came over where I was putting up the tools in a shed near the first tee. He said he had lost his golf clubs under the most mysterious circumstances. Apparently he had held the clubs in his hand one moment and they were gone the next. He had stopped to get a drink of water out of a spigot and the clubs vanished while he had his back turned. For almost two months after that we searched high and low for those clubs. We emptied the tool house; we searched under the floor of a little old shelter just back of the tee; we looked up and down the road, and searched every fairway on the course. We all but waded barefoot through our productive water holes looking for those clubs. The exasperating thing was that Bill had had them in his hands and they had disappeared in less than a minute. So far as he knew there was no one else around. Willie and I began to think he suspected us of some antic. I left the University in the early summer of 1928 to attend summer school at the University of Virginia without having found Faulkner's clubs. He was out of play until he could recover them because he was too poor, he said, to buy others.

I left my chores as caretaker of the sandy old golf course in June that year with genuine nostalgia; I parted with Bill Faulkner and Willie with a touch of real sadness. There was still the unsolved mystery of the lost clubs, a story which was not ended with my departure for Virginia. In high school I had become enamored of the idea of fox hunting and set out to assemble a pack of fox hounds. This involved me in a fascinating bit of correspondence with both white and Negro potlikker hound-raisers. The first dogs I bought developed running fits, and within twenty-four hours they had all run off and died. Because of this misfortune I became disenchanted with the sport, but I could not stop the hound-dog raisers from writing me. All through college I would get greasy, smoky little old envelopes containing illiterate notes telling me that an old bitch down near Ackerman, Weir, or Louisville had whelped and I could have the lot for a cheap price. Soon after I arrived in Charlottesville there was another crumpled and soiled little old envelope, and I knew the hound dogs in Mississippi were still thriving. I was startled when I tore it open to find that it was from Bill Faulkner, and it was not a nostalgic greeting from an old friend either.

Bill had found his golf clubs. He had spotted them in the hands of a geology professor, and when Bill challenged the professor directly he was at a loss to explain how he had come by the clubs. Then he thought he remembered that I had loaned them to him. In a righteous fit of anger Bill accused me of double-crossing him, and even suggested that perhaps I had loaned the professor his clubs at a price. That letter angered me as much as Bill's finding the clubs had angered him, and while the bloom of temper was in full burst I gave him a piece of my mind. I felt that I was being assaulted by a fellow that I had gone way out of line of duty to try to help. I wish I could recall really what I did say, but whatever it was I singed him. I did, however, try to tell him that if I had ever said more than "thank you" to the professor when he paid his dues I did not then recall it. One thing was clear: I had not loaned him Bill Faulkner's golf clubs. I then wrote the professor in high dudgeon. In about ten days I received a second letter from Faulkner. This time he was most apologetic about the first letter. After talking with the geology professor further he discovered that he had picked up his clubs while Bill was over getting a drink of water and could never exactly account for the fact that somehow or other he had come by a strange set of golf clubs. All these years I have wondered where the professor left his own clubs.

In the fall of 1929, after I had enrolled in the Graduate School at Duke University, I went over to Chapel Hill to call on Arthur Palmer Hudson and his family. Mr. Hudson was one of my favorite professors at Ole Miss, and he had helped me more possibly than he was able to help Bill Faulkner. In his living room I saw a copy of the *Atlantic Monthly*, and on the back of it was a book advertisement with a very good picture of Bill Faulkner. I would not have been more surprised if I had seen Willie's picture on that magazine cover. In fact I might have thought at times that Willie had a better go at fame than Bill because Willie was a genius at finding lost balls, and an even better one when it came to getting his price for them. I knew then that somehow Bill Faulkner had arrived, and soon there were many reviews and comments on his books.

The next summer I was back in Oxford for a brief visit with Charles S. Sydnor of the Department of History, and for old time's sake I played a round of golf on that barren waste that I had cut on, scraped, replaced, and mowed so many times. Going over the high hogback along the "high and windy" branch of the Illinois Central Railroad to the fourth "green" I met the famous old University foursome of deans. I remarked that I had seen where our Bill was becoming famous; he was getting his picture in all sorts of highbrow publications. One of them stepped over to me and, shielding his mouth with his hand, said, "We don't talk about him around here."

I saw Bill Faulkner only once after I left the University in 1928. In 1955, Philip Davidson, president of the University of Louisville, and I presided over a general dinner meeting of the Southern Historical Association in Memphis in a comical program arrangement. There was a great deal of tension over the race question following the Supreme Court decision of 1954. On the program were a Nashville attorney, Cecil Simms; Benjamin Mays, president of Morehouse College in Atlanta; and Bill Faulkner. Faulkner had stirred resentment over some letters he had recently published in the Memphis *Commercial Appeal*, and Benjamin Mays, a Negro, was to sit down to dinner at a public meeting in the Peabody Hotel. There was a rumor that the hotel looked on this with disfavor and that there would be an invasion of "minute women" from somewhere. It seemed that we would never get clearance to proceed with the meeting. Bill Faulkner was there on the mezzanine and in a lull in the excitement I introduced myself to him and tried to tell him that I had worked with him for three years on the golf course at Ole Miss. He gave me a vacant stare, and I quickly saw that we were back on the golf course in Oxford on a hazy Indian summer afternoon and that Bill was off somewhere in a "deep brown study." As for his speech that evening, I think both Willie and I would have agreed that he was a lot more interesting when we talked of such simple things as sand, leaves, weeds, and the price of second-hand golf balls. He was, it seemed to me, disjointedly in love with his fellow men collectively and blithely indifferent to them as individuals.

WILLIAM EVANS STONE, V

Our Cotehouse

*S*oldiers' Pay, *published with the help of Sherwood Anderson, appeared in February of 1926. Later that year Faulkner wrote* Mosquitoes, *his second novel, which was published in the spring of 1927. He spent some time on the Mississippi coast and paid another visit to New Orleans.*

In "Our Cotehouse," William Evans (Jack) Stone, V, then a boy in North Mississippi, now a banker in Meridian, recalls those years—and especially the visits of William Faulkner and his Uncle Phil.

Mr. Stone left Ole Miss during World War II to serve in the artillery, but transferred to flying and attained the rank of captain. His plane was shot down over Germany and he was a prisoner of war for two years. Even though he had not been born when World War I erupted, Mr. Stone, as a member of the Cross and Cockade Society of World War One Historians, is making a study of Faulkner's experiences during that war.

ℰ I last saw Bill Faulkner in the Gathright-Reed Drug Store in late 1960. I was in Oxford on a visit and in the evening after supper had gone to visit with Mac Reed at the drugstore, which had been my custom when I lived in Oxford. Mac and I would converse and, while he was waiting on customers, I would browse among the newspapers and magazines. At that time there was a comic strip in the Jackson *Daily News* called "Captain Easy and Wash Tubbs." Evidently the artist had been making a trip through the Southland collecting authentic background for the strip. On this particular evening, as I was looking at the strip and Mac was waiting on a customer, I recognized in the background our Oxford courthouse. I showed the picture to Mac, and he agreed that it must be our courthouse.

Mac went back to customers and I to my reading. Shortly afterward Bill walked in. It was a cold, misty night. He was wearing his trench coat, a favorite garment since his Royal Canadian Air Force days. He was talking to Mac about some purchase or other as I walked over to speak. . . . I showed him the comic strip and he commented in his soft voice, "Why that does look like our cotehouse!" Contrary to what many people think, nothing about Bill was affected—certainly not his Southern pronunciation. He lived and spoke the way he wanted to live and speak. He had that natural quality long before he was exposed to the light of fame.

My last meeting with Bill, for nostalgic reasons, couldn't have been in a better place, Mac Reed's drugstore; nor could we have discussed a better subject, our "cotehouse" just across the square.

My first remembrance of Bill was his visiting with us in Charleston, Mississippi. He would come over from Oxford with my Uncle Phil Stone in Uncle Phil's Model T Ford, the real sports car of its day, equipped with white wire wheels. In those days of gravel roads, around 1926-27, that was quite a trip; so they usually spent a night or two. Bill was then about twenty-nine. Because he was a family friend, I was encouraged to call him Bill.

Bill had been in the Royal Air Force Canada during World War I and had been in an airplane accident. The story I remember from my Uncle Phil is that, as a result of the accident, he had a silver plate in his head; this fact made a lifelong impression on me, then a child of five.*

* Much Faulkner apocrypha is built upon stories such as this. Probably Phil Stone, to entertain his young nephew, improved on the fact that Faulkner, while still in training in Canada during World War I, crashed a plane into a hangar.

On these visits, my uncle and my father, law partners, would discuss the business of the firm while Bill would entertain my sisters and me by telling us stories; or he would play golf on the local links. The golf course has long ago been plowed up and turned into pasture, but in those days it was quite a center of attraction. It was sponsored by a large lumber mill then in operation in Charleston. Bill also did some golfing on the University golf course, but the links at Charleston gave him variety in his game.

Another vivid impression that I still have is that of Bill sitting at my mother's dinner table in a rust-colored Harris tweed jacket with a red bandana in his pocket. In those early years, I doubt whether I should have known an Englishman from a Hottentot, but I think that Bill was wavering between clothing himself as an English country gentleman and a Mississippi hill farmer. I know that in later life I often saw him in a once-expensive tweed jacket with leather patches at the elbows—and a pair of khaki pants. I am sure that most people thought this incongruous outfit to be an affectation, but I am rather of the opinion that it was Bill's method of identifying himself with the aristocracy—and he was to the manner born—and also with the hill farmers of North Mississippi, for whom he had great compassion. He considered himself to be foremost a farmer. Bill, at various times in his early years, had contact with the English, and I think that he was something of an Anglophile. His first association with the English and their way of life was with the Royal Air Force in Canada and later on a trip to Europe. Such contact, together with his wide range of reading, most likely cultivated his fondness for tweeds, pipes, and riding to the hounds. His courtly and refined manner was a heritage from his Southern aristocratic forebears, and I think his mode of life would have been the same without his British associations. It is a matter of historical record that most of the landed gentry of the South were descendants of the original colonists from the British Isles; they would, therefore, follow British customs and manners, and love the land, and have pride of family.

Until my teens I spent every summer in Pascagoula, Mississippi, with my family. In those days the trip from North Mississippi to the Mississippi Gulf Coast took two days of hard travel. As the family was large and because we took lots of baggage for a long summer's stay, sometimes we made the trip in two cars. Bill went with us several summers. My memories of him at this period are more vivid than they are of his visits to Charleston. This is the first time that I knew him to be a writer or thought of him as such.

The people of Charleston, Oxford, and Pascagoula were not so cosmopolitan as they are now, and, if a man did not have a regular job, they thought it a bit odd. Except for the local paper editors and the university professors, nobody had an excuse for writing just for the sake of writing. Even the editors and professors were considered to have a more primary purpose in life than that of writing. As a child, however, as I watched Bill work, it seemed to me to be the most natural thing in the world. My only thought was not that it was strange for him to write but that he was a guest of the family—a part of the family—and a good companion.

Bill would take our friends and my sisters and me on walks along the beach to look for soft shell crabs. In the evening families and friends would visit each other. When visitors came to our place, Bill would take all the children to one end of the porch, while the grown folks visited, and keep us spellbound with stories such as only he could tell. Some of the stories were well-known childhood fairy tales, but others, I am sure, were of his own making. He told them in a manner that kept us wide-eyed until bedtime and dreaming into the night of high adventure. I shall never forget his rendition of Washington Irving's "The Headless Horseman." I still read it from time to time, but it will never be the same without Bill's magic of presentation and the wonderful time of childhood as the setting.

The beach at Pascagoula is now built up with a seawall and homes costing in the thousands, and the land sells by the front foot. In those happy days most of the homes, called camps, were of rough frame construction with windows all around. The windows were kept open to admit the breeze but fixed so they could be quickly shut when the sudden summer rain squalls appeared. The plumbing was of the rustic outdoor type, but we had running water and electricity. A few families who lived on the beach all year long had permanent, indoor plumbing. One summer, the camps having all been taken, we rented one of the larger permanent homes, a large frame one-story affair with screened porch on two sides. The house was about a hundred feet from the beach, and the front yard was filled with live oak trees and oleanders, making the yard shady most of the day. The house was known as the Baird Place, named for a family from New Orleans who had built it as a summer place. Pete Baird, long-time feature and editorial writer on the New Orleans *Times-Picayune*, was a member of the family. Bill had known the Bairds previously in New Orleans and Pascagoula and had dedicated one of his books, *Mosquitoes*, to Helen Baird, Pete's sister.

The live oaks in the front yard had wooden benches built around their trunks. Bill used one of the benches as a writing surface; he sat on a camp stool. His best time to work was in the early afternoon when the children were all taking a nap and were not around clamoring for his attention. I remember one conversation —I must have been about six or seven—while he was writing. I asked him whether he got any money for what he was doing. He told me that sometimes he got a nickel and sometimes a dime. In those days, to a child of six or seven, a nickel or a dime conjured up visions of candy bars, ice cream, or fare to the picture show. To me at least, the reward seemed well worth the effort.

Bill, like any other human being, had faults along with good qualities. Because he was a man of renown, it was easy for some to magnify his faults and play down his strengths. Such is human nature. Having known him when I was a child, having observed him as a family friend for some forty years, and having seen him with my own children, I can say authoritatively that I have never known a man with a gentler approach to, and appreciation of, children. He was the personification of the Christian doctrine,

"Suffer little children to come unto me." My happy childhood was enriched for knowing him.

The Falkners and the Stones have known each other for some four generations. My grandfather, General James Stone, had known Bill's grandfather, J. W. T. Falkner, the "Young Colonel," and Bill's father Murry. My father, W. E. Stone, Uncle Jim, and Uncle Phil had known Bill and his brothers, Jack (Murry), John, and Dean. My grandfather was a lawyer who rode a white horse to his office each morning. He was born in Batesville in Panola County, adjoining Lafayette County. After studying law at the University, he moved to Oxford, while still a young man, to practice. He purchased a large, two-story, white-columned home on the edge of town on what was then the College Hill Road. The home had been built by a family named Avant long before the War Between the States; the land is adjacent to the University campus. The house had been spared during the burning of Oxford because it was being used by Federal troops as a headquarters. Mute testimony of this was an inscription of a name and date on a window pane in one of the bedrooms, said to have been scratched with a diamond. As I remember, the last name was Grant. I always said that this was a relative of U. S. Grant—it makes a good story anyhow. In the 1940's the house was destroyed by fire. Now there is nothing but the charred remains of a glorious era.

The Stones had come from Georgia and South Carolina long before the War and had settled in Panola County. General Stone owned some of the original Stone-settled land in the rich bottom of the Tallahatchie River and maintained a hunting camp there. In the middle twenties and early thirties it was reached by travel over a rail line that had been laid earlier to get out the virgin hardwood growing in the rich bottomlands. At this time, however, the good timber had been cut out and the railroad equipment used for hauling timber had been abandoned. Still operating was a gasoline engine bus on railroad wheels that served the farm settlers and hunters going into the bottomlands. The whole area was still

populated with wild game: squirrel, possum, coon, deer, bear, wild-
cat, and panther.

General Stone gave a deer hunt each year at this camp. The
place at which we got off the bus-train was called Stone Stop. It
consisted of nothing but the beginning of a road that led from
the railroad to the camphouse about a mile away. The journey
to the camphouse down this road was by mule and wagon. At this
time of the year, late fall and early winter, the road was almost
always muddy.

Bill went on a number of these hunts. I remember his being
there on the one or two occasions that my father took me. After
my grandfather and Uncle Jim died, the hunts were abandoned.
The land has now been cleared of timber and planted in crops.
The annual floods have been controlled by government program;
communities are served by paved roads and electricity; and there
is not a panther within 150 miles. Some of Bill's stories are of
hunts in the Mississippi Delta. Hunters, he says, must look for
new hunting grounds as the land is settled, cleared, and farmed.
I've read somewhere—no one in my family told me—that the
annual deer hunt of my grandfather was the inspiration for the
deer hunts of Bill's Major DeSpain.

The closest Falkner-Stone friendship was that between Bill
and my Uncle Phil. There was a difference of several years in their
ages, which created a larger gap in their youth than it did later.
The tremendous mental power possessed by each of these men,
however, overcame the age gap.

All the Falkner boys were SAE's, including Bill. Uncle Jim,
John Faulkner, and Bill attended many a sub-rosa meeting of the
brotherhood during the period that fraternities were banned at
Ole Miss.* Sometimes these meetings were held by the light of
the moon in one of Uncle Jim's cornfields, and I am not sure that
a rousing possum or coon hunt did not take place following the
formal rituals.

* Lee M. Russell, a one-time law partner of the Falkner boys' grandfather, banned
fraternities after he became governor of Mississippi in 1920. The SAE's went underground.

I had known Bill's nephews, Jimmy and M. C. (Chooky) Faulkner, while living in Oxford, but my closest friendship with the family was with Malcolm Franklin, Bill's stepson. Bill had married Miss Estelle in 1929 and came to Pascagoula with her and her two children, Malcolm and Victoria (ChoCho) to spend the summer. My family and I were spending the summer there. This was several years after the summer at the Baird Place. The families saw a lot of each other, especially the children. I had an older sister the same age as Malcolm's sister ChoCho, and, though Malcolm was a few years younger than I, we started what has remained a lifelong friendship. Bill and his family did not return to Pascagoula the next summer; so I did not see Malcolm again until I moved to Oxford in 1936. Jimmy and Chooky still live in or near Oxford, but Malcolm has left and I have left. The fourth generation of friendships of Falkners and Stones will be like the annual hunts at General Stone's camp, lost in time and dimmed by fading memories. . . .

When we first moved to Oxford we lived in the old Stone home with my Grandmother Stone, my Uncle Phil, and his wife. My grandfather had died just before we moved to Oxford. In this house I saw my favorite picture of Bill. It had been taken on a trip to Europe when he was a young man. This snapshot, reproduced many times in magazines and books about him, depicts Bill sitting on a bench—in Paris, I think—dressed in tweeds, sporting a full beard, and smoking his pipe.

Uncle Phil once told me a story about Bill and that European trip. It seems that before Bill left home, his mother, Miss Maud, sewed a twenty-dollar gold piece in the lining of his coat and told him that she had done so, so that he might have something to fall back on if he got hungry. After his return he told his mother that on several occasions he had been without funds and had gone hungry. She asked him whether he had used the twenty-dollar gold piece that she had sewn in his coat lining. Bill, who was wearing the same coat, felt the lining, and there was the gold coin. He had forgotten all about it. . . .

Later we moved from the old Stone house to a house on Second South Street. On Bill's way to town I would see him when he passed by our house. Sometimes he was preoccupied and would acknowledge my greeting with no more than a nod, and at other times he would stop and exchange pleasantries. On most of these trips to town, Bill would be on his way to Mac Reed's drugstore. Mac was an old friend of the Falkners and Stones. I think Mac and my Uncle Phil were closer to Bill than anyone outside his family. Bill as a young man, according to one story, would go to town, stop at Gathright-Reed's, "hunker down" in front of the magazine rack, and while away the hours in reading, oblivious of the comings and goings of the countless customers. I know the pleasure he must have derived from this because I have had the same experience, and count, right along with the University library, Mac Reed's magazine rack as one of the founts of knowledge of my youth.

Bill and my Uncle Phil smoked pipes. I remember, as a little boy, seeing them load and tamp their pipes with a mixture, popular then, called Blue Boar. I remember this brand mostly because it came packed in a heavy, lead-foil wrapper which my uncle would give me when he had used up a package. After World War II, when I was discussing pipe tobacco mixtures with Mac Reed, he reached up on a shelf and took down a round tin of tobacco and told me to give it a trial. He said that Bill had asked him to stock it; several University students were also buying it. The name of the tobacco was Balkan Sobranie; it was, as I remember, an imported English mixture. At another time when I was visiting Malcolm and we were talking to Bill in his study—I think he referred to it as his office—he had a piece of newspaper spread on the table and was blending his own mixture.

During the four years that I lived in Oxford, Bill's fame was becoming more widespread and he was being recognized by more people. In Oxford he was still just a friend and neighbor whose efforts were coming into their own, and we were glad for him. . . .

Bill has gone now, and many of his friends and contemporaries have passed on. They still remember him in Oxford, though, and will for a long time—at least as long as our "cotehouse" stands in the middle of the square, itself a symbolic connection with the past, the future, and William Faulkner.

JOHN REED HOLLEY

Halloweens at Rowan Oak

*J*n 1929 William Faulkner published two major works: Sartoris, the first of the Yoknapatawpha novels, and The Sound and the Fury. Both were rejected before he finally found a publisher; neither sold, but The Sound and the Fury earned him his first serious attention.

In the summer of that year Faulkner married the girl he had courted a dozen years or so earlier. The Falkners and the Oldhams had lived just down the street from each other before Murry Falkner moved his family out to the Ole Miss campus. When William married Estelle Oldham Franklin, he also became the father of Estelle's two children by her first marriage.

"Halloweens at Rowan Oak" is the reminiscence of a native of Oxford who was in the same age group as Malcolm and Victoria (Cho-Cho) Franklin. John Reed Holley is assistant director of intercollegiate athletics at the University of Mississippi.

This interview was taped on September 11, 1964.

❦ My first recollection of Mr. Bill Faulkner is of the days when he and Miss Estelle were courting. I don't know my exact age at that time. I was right in between Malcolm and ChoCho; we were all in the same playout group after supper. And my first recollection, I guess, of Mr. Bill is of the stories that he and Miss Estelle would both tell us—just entertaining the children, to keep us from running around out in the street after dark. Most of the time they were ghost stories. I think that's what the kids would call them. And I'll say this: Miss Estelle was, in my estimation, just as good a storyteller as Mr. Bill.

At that time all of us lived on South Street, and I guess I was about eight or ten years old. I'm just guessing because, as I say, I don't remember the exact stories or the exact time, but it was customary during those days, when we didn't have television or radio, for all the kids to congregate in somebody's yard, and we congregated in the Oldham yard or in the old Oldham house. Miss Estelle was living there with her mother and father and her two children by her first marriage. There were semicircular steps up to the main part of the house with columns, and we sat on those steps, and they would try to entertain us after we had probably run ourselves to death. I imagine that if we got too hot or it was getting later in the evening, there'd just be ten or twelve of us around, kids I knew.

I guess we all admired, or thought about, Mr. Bill—as kids will do—because he had been in the RAF and was a pilot. And a pilot in those days, a man who flew, was something that I think even the general public looked on as not a curiosity but something that was different from the man who drove the T-model Ford. He told us stories of his experiences in the RAF and about flying, which we were all interested in. Mr. Bill talked a lot about flying in those days, but I think he probably shied away from it after Dean's death.

Mr. Bill and Miss Estelle weren't married at this time—I mean in the twenties. And that's my first recollection of him. Of course, after they got married, then we were together again as children and they always had a big Halloween party down at their big house.

Outside and inside they went to a great deal of preparation for the kids and to impress us, and, of course, it was always dark, winding in the roads. There weren't any streetlights. It was quite an event for all of the kids in town, really, to go down there. I remember that Mr. Bill told a story sitting on the steps just inside the door, the story that every Halloween night the bride came down the steps and the chains rattled, and, of course, we heard the chain rattling. Then he asked if any of us would like to go out and see the grave. And those of us who had nerve enough to go followed along and went out and he showed a so-called grave (I don't knew whether it was a grave or not) under two cedar trees out beyond the horse lot, quite a way from the house. I think I walked out there with Mr. Bill and several of the boys. None of the girls in the crowd went out that I remember.

The stories he told were vivid: I believed them. That's what I mean by "good storyteller." The ghost story on Halloween night was dramatized. The showmanship and everything else was there because the chains rattled and we saw a white sheet out under the magnolia trees to represent a ghost, and it would move. I guess that was one of the Negroes dressed up. But the animation was there. Some of a story comes back about a soldier from the North and a girl from the South who fell in love but couldn't marry. One grave at Rowan Oak is that of the man, but the girl was buried there too. In other words, there were two graves.

Right after Gena and I had gotten married, Joan Williams, who has written a novel and is now Mrs. Ezra Bowen, drove down with her date to visit us. She was very much interested in writing,* and I really think that the main reason for the visit was to meet Bill Faulkner. It was a dreary fall day, beginning to drizzle as it does in Oxford, and after lunch she asked me if I knew William Faulkner and if I would call him and introduce her to him. I, of course, knew Mr. Bill's feeling on introductions and how much he stayed away from the public eye, but I called him anyhow. He told me that he was going to the lake to sail. I don't believe it was raining at the time. I called him later on in the afternoon, I'd

* Joan Williams is the author of The Morning and the Evening.

say at three or four o'clock. The drizzle was on and Mr. Bill told me that he would be happy to meet Joan and her date but that he'd already made plans to go—in fact, was on his way out to the lake at that time.

Joan was then planning to go to college and was trying to select her school but hadn't yet decided. We got to the telephone conversation, and I told her what Mr. Bill had said, that he might be going to the lake, and might not be, but that we would wait until four or five o'clock and if he got back we'd go down. When four or five o'clock came around and he hadn't called me, they decided they wanted to ride around and go down to see the house. We got in the car and I just drove on in, drove up to the house so she could see it, although the sign "No Trespassing" was there.

I happened to look out in the horse lot and there was Mr. Bill in his T-shirt playing with the horses, I guess, or tending them. When I saw him out there, I got out of the car and, in the drizzle, walked over to the lot. He met me at the fence, and I told him that Joan was in the car and I would appreciate it if he would come over and speak to her. He was most cordial and said he would, but, on the way over to the car, he said, "Well, what does she want to see? Why does she want to meet me? Does she want to see if I have two heads?" "I don't think so," I replied with a laugh. "She would just like to meet you." Well, he stood at the car and talked to Joan and all of us, and he asked Gena about our baby, and we left.

On the way back home, I told Joan what Mr. Bill had said on the way to the car. She got a big kick out of it, and when she got back to Memphis she wrote him a letter and said that she, by no means, came to Oxford to see if he had two heads; she just wanted to meet him. He answered her letter and they carried on a correspondence. When he went to Memphis, he called Joan and went out to the house, and, on another occasion, he had Joan and her mother for dinner when he was in Memphis. Joan told me on this last trip that when Mr. Bill was in New York he had called her and Ezra and had gone out to the house to visit them. So they struck up quite a friendly relationship from the visit down here, and I think that he probably advised Joan on pursuing her writing. I've never heard her say whether she sent him a copy of her novel or whether he read it. I don't think she sent him the manuscript. I don't believe that Mr. Bill would have read it. Knowing him, I don't believe he would. Yet there were manuscripts in his office on his desk that he had not read, or had not returned, that he probably had kept for ten years.

That was quite an experience. Mr. Bill never did mention it any more to me.

When I've seen him on the street, sometimes he would speak and want to chat, but the next time he didn't even see me when I spoke to him. I've seen him going to the Oxford post office when I was going there to get my mail—sometimes two or three times a week. One time he'd want to stop on the steps and talk, but the next time he just ignored me. But that never bothered me. I have never thought of him as a writer or a town character or anything else. He was just Bill Faulkner.

J. W. (BILL) HARMON

Hometown Actor

What a man of William Faulkner's retiring nature would have taken part in a theatrical production, even a hometown theatrical production, would seem a patent contradiction. But, then, Faulkner was a man of contradictions. It might also be noted that while enrolled at Ole Miss in 1920 he had been associated with a student dramatic group.

In the sketch which follows, a friend who saw several sides of him
recalls that Faulkner once played the lead in a play called Corporal
Egan. J. W. (Bill) Harmon, a graduate of Ole Miss who served with
the American Red Cross during World War II, for a time owned a
men's shop which Faulkner patronized. He is now a member of the
Oxford Insurance Agency.

The interview with Mr. Harmon was taped on September 11, 1964,
and was somewhat amplified by conversations with J. Byron Gathright,
one of those who played supporting roles to Faulkner's "Corporal
Egan." Mr. Gathright is a partner in the Gathright-Reed Drug Store.

꙰ It was a long time ago—and it's difficult to recall the circumstances—when Bill Faulkner was in a play in Oxford. The play
was Corporal Egan. It was one of those things for which you get
a franchise. They made use of local talent—and Bill played Corporal Egan, which was the leading part. It's been so long ago that
I can't remember who was in it. George Buffaloe was one of the
characters. I can't even remember the year the play was put on.
I would give an approximate date sometime around 1929. Bill
bought Rowan Oak in 1930 and was busy restoring the place
about then.

The first night's performance went off on schedule, but a deluge
of rain on the second night made it appear that Corporal Egan
would be a financial failure. The lady who had come to Oxford
to produce the play was, therefore, asked to remain in town and
give the play on a third night. She did so.

The auditorium in the Oxford Elementary School, where the
play was presented, has a dressing room with a window in each
wing, one on the east and another on the west. One window was
kept open and a ladder was placed outside. At the back of the
building, outside steps led to a concrete platform at the entrance
to the boiler room. Sometime before the play was to begin, Ernest,
the shoeshine boy at the barber shop, took a gallon jug of corn

liquor to the platform, where he set up a bar with cups and ice. Before, during, and after each scene and act, the players kept the ladder hot in going to and returning from the bar. During the entire evening Corporal Egan and all the other players ad-libbed and were hilarious. The play was a glorious success. I remember that we all commented on how well Bill Faulkner played his part.

There was a ballet chorus to get the interest of local girls. I don't remember the theme of the play, but I do remember one thing: George Buffaloe, who was very thin, was supposed to be hiding under a pile of stovewood. Corporal Egan (Faulkner) looked at it very hard and made some comment about the "nigger in the woodpile." Faulkner then extemporaneously made the re- mark that there was no woodpile and, in the second place, there was no nigger there—or something like that, which almost brought the house down with laughter.

Bill was an unusual man. I remember he had insurance with my company on his automobile—on the jeep—and liability insurance on his property. The jeep was sitting down by the house. A hail- storm beat down on the top and almost ruined it while he was away as writer-in-residence at the University of Virginia. Someone submitted a claim. We paid him the damage, about sixty dollars, as I recall. On his first trip home several weeks after that, he brought the check into the office and said, "Bill, I got this but that top was all worn out before the hail." I told him that we took that fact into account when we paid him—that the hail actually did damage. We finally convinced him that the check was rightly his, although he kept it reluctantly.

At the time I had the clothing store, Bill was one of my cus- tomers. Once he sent a note, written in his own handwriting, that I kept for several years. Where it went I don't know. He wrote that he was sending his colored boy up there and told me to sell him a white coat, trousers—all suitable for waiting on the table. It was written very informally, you know.

Bill was hard to fit because he didn't wear what we would call conventional clothing. He wore heavy Harris tweeds, but they were too heavy for this part of the country. He wore just what he wanted to wear. He wore a cap lots of times—years ago; he didn't later in life. Used to carry a walking cane too—or a parasol. But he wore good clothes. Lots of times he put on cotton slacks with the tweed jacket, and he wore blazers and things that were two or three years ahead of the style generally worn in this part of the country—not that we are so very far behind, but he traveled in a different atmosphere up there in New York—and in lots of places he went. He was not a clothes horse at all. He wore that old trench coat from World War I until it almost fell to pieces.

I remember once when he went to New York to work and Estelle decided to go and visit him. She took his evening clothes and other things so that he could accept some of the invitations to parties. He told her that he went up to work and write and not to play—and he came home the next day and left her up there. I know that for a fact. He was sincere in his desire to be honest.

I've talked with him many times—but I do remember one instance when I was in the store: he stopped by and said, "Bill, I need a belt." I had just recently read a story in the *Saturday Evening Post* that he wrote, and I said, "Bill, I believe you've gained some weight." And I put a tape measure around him and, while measuring him, I remarked about how much I had enjoyed that recent story in the *Post*—and he said, "What size belt do I wear?"

Bill Faulkner was tremendous as a scoutmaster—no question about it. He had a big heart, a kind heart. He loved young people and spent much time with them: building boats, repairing guns, shooting the bow and arrow. He had great patience in teaching them how to build a boat or sail. For about five years he spent a lot of time with Boy Scouts. They usually met out near College Hill, near Dr. W. D. Hedleston's. The home of Dr. Billy Guyton, the eye specialist, was quite a hangout too. That's where they built a sailboat—spent months at it. Exactly where they camped out I don't know. That was before Camp Yokona was established.

Often you would see Bill come down the east side of the square and get his mail and walk to the west side of the square and frequently stop by Gathright-Reed's. Some mornings he would have mail in his hand. On occasion he would enter easily into conversation with certain ones. Again you would see him with his mail stuck under his arm and reading something of interest—preoccupied. You might speak to him all day long and he wouldn't recognize the fact that you were around. Sometimes he didn't greet his best friends on the street. He didn't mean to be rude—just preoccupied. His friends understood him and knew that he was in no mood to talk. They accepted that fact. There was nothing high-hat about William Faulkner—no pretense.

If a lady spoke to him, he would almost drop his pipe grabbing his hat—old fashioned—the old school type—not stilted, usually calm and easy. He had a manner—I mean he was reserved—didn't gush—you know what I mean. At home he was the perfect host. He could put you at ease there.

When I served as publicity chairman for several years for the city and we frequently got out brochures on Oxford, naturally we wanted a picture of him. I made several attempts to get him to go to the studio. He would promise graciously to go the next morning. "I can't go this morning because I need a shave," he'd say. The next morning he had something else to do and never got around to it. We never got the picture. I wasn't the only one who worked on this project either. "Who wants to see my picture?" he would say. That was his attitude.

One rainy Sunday afternoon back in the twenties I was walking past what is now Morgan and Lindsay's, where the plate-glass front of the store was recessed. As I was about to pass, something hit me in the back. I looked around and it was Bill Faulkner with his little cane. He had tapped me with it. He asked me if I was in a hurry and I said no. "Well, let's go have a little drink." "Where are we going?" I asked. I roomed with Dan Roy at this time and we went and called Dan up and borrowed his car. I don't remember where we went to get a drink, but we got one and then headed down Highway 7 South. We went down past the old Markette place where the woods start and where you can look over an expanse of country there. Bill was full of stories and songs. I remember when he started singing a little song, very morbid—something to do with people who put on airs as if they were the only ones in the world who mattered.* "There," he said, "is a beautiful spot. I'd like to be buried in a spot like that—right there," and he continued, "You know, after all, they put you in a pine box and in a few days the worms have you. Someone might cry for a day or two and after that they've forgotten all about you."

Bill had very fixed opinions. I don't mean that he imposed his opinions on anyone else, but he either approved or disapproved of something. He never went down the middle of the road, and I never heard him express an opinion about something he didn't know what he was talking about either. He was sincere in the way he looked at things.

Bill Faulkner had his dark moments—even morbid at times— as I have noticed several times in his writings. On the matter of death he said he had rather be hauled to the cemetery by a wagon and mules—a team—than to be taken in a Cadillac limousine. This was back in 1928 or 1929 and I've thought about it lots of times—when I've seen that nice stone out there. I bet he would have been satisfied with a pine box.

* In the fall of 1931 Faulkner stopped off at the University of Virginia, where a writers' conference was in progress, and, according to the New York Herald Tribune, astonished his admirers by "gently crooning 'Carry Me Back to Old Virginia,' in an automobile between Charlottesville and Farmington."

EMILY WHITEHURST STONE

Some Arts of Self-Defense

In the fall following her graduation from college in the spring of 1930, Emily Whitehurst came to Oxford from Georgia to teach English. She associated herself with a group of talented young writers who were publishing several literary magazines.

After her marriage to Phil Stone in 1935 she saw more of William Faulkner than she had previously seen of him, and she came to understand him, as "Some Arts of Self-Defense" attests.

Mrs. Stone left the faculty of the University of Mississippi in 1964 to teach English at All Saints Episcopal School in Vicksburg. She writes in her spare time.

❦ The first time I ever saw William Faulkner was sometime during my first year in Oxford. I started teaching at the University High School in 1930, and somebody had arranged during the term for a statewide meeting of high school journalism students there. Among those who came was George Marion O'Donnell, who was eager to interview Faulkner. Marion was later to make a name for himself as a poet, and his 1939 essay on Faulkner as a moralist is still an important one.

Everybody said that Faulkner would not see any strangers, much less high school reporters. But he did. He was always kind to young people.

None of the arrangements do I remember. All I recall is that although I would never have had the nerve to open my mouth to a real, live author (I had never so much as laid eyes on one), still I knew that wild horses could not have dragged me from going along too if somebody else was to do the talking so that I could look and listen.

And that was exactly what I did. If I opened my mouth, I have no recollection of it. I don't think I could have. I would as soon have addressed the Archangel Gabriel as say anything to a person who had had a real book published, much less a novel which had knocked me between the eyes as *The Sound and the Fury* had done. That had happened when I was in college over in Georgia. It had set me walking the floor because, although I had not understood then what it was all about and certainly not why it had been done as it was, I still knew it was terrific.

So I was not a bit surprised to see that Faulkner was a person of presence, that his eyes, even then when he was young, burned through the flesh and bone of everybody in front of him and saw clearly down into the ultimate emptiness that is in most of us. I had expected nothing else but that. He was a writer, wasn't he?

The house looked right, but it had an unfinished bareness somehow which, even in my dazed state, I understood when he said he had recently bought it and moved in: there was simply not enough yet to fill it up. A long crack in the plaster, which I think was then unpainted, he said he had made when he wired the house.

I was scared, and besides, I would have been ashamed to ask the questions Marion asked, and for having come along I paid the price of humiliation at being a party to a writer's being asked questions about himself. Indeed, as a consequence of my guilty embarrassment, I have forgotten most of what Marion did ask.

But I well remember some of the things Faulkner said. He was talking about his days in the Royal Air Force in Canada. "We crashed," he said, "through the hangar roof, upside down. There we were, hanging from our belts with our heads down in the plane, craning our heads back and looking down at the ground." We stared at him. "That was awful," Marion said glibly. "You were terribly scared, weren't you?"

"No," Faulkner said, lifting his chin the way he did and looking out the window while we watched those gimlet eyes turned back to that moment he said he was remembering. "There wasn't but one thing worried us about the fix we were in up there and that was . . . " He looked at us again—two young high school teachers and three or four high school students. "Did you ever try to drink whiskey while you were hanging upside down? It's a sort of a hard thing to do if you think about it when the landing place for the whiskey is on top of the going-in place in you. We just couldn't hardly make that whiskey go up, that was what the trouble was. That was what bothered us up there."

We stared at him and after a while he went on. "There was one thing, though." It seemed an inconsequential afterthought. "I died that time."

We goggled. "Died?" Marion finally got out. He was not glib then.

"When we landed." He was not looking at us at all. We might as well not have been there.

"How . . . how do you know you did?" It was Marion, of course.

Faulkner leaned back, there in the bright morning, his hands between his crossed knees, and started talking. His face was stony grave, but his voice had a little sardonic merriment in it, and he talked fast, and the variations in his tones were over a narrow span; but we believed every word of it. "Well, you know when you walk down the street and you see, say, a telephone post or a fence paling or something like that, and then you walk on and all at once you see another one and you know you've seen some more in between but you don't remember them at all. Still you know. Or you go to sleep in the dark and you wake up in the dark. Everything looks the same, but you know some time has passed since you went to sleep. You don't know how you can tell it, but you can. Well, it wasn't like that when we landed in the roof. When I came to, fumbling for that whiskey bottle, I didn't know any time had passed at all. So I knew I had died." He was matter-of-fact and his chin was pointed up again and he was looking out the window as though he had been talking to himself and was not needing any audience at all.

Well, after all, why shouldn't I have believed every word he said? He was a writer, wasn't he? Any wonderful thing can happen inside a writer, can't it? And usually does.

At first, after Phil and I were married, Faulkner did not armor himself—he gave me the benefit of the doubt. It was during the early part of our first winter that he came out to read part of what he was working on. (I do not remember one thing that he read. I just see the deadpan look on his face and hear the deadpan sound in his voice too as he read, fast, fast.)

I had made an upstairs living room for Phil and me. Phil's father and mother, General Stone and Miss Rosie, lived downstairs, and Miss Rosie met Bill at the door and I waited for him at the top of the stairs and we walked together down the book-lined hall, I explaining the reason we had brought him up there and the changes I had made in our part of the house.

"Yes," he said. "I can see another hand than Miss Rosie's here."

"You surprise me," I said. "Phil says you never see anything."

"I see everything," he said.

It was the first time I had ever heard anybody contradict Phil. I did not believe him at all. And that was where I was wrong.

It was there, then, that it started. So he was just using his usual method, his way of protecting himself, when he did not tell me anything real. And why should he have?

It was when he was working on *The Hamlet* that I spent a summer politicking out in the part of Lafayette County which Faulkner made particularly his own. With me went a rather old lady (at least, I thought she was old) who had moved into town from that neighborhood. We were trying to help elect as governor a man who wanted to bring industry to Mississippi, and we wandered far out in the backwoods and bushes. One afternoon she told me, with proper and profuse preliminary apologies, about the only son of the Widow Somebody who had, as she put it, "taken up with a cow." And she added, "Do you know, Miss Emily, that pore boy ain't had a lick of sense from that good day to this. It ruint him. Plumb ruint him."

"That," said Phil, "is made to order for Bill. I can't wait to tell him." And he did, and when Bill brought Phil the manuscript of *The Hamlet* to read, there, right in the middle practically, was the story of the idiot and the cow.

He never opened his mouth about having published an earlier version of that story several years before, and it was not until years later that I knew he had. Of course, he had known about that incident long before I had. Everybody out that way was bound to have known it, and certainly he did. Maybe my thinking he had learned about it while he was writing the novel was part of the reason I thought it was just stuck in. For I did think so. I thought there was no design about it at all. How could there have been when he had just pitched it in because he was taken with the tale?

So I was a long time seeing. At that time it did not even occur to me that the idiot section is a long metaphor, a dramatization of the whole idea-feeling of the book, and is not only integral to it but is a part of the germ of the whole work of art.

All right. I can't, as they say hereabouts, fault him for keeping that to himself. But there was one time at least when he did not see. And that was before the one time in my life that I ever tried deliberately to pick him—when he was out home one night and I asked him what he knew about Jung and Freud and he said out of his deadpan face, "Never heard of 'em," and I could feel, but would not admit it to myself then, that he was lying.

Anyway, there was once that he did not see. And as for me, I said what I did in all innocence. There was nothing, not even stupidity, from which he had to protect himself, and so he did not need to do what he did. It was sometime in the forties when Phil and I drove out to Bill's house one afternoon to take him

Phil's Christmas present, a diagonally striped tie which was actually a memorial to their past, for in their young days that was what he had always given Bill.

The afternoon was balmy for December and Bill was out in the yard. We did not get out of the car. "Wait a minute," he said, and he went into the house and came back with a copy of André Malraux's Man's Fate, which he had written in for us for Christmas. "He's the best one of us all," he said, and Phil and I laughed to one another afterward about his characteristic lack of modesty. Nobody had asked him who he thought was the best, so he may as well have meant it as not. I assume he did.

I had just finished reading Thomas Mann's Joseph and His Brothers, and I asked him if he had read it. Maybe with all the prodding he had had from so many people, he acted automatically and so could not see. A curtain certainly came down over his face. "Who?" he said in his wooden way.

"I think it's great," I said. "In spite of that German heavy-footedness. Or maybe that's the translation. Joseph and His Brothers. Thomas Mann."

"Never heard of him," he said. He turned and went into the house.

Well, even if he did or did not see, he could not have been expected to conclude that one swallow means even springtime. But I believed him, and it was a long time before I found out that he thought Mann a great writer.

But that was not the only thing against which he needed armor.

An artist needs to keep to himself the secret of his design more than he needs not to be bothered even by innocents. For his design is the personal part. It is the order to which he has subjected and disciplined his passion, and it is not to be trampled upon, if he can prevent it, by anybody.

LOUIS COCHRAN

A Front Steps Interview

*J*n "A Front Steps Interview" Louis Cochran, a professional writer
living in Santa Monica, California, recalls his early association with
William Faulkner at Ole Miss and their later, and last, meeting when
he went to interview Faulkner at his home in Oxford in 1931.
    This was the year that Sanctuary came out and the year that its au-
thor became a celebrity. He said he had written the book to make
money. If so, he succeeded. The book was published in February and
by the following July had gone through six printings.
    After graduating from Ole Miss in 1920, Mr. Cochran became a
school superintendent, studied religion at Vanderbilt University, practiced law in Mississippi, and in 1935 joined the FBI, where he became
acquainted with Faulkner's brother Murry. Of Cochran's nine novels,
the ones with roots deepest in Mississippi are Son of Haman, Boss
Man, and Row's End (a trilogy) and Hallelujah, Mississippi. His latest
are The Fool of God and Raccoon John Smith.

❧ About 1926 I was beginning the practice of law at Belzoni, a
small town in the Mississippi Delta. I noticed in the Memphis
Commerical Appeal a news item from Oxford to the effect that
William Faulkner had just published his first novel, Soldiers' Pay,

and was then "resting up on the golf course." I had known Faulkner a few years earlier at Ole Miss, and I promptly ordered a copy.

The year that I knew Faulkner best, 1919-20, I was a senior and
editor of the yearbook, Ole Miss. Murry Falkner, the father of
William, was business manager, or "provost," of the University.
William was a "special student," taking courses in English and
French. The story was that he never bothered to take examinations, and would have been dropped except for the fact that his
father (whom everybody liked) was an administrative officer and
that the Falkners were an old-time Mississippi family and among
the leading lights in that part of the state.

William was at that time known to be something of an artist.
He also wrote poetry. I had somewhere or other seen some of his
drawings and liked them, and I needed artists for the yearbook.*
One day I stopped William on the campus and asked him if he
would submit some drawings for the 1920 Ole Miss. I asked him
to submit a drawing for the section called "Classes," one for "Or-
ganizations," one for "Social Activities," one for the "Red and
Blue Club" (an organization limited to seniors which gave two
big dances a year), and one for the "AEF Club" (American Ex-
peditionary Force veterans of World War I). He did. I liked them
every one, and still do. Faulkner could have been a successful commercial and magazine artist had he chosen to be.

Later I needed a poem to extol for posterity the beauty and
manifold charms of the Ole Miss co-ed. I asked him to give me
a poem titled "To a Co-ed" and he did. I liked the poem. That
some of the allusions were beyond my simple mind was additional
proof that it had in it the true essence of the Muse, a reckoning
which was confirmed beyond the slightest doubt by Faulkner's
future editors and the literary critics of the world. I mean this.
I thought William Faulkner had a lot of talent, although I did not
then suspect he had greatness in him.

Our "conferences" were limited strictly to somewhat chance
meetings on the campus. I would arrange to meet him as he
walked to his home in the afternoon after a class. He would tell

* Faulkner's drawings had appeared in two earlier yearbooks.

me when he would have the drawing, or the poem, ready for delivery to me. My recollection is that he was punctual. He did exactly what he said he would do. He was dependable. In return, I did for him the only thing I could do. In my capacity as editor-in-chief I listed him as an "Art Editor" of the 1920 Ole Miss and included his photograph (in the uniform of an officer in the Royal Air Force, smoking a cigarette) along with those of other members of the Ole Miss staff.

Although our relations were always friendly, they were always "strictly business," as I recall. There was little small talk between us. That same relationship existed between Faulkner and the other Ole Miss students with the exception of a few intimates, generally those he had known for years in Oxford. He rarely spoke to anyone on the campus unless first spoken to directly; then he would stop, discuss the matter at hand briefly and pleasantly, and to the point, and continue on his way.

Often during that year when I knew him best he would appear on the campus in his wartime uniform and carrying a swagger stick. Some of the students attributed his mannerisms to arrogance, which was untrue. I believe then, and I now believe, that during that period of his life Faulkner was almost painfully shy; he felt that many of the other students did not like him, and he retaliated by affecting a total indifference he did not totally feel. Our own relations, though never intimate, were always pleasant and agreeable.

So when I read some six years later that he had published a book, I promptly ordered a copy. I read all the novels as they came out. When Sanctuary was published—in 1931, I believe—the Depression was upon us and I was practicing law in Jackson, though most of my time was spent in writing. I read Sanctuary. Literary fame had come at last to a native Mississippian! I conceived the idea of writing a "personality sketch" of William Faulkner.

I went to Oxford and for the last time we met face to face. He had recently purchased the antebellum place on the outskirts of the town which was later to become almost as famous as its owner. He had no telephone (or an unlisted number) and so I drove out to his home, not knowing whether I would see him. I recall there was a single straight-backed chair on the front porch, and a couple of children's playthings. There was a silence about the old house, and a sort of unkept look, as though the family had but recently moved there and had not yet had the time to straighten things out as they may have wished.

As I knocked at the front door I heard from somewhere in the rear rooms sounds as of a hammer driving a stubborn nail through hard wood. Then steps, as of a man walking through an almost deserted hallway, and William opened the door. He was in work clothes, and quite affable and relaxed, though he looked surprised to see me. We shook hands and I explained that I had come to ask his permission to do an article on him and, if agreeable, to "conduct an interview." He smiled and, closing the door behind him, invited me to sit with him on the front steps and "talk a little."

This we did for perhaps half an hour, and though he readily gave me permission to do the article, he seemed perhaps modestly reluctant to talk about himself. He explained that he was "doing some carpentry work about the house" and was going to do a paint job when he had the time. He spoke of a recent trip to New York. My strong impression is that he did not care for the place; that, in fact, he disliked it. It appears that he had attended some rather fatuous literary parties and that he did not like them; that he had never been so tired of literary people in his life, and cared not at all for a city "where everybody talks about what they are going to write, and no one writes anything." It is also my impression that he had recently returned from Hollywood, where he had "made some money," as he phrased it, in connection with the forthcoming filming of Sanctuary.* He appeared justifiably pleased at this turn of events and in as good spirits as I had ever seen him.

Faulkner told me he thought I knew him pretty well, and that whatever I wrote about him would be all right with him. He did

* The picture, starring Miriam Hopkins, was released in 1933 as The Story of Temple Drake.

suggest, however, that I could talk with Phil Stone if I liked. He said that Stone knew him and his ideas about writing probably better than anybody else, and had been of much help to him. He then asked me about my own writing, and when I told him I was trying to write a novel of a sharecropper who had risen to become a big Delta landlord, he said it sounded like a good idea and that he would write his publisher, Harrison Smith, about it. (True to his word, he did write his publishers, and sometime later I received a polite query from Harrison Smith about the novel, the publisher advising that he was writing me at Faulkner's suggestion.) We also chatted a little about our student days at Ole Miss, and then I left, anxious to talk with Phil Stone before the day was done.

As we shook hands I recall I told Faulkner (of course, we were on a first-name basis and I called him Bill, like everyone else) I would be glad to submit whatever I wrote to him for his approval, but he told me, smiling, that he didn't want to be bothered; that if I wanted to submit my article to anyone I should send the draft to Phil Stone; that Phil was his "attorney, as well as friend." This I said I would do. We parted cordially, and we never met again.

Within a few minutes I was in Phil Stone's office just off the square in Oxford. We talked for over an hour, principally, as I recall, about Phil's ideas on writing and literature, and when I left it was with the understanding I would send a draft of my article to him for any correction and comment he cared to make before I submitted it to an editor.

I drove back to Jackson and wrote the article. I recall clearly that it was a Sunday afternoon in December; I went to the office I shared with another young lawyer and hammered it out on my typewriter in about three hours. Shortly afterwards, probably the following Tuesday or Wednesday, I had the piece typed, and mailed the draft to Phil Stone for his comments.*

I hoped to place the sketch with some Southern magazine. I felt that it was high time the South should begin to recognize its own. And so I sent it first to the *Virginia Quarterly Review*, but it

---

* Cochran mailed the early draft of his article to Stone on December 23, 1931, and Stone responded in a letter dated December 28. See Appendix.

was not a "scholarly" piece, and not for them. Next I sent it to
Holland's Magazine. In fact, *Holland's* considered it twice, and
the editor there liked it and was going to publish it. But after
holding it for several months he returned it. *Holland's* was a very
genteel Southern magazine, and Faulkner could never have been
a favorite author of the *Holland's* readers! I then sent the piece
to the Memphis *Commercial Appeal*, which accepted it and published it in the Sunday magazine section of November 6, 1932—
approximately eleven months after the first draft was written.

In submitting the final draft of my Faulkner article to the
Commerical Appeal, I told the editor I had been authorized by
Faulkner to "write anything I wanted" and that the facts in the
article, aside from my own personal recollections, had been given
me by Faulkner and by Phil Stone. I suggested that because Faulkner practically never answered letters, the proofs should be sent
to Stone, if approval were desired before publication. Nearly a
month passed before I received a reply from Leroy Pope, Sunday
editor of the *Commerical Appeal*. The proofs had been sent direct
to Faulkner. "You may be somewhat surprised and certainly grati-
fied to learn that I received a letter from Mr. Faulkner this morning
expressing his pleasure at your article and declaring it entirely satis-
factory." A few days later the newspaper sent me a check for ten
dollars with the notation on the stub: "Magazine story to appear
Nov. 6."

Immediately after the article appeared I received a number of letters from friends I had known (and who had known Faulkner) at
Ole Miss. One wrote: "Although I have never been able to appreciate 'The Count,' nor his novels, I do want to congratulate you on
the splendid manner in which you handled the subject." And another: "Your description of The Count covering the period that I
lived in Oxford coincides with my recollection of him, . . . you
have only given the devil his due. Tell me, Louis, do you really
think that Faulkner has arrived, in a real sense?"

On November 12, 1932, I sent to Harrison Smith, of Harrison
Smith and Robert Haas, Inc., Faulkner's publishers, a copy of the
article, which I said "was written solely to prove that a 'prophet'

need not necessarily be 'without honor in his own country.'" I
also said, "Knowing Bill's modesty as well as I do, I doubt that you
would see the article if someone other than Faulkner did not
send it." On November 17 Smith wrote me that the article made
"excellent reading and I hope it will wake up the South to the ex-
traordinary talent it possesses. I wish Bill wasn't quite so modest; I
can't even get a letter out of him."

But there were some who had seen that talent, as I recalled to
another former student editor, John E. Fontaine, on July 25, 1962,
soon after the death of Faulkner: "It is to our credit (it couldn't
have mattered less to Faulkner in so far as his future fame was concerned!) that we, as editors of the Ole Miss student publications,
at least recognized that he had talent above the others, and solicited
him for our pages."

J. R. COFIELD

Many Faces, Many Moods

*The author of "Many Faces, Many Moods," J. R. Cofield, has been
a photographer in Oxford for thirty-seven years. He has been prodigal
of his limited time and unlimited talent in photographing the trinity to
which he is devoted: Oxford, Ole Miss, and William Faulkner.*

*Mr. Cofield has made so many photographs of Faulkner that he can-
not even estimate the number, but it must be considerably more than
a hundred. One entire wall of his studio is hung with Faulkner photographs; in the rear section, much larger, almost any of the cabinets may*

108

WILLIAM FAULKNER

be opened for a view of additional Faulkner photographs on the inside
of the double doors. Many of the illustrations in this book came from
that valuable collection of photographs.

Cofield saw the multifaceted Faulkner as few others could see him:
in garb shoddy and elegant, in various places and poses, and in varying
moods.

🦌 'Twas in the early spring of 1928 and I had not been in Oxford over a few weeks and had bought out an old codger (name of
Tom Majure) who ran the only studio in town. Bill Faulkner was
still known as Count No-Count hereabouts and was a handyman,
and a very mediocre one at that. I think he tried his hand at most
everything, including sign painting. Well, I stepped upstairs one
day—back of the old First National Bank—to see Judge John
W. T. Falkner, something about the studio biz, as he had handled the sale for Majure, and in the conversation I casually asked
the Judge if he happened to be any kin to William Faulkner. He
blatted out, "What, that nut! I'm sorry to say he's my nephew."
A few years later he lived to eat those words, eh?

My second introduction to this man I didn't know, soon after
the introduction by the Judge, happened in a barber shop on the
west side of the square. Mr. Brooks Patton ran the shop and
wielded about the wickedest pair of shears in this burg—at least,
the Ole Miss swains of that day thought so. Well, I was in there
waiting my turn on a Saturday afternoon when a little sawed-off
squirt of a preacher got up (finally) from the barber chair. In
the discussion amongst us males, Faulkner's name was mentioned.
This little squirt went into a tirade and expounded thusly: "Why,
that reprobate should be driven out of town. He does nothing but
ride around and carouse in that old gray Hupmobile that looks
like the wreck of the Hesperus." The men guffawed, natch.

Not long after that, Bill came upstairs to my studio in the Guyton Building and brought me the first of many assignments for

him. It was a tiny Kodak photo his mother had saved of him made back in World War I days in his RAF uniform, looking very casual. He wanted me to copy it. I always said Bill should have been in Hollywood as an actor, not a writer, because I never saw him fazed by a mere camera. He was so natural that I never had to pose him for any photograph. Everything just fell into place without any sweating over getting the right angles.

I'll never forget the incident of taking his first—his very first—portrait. The Associated Press and some periodicals had about worn out the wire between Oxford and New York trying to get some decent pictures of the man. This was in the early thirties, when *Sanctuary* hit the presses, but Bill says, "No dice." That is, till Stell and I ganged up on him. Finally he broke down and told her, "All right, all right. I'll go down and let Cofield snap a few of me, dammit—but I ain't gonna dress up for it." Subsequently he showed up (with Stell, of course) for the appointment. His attire consisted of the old tweed hoss coat, with a red bandanna stuffed in the pocket; and his pants—that luckily did not show in the picture (I also cut out the bandanna)—were white seersucker, washable, with red paint splattered all over them. He was unshaven and his hair was unruly, very much so. But do you think I would have had him any other way? It turned out to be the perfect, plain Bill Faulkner, the home-lovin' man.

Although he liked this picture (and always did, and told me so) it took twenty-five years to get his autograph on it. There was a bit of bribery connected with my getting it. He had asked me to come out to take some shots of his jumping Old Tempy. On inspiration I carried the picture, along with my fountain pen. He spied me coming with the picture under my arm and didn't say a word, just reached for it, and I handed him the pen. He knew I had him over a barrel: no signature, no hoss picture. He autographed it on the back paddock fence gate, with one foot propped on the lower rail.

In the mid-thirties Bill was a devout camera fiend. In his rambles in Europe he had picked up a genuine old Zeiss camera with one of the finest German mechanisms ever made. The only drawback was that you practically had to hold a Georgia Tech degree in order to operate the thing. He'd rush out wildly and shoot up a film and bring it in to me to develop. It usually turned out to be a hodgepodge of double exposures, overtimed or undertimed, general mediocre craftsmanship that most any dunderhead with a $1.50 Hawkeye box Kodak could beat a mile.

He finally gave it up in disgust, even though cameras always did fascinate him. I never took a shot that he was not at my elbow taking in the complete procedure. I've often wondered what went with that little old camera. Once he owned anything, Bill never did throw it away, no matter how useless or outmoded it had become. He may have left it in Memphis in some Beale Street pawn shop.

Sometime in the spring, or maybe it was the fall, of 1938 Bill called one Sunday morning and asked me to please come out and take some shots of his now famous Hunting Party. I found the elite of our fair city and campus attending, and all in very gleeful mood. They insisted that I lay everything down and take a straight shot of Old Forester—not on the rocks and no chaser of any kind, not even Wrigley's. The old colored butler, in full regalia, was serving at fifteen-minute intervals.

I took some splendid shots. Then they began to ply me so dern regular with Bill's poteen that I hollered for the calf rope, and I whispered to Bill that I was beginning to see double images on the "groundglass." So he told the gang, "Pass Cofield up as of right now." He wanted some good pictures of this eventful affair.*

"Civilization," mused Bill once, "started with distillation."

"True," says I. "After all, was not the main purpose of all conquest simply for the other fellow's store of wine, or his cache of gold (to buy wine with), or his gaggle of gals?"

"There is no such thing," meditated Bill, "as bad whiskey. Some whiskeys just happen to be better than others. But a man shouldn't fool with booze until he's fifty; then he's a damnfool if he doesn't."

* One of these photographs, and other photographs which Mr. Cofield took and which he tells about, appear in the gallery of illustrations following page 114.

A worshipper of Faulkner at a distance, an Ole Miss student who had never seen him, suddenly saw him face to face and followed him up the high steps of the Oxford post office. "He was faultlessly dressed in a fine sports jacket, bow tie, and expensive shoes, but . . ." and the boy was horrified, "he had no socks on!"

Many a time I've seen Bill in outlandish combinations. He had a wardrobe, I know, that would equal, if not surpass, that of the former Prince of Wales, but he wore his clothes as the mood suited. A mixture of tastes made no difference. I've seen him uptown in the seediest looking outfits—old coats that a dog wouldn't lie on. I don't believe he ever threw away a single garment that he ever owned. On the same day, maybe within hours, I'd spot him in a regular Madison Avenue outfit; and then again, maybe within hours, I'd see him wearing a genuine Irish linen suit in the dead of the winter if the day was warm. And it was nothing to see him immaculately dressed from the waist up, but from the belt down an old pair of khaki farm pants, unpressed and smeared with axle grease.

One time Bill took his riding breeches to the cleaner, who also makes repairs, to have leather patches sewn around the knees. The breeches hadn't been cleaned for several years. After the patches had been put on, by mistake an employee sent the breeches through the cleaning process. When the owner of the establishment discovered the mistake, he took the breeches to the stable of a friend in the country and left them hanging there for a week, in the meantime putting Bill off with excuses. When the pants had soaked up enough of that good old hossy smell, they were sent back to Bill, who didn't notice the difference.

Bill remained a jockey at heart to the last. He received injuries in four different falls. In one of them, in Virginia, he broke his arm, but he said that the broken arm was no worse than a hangnail. One Saturday on the square when I talked with Andrew Price, the man who tended his stable, he told me, "I kept telling Mr. Bill that old hoss was gonna hurt him."

That old white hoss may be accountable for his death. After old Stonewall had pitched him over his head, Bill got up and walked for a mile or so and then caught the hoss and put him through all his paces before he would even consider being examined medically.

Early one morning I went out to Bill's home, Rowan Oak, to take a shot of it with the rays of the sun peeping through those ancient cedars. I wanted the picture to be a surprise to Stell and Bill. But, quiet as I was at four-thirty or five, Bill came out and greeted me with a smile and was standing right side of the camera when I clicked this now famous scene. I made him up one, an extremely large one in a nice frame, and sent it to him in Charlottesville. It now graces his Virginia home.* "I want you," I wrote on my last view of him, "to have a part of your beloved Rowan Oak while exiling yourself away from Oxford."

Just before Christmas, 1960, he made a special trip down to make an appointment for January 3, 1961, and then later called me once or twice to remind me. He was a stickler for exact appointments because at least four times I had been forced to turn him down when he wanted an appointment because of the deadline on the Ole Miss yearbook.

At that time I took the very best character shot of my career—the famous "Riding Habit" portrait, the one that hangs in the chancellor's office at the University, and at Rowan Oak, and now one hangs on the walls of the Faulkner Room in the new library at the Military Academy at West Point. When I was making this special pink-coat shot, he said, "I suppose you wonder at the vivid hue of this garment. Well, it is purposely colored: in case one should topple off his hoss, he can be found easily." Anyone who knows how the bourbon floweth at those Virginia fox hunts would say it's a danged good idea.

When he came down to settle his bill, rather stupendous because he had ordered seventeen of the smaller (8 x 10) portraits, all in color, to be sent to friends all over the world, he insisted upon paying for the large portraits, two of which I had made at

* Faulkner became writer-in-residence at the University of Virginia in 1957. Later, in order to be near his daughter Jill, he purchased a home in Charlottesville. Jill is Mrs. Paul Summers, the wife of a Charlottesville attorney.

first—one for him and one for me. I said, "No, it was my pleasure and my gift to you."

"Mine that hangs in my home," he replied, "I accept graciously. But you have not read my autograph on your portrait. Therefore, I insist on paying for it." The autograph reads: "To J. R. Cofield, from his friend William Faulkner, 15/Feb./1961."

Soon after I had made the portrait, I got a request from Bennett Cerf of Random House for a color transparency copy of it for publication. When I spoke to Bill about it, he said, "Send 'em a plain black-and-white copy; otherwise someone may think that I am already dead."

Later I thought about that remark, and about a little note he wrote me not long before he died. He came into the studio to see me about the sitting for the artist to paint from—for that portrait that now hangs in the Mississippi Room at the Ole Miss library. I was busy at the time in my darkroom lab, and hollered out that I would be out "in a few minutes." He evidently got tired of waiting and left, but I found his little (unsigned) note hanging on the lampcord in the lobby of the studio. "Don't be too late," it said. "You may be too late."

TOM S. HINES, JR.

The Crusader

William Faulkner, who at an early age, as he later told it, "learned the medicinal value" of his grandfather's liquor, in 1933 lent his name to a pro-repeal organization which was active at that time. In the piece which follows, Tom S. Hines, Jr., author of a study on prohibition in Mississippi, gives an interesting footnote to the episode.

Mr. Hines is a native of Oxford. His paternal grandmother was related to the Falkners, and his great-grandfather, Chesley Hines, was a business associate of William Faulkner's great-grandfather. His father was born in the room in which Colonel Falkner died.

William's niece, the daughter of his brother Dean, was a close friend of Tom Hines.

ꙮ When I was doing a study of Mississippi and the prohibition question, I discovered that William Faulkner had been a member of a pro-repeal organization known as The Crusaders back in the early thirties. In fact, when the state organization was chartered in 1933 he was listed as one of the executive directors. One evening more than twenty-five years later I stopped in Aubrey Seay's restaurant, The Mansion, for a cup of coffee and noticed Mr. Faulkner there having dinner. We chatted for a few minutes and I asked him to tell me about his experiences with The Crusaders. He replied that, frankly, he couldn't remember much that I didn't already know: he had become excited over the organization and had even signed his name to the membership roll—but that was "one hot summer night over a bottle of gin."

The prohibition amendment was repealed, of course, but Mississippi remained dry—a fact that continued to bother Mr. Faulkner over the years.

It was my friendship with his niece Dean that took me to Rowan Oak on a number of occasions and that gave me the privilege of seeing as much of Mr. Faulkner as I did. The Saturday morning before Dean's wedding on Sunday, the Faulkners entertained the wedding party at a brunch. On the afternoon of that same Saturday, Ole Miss was playing its homecoming football game, and the wedding party was planning to sit together in a group. We had several extra tickets, and I asked Mr. Faulkner why he didn't come

The four Falkner boys, about 1910. Left to right, Murry (Jack), William, and John; standing in front of them, Dean.

William, Murry, and John on their ponies, about 1905. This is the house in which the Falkners first lived after moving to Oxford.

Left, 1899 photograph of Maud Butler Falkner with her two oldest boys—William, then two, and Murry. Right, Mammy Callie, the Falkner family nurse, holding Dean Falkner's baby daughter Dean.

Three early Oxford scenes. Top, courthouse square as it looked to the young Faulkner. The exterior of the courthouse was then of red brick. Center, South Lamar, the street on which the Falkners once lived, looking south from the courthouse, before it was paved in the late 1920's. Bottom, scene on the University of Mississippi campus. The Lyceum Building is in the center of the picture.

The "cotehouse," hub of Oxford and of Lafayette County, and in turn of Jefferson and Yoknapatawpha. Plaster and white paint cover the original brick. Cofield took this picture from the south side of the square.

Right, William Faulkner in the uniform of an RAF officer after World War I. Below, home on the Ole Miss campus in which the Falkners lived during the time that William's father was a University official. Bottom of page, the building in which William served as University postmaster from 1921 to 1924.

J. R. COFIELD COLLECTION

ED MEEK

Ole Miss SAE's in 1919, not long before the fraternity went underground. Faulkner is at far right on the back row.

Cofield photograph of the 1938 "hunt breakfast" at the Faulkner home. William and Estelle Faulkner, in riding costume, stand on the top step of Rowan Oak. The gentleman in the coat of m-a-i-l is historian Bell Wiley.

Faulkner with his friend Phil Stone, in Stone's law office.

Faulkner with hunting friends, including Red Brite (left), Mr. Ike Roberts (in dark hat), John Cullen (back to camera), and Bob Evans.

Faulkner with Mac Reed, at the Gathright-Reed Drug Store.

Faulkner with Andrew Price and the spirited jumping horse Tempy.

ED MEEK

COURTESY MURRY C. FALKNER

Contributors to this volume include (on the page opposite) Earl Wortham, pictured in front of his blacksmith shop with one of his granddaughters; Dr. Felix Linder, shown in a candid shot taken several years ago; and Murry (Jack) Falkner with his French-born wife Suzanne, 1946. Left above, Tad Smith. Right above, Emily and Phil Stone, pictured in 1940. Below, J. R. Cofield in his Oxford studio.

The famous riding-habit photograph of Faulkner which Colonel
Cofield calls "my all-time best." Soon after Cofield made the portrait
he got a request from Random House publisher Bennett Cerf for
a color transparency. "When I spoke to Bill about it," the photographer recalls, "he said, 'Send 'em a plain black-and-white copy;
otherwise someone may think that I am already dead.'"

Faulkner, at sixty, takes a jump. He also took some falls.

The houseboat built by Faulkner and his Oxford friends.

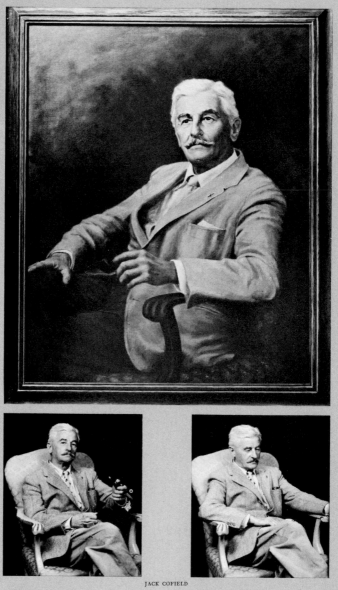

Top, the Goldsborough portrait of Faulkner. Bottom, two of the photographs used by the painter. These were taken in 1962 and were the last formal portraits for which Faulkner sat.

The Faulkner home, Rowan Oak. The author bought this home in 1930 and spent the next several years restoring it.

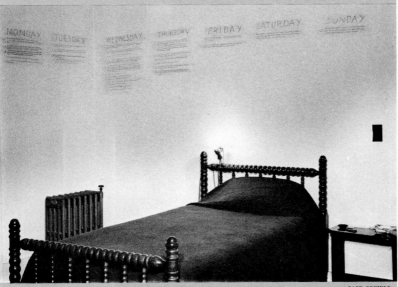

Faulkner's study, in which he did most of his writing. Written around two walls of the room, in the author's hand-lettering, is a day-by-day plot outline of A Fable.

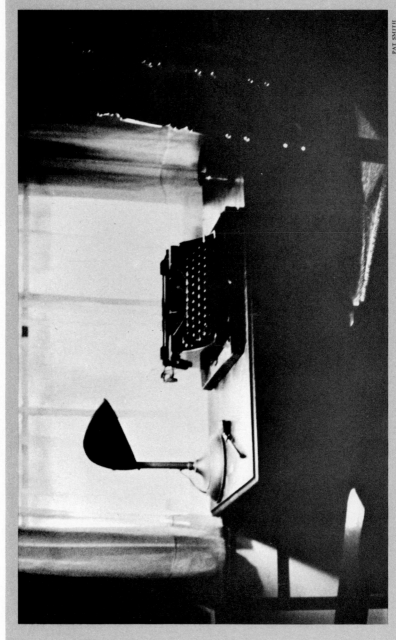

The table where Faulkner wrote. This photograph was taken shortly after his death.

on and go with us. "Well, thank you, Tom," he replied, "but I've never liked professional football or amateur show business."

After Dean left I stopped by Mr. Faulkner's mother's house fairly often to take her books from the University library that she specifically requested. She read widely and deeply and possessed an intellect that too few people have appreciated. She was also a great student of the works of William Faulkner and his critics, and seemed to delight in finding errors in the critics' pieces. One of them spoke of Maud Falkner as the writer's grandmother. Though Miss Maud was usually very quiet, her voice rose when she laughed at that. "Of course, William Faulkner," she said, "is an old man, and whenever anyone speaks of William Faulkner's mother, they say, 'Faulkner's MOTHER? Is SHE still alive?' But now this man's trying to make me even older than I am."

Miss Maud told me a story about the time William, as a small boy, was lost. He and William Hines, my father's oldest brother, went off one afternoon—around 1902 to 1905—to play together. At sunset they had not returned and the families became very much worried. After cursory searches had revealed no boys, a formal searching party was organized and the two young Williams were eventually found in an old culvert, sound asleep, apparently exhausted from the day's play. Miss Maud said she would never forget the anxiety she and my grandmother felt in the belief that something had happened to their oldest sons.

I don't know how much the years have added to the "awesomeness" of this incident. It's a trivial anecdote, but the world might owe a lot to that searching party.

HAROLD BURSON

Mr. Faulkner Sees a Cub

*J*n the 1930's Faulkner brought out ten books, including two col-
lections of stories and a volume of poetry.* During the period 1932 to
1938 (after Sanctuary had first caught the eye of Hollywood), he also
did a good deal of motion picture writing, beginning with the screen
treatment for Today We Live (1933).

It was toward the end of this period that Harold Burson, an Ole
Miss student who was also a stringer for one of the Memphis newspapers, managed an interview with him. Faulkner had submitted to
interviews earlier, but by then he had made himself largely unavailable
to inquiring reporters.

In the piece which follows, Harold Burson, now head of the New
York public relations firm of Burson-Marsteller Associates, tells how
he got his story. Burson is a native of Memphis.

❦ I first met Wiliam Faulkner in the winter of 1937–38 and it
came about because of a misunderstanding. As a student at the
University of Mississippi, I was campus correspondent for the
Memphis *Commercial Appeal*. Even then, Faulkner was the local

---

* In addition, two of his stories, Idyll in the Desert and Miss Zilphia Gant, were
published as books.

celebrity and one of the assignments I gave myself was an interview with him. For several months he was in Hollywood. When he returned, he turned me down over the telephone with the simple explanation that nothing he had to say would be of interest to anyone.

Some days later, I heard a rumor that a "Mr. Devine" had returned to Oxford with Faulkner and was, in fact, his house guest. My mind ran to Andy Devine, who was, in those days, a fairly popular screen figure. I felt he was worth an interview—and, if he agreed to it, I would at least get inside Faulkner's home. I phoned; Mr. Devine was indeed there; he would be happy to talk with me but he couldn't for the life of him imagine why.

I remember driving along the quarter mile of cedars that lead from the front gate to the Faulkner home. I rang the doorbell, was received by a maid, and was told Mr. Devine expected me in the parlor. You can well appreciate my dismay when a short roly-poly type with a deep bass voice greeted me with "Devine's the name, Jim Devine, what can I do for you?" I was flabbergasted. The only out I had was to tell him the truth.

"Hell," he said, "even if I were Andy Devine I wouldn't be the guy you should interview. You ought to be talking to Bill Faulkner." I confessed it was a noble thought and recounted my frustrations in that direction. "Maybe I can do something about it and avoid a wasted trip," he volunteered before taking off to the rear of the house.

A long five minutes later, Mr. Devine returned. He had with him the slight, sparse figure whose photos I had seen from time to time on book jackets. My first reaction was "what a peculiar way to dress this time of the year!" It was January or February and I remember a cold, bitter, windy day. Faulkner had on white duck pants and tennis shoes. No jacket or other outer covering, his shirt open at the neck. And it was obvious he had come from the out-of-doors to see me.

Devine introduced us. Faulkner appeared ill at ease even in his own home; I could rationalize only that he wanted to have nothing to do with a newspaper reporter, but had given in to Devine's plea that "it's only some young kid from the University."

This was at a time in Faulkner's life when he had not published a new novel in a couple of years (the facts are vague at this point).* He had spent a good deal of time in Hollywood writing screen-plays and there was considerable speculation in literary circles about his future writing plans. I questioned him in this vein. He told me that he had just assembled a selection of his short stories that had, in the main, appeared in the *Saturday Evening Post* and that this would be published as *The Unvanquished*. He then re-vealed that he had finished a new book and that it would be pub-lished some six months hence. The book was *The Wild Palms*.

Since it was at that time in history that *Gone with the Wind* was making its impact, I asked if he had read it. "No story is good enough to justify that many pages," he answered.

Did he like Hollywood and what were his future plans in that direction? No, he positively and vehemently didn't like Holly-wood but needed the money and they paid well. He didn't have any plans for returning beyond his present commitments, but he supposed he would need money in the future and they seemed to think his name on a picture was worth more than he could earn elsewhere so he probably would return some day.

He then narrated a story to me which has since been quoted else-where. It seems he was in Oxford at his own home by virtue of a ruse which he had perpetrated on his Hollywood boss. He was in the midst of writing a scenario and had been working in a fancy office with all the trimmings one once expected of the movies and he didn't believe the surroundings were conducive to creativity as far as he was concerned. He asked for permission to do his work at home and report to the studio from time to time. Permission was granted.

"They haven't yet discovered that I meant my home in Oxford and not the garish apartment they furnished me in the Hollywood environs."

* *Absalom, Absalom!* had appeared in the fall of 1936.

I hastened back to the campus, informed my superior at the *Commercial Appeal* I had interviewed Faulkner. He wired back congratulations and went totally out of character by advising "file all you've got."

The story appeared next morning in the *Commercial Appeal*. By noon I had had two telegrams. One from the Associated Press asking if I could provide them a 500-word version of the interview; the second from Herschel Brickell, then book editor of the New York *Evening Post* (I believe this was his title), with a similar request. In retrospect, this was something of a literary triumph for me. But at the time, I was more interested in the commercial aspects. I was paying my way through Ole Miss by writing for the *Commercial Appeal* at fourteen cents per column inch, and here was an opportunity to sell the same story three times. As I recall, the AP paid me ten dollars and the New York paper twenty dollars. It had been a big morning for me.

Also during the next day, I got another telephone call. "Devine here," the voice announced. "Just want to tell you I thought our little session worked out very well. Even Bill Faulkner found nothing objectionable about what you said in this morning's paper."

MAGGIE BROWN

Hunt Breakfast, Faulkner Style

The sense of humor which Faulkner brought to the printed page manifested itself in other ways. There was, for example, the hunt

breakfast which the author staged in the late thirties and which one of
the participants here recalls.

Mrs. William Ross Brown, or Maggie Brown as her Oxford friends
call her, is fond of all other human beings, and all other human beings,
in turn, are fond of her. The association of the Browns and Faulkners
was, for many years, a close one. The two families, with two others,
embarked on a boat-building project and spent happy hours on the
Minmagary after launching it.

While her husband was quite ill at home, Mrs. Brown agreed to talk,
without previous thought, about William Faulkner and to show her
Faulkner treasures to the editors. She also permitted them to make
copies of two documents relating to the Minmagary made by Faulkner's
hand.

❧ In the late thirties (1938, I think it was) Bill Faulkner, Colonel Hugh Evans, and my husband Ross had been on a hunting
trip at Grand Gulf near Port Gibson, Mississippi, and had killed
a deer. Bill told us that Estelle knew how to cook venison and suggested that we have a breakfast at his house. Knowing that Bill
loved to dress up, we were not surprised to have him ask us to
come in costume. He was to make arrangements for the breakfast,
but things got very much involved because we all rushed to our
attics trying to find costumes.

Hugh Evans showed up in a blue velvet jacket—a sort of Henry
VIII costume—with a plume in his cap. Mary Evans had on parts
of old Army uniforms discarded by Colonel Evans, but she, too,
wore a plume. Another guest wore a coat of mail—m-a-i-l. That
coat of mail—U.S. mail—consisted of letters which he had received and stuck all over himself. He had placed on his head a
helmet with a crest on top and had closed the visor. His wife wore
jodhpurs. Bill wore boots, riding trousers, and a pink coat. He had
made the pink coat. It had no buttons, but he had pinned it with
very large safety pins all the way down. Another guest wore a
formal riding habit, and his wife a riding outfit with a fur cape.

One of the men wore a hunting outfit, I believe, and his wife, because it was cold, wore her husband's long underwear. The underwear was white, and I think she was the only guest resembling Lady Godiva encased in long underwear. Unlike Lady Godiva, she's afraid of horses; so she rode her daughter's Shetland pony. She practically walked with her feet dragging the ground. Ross wore a derby that didn't fit him; he really looked like Stan Laurel. I had no horse because Ross and Bill had given out of horses when they got around to me. So I rode a white mule, sidesaddle—on my grandmother's sidesaddle. I'd never ridden a sidesaddle or a mule before.

We all met right outside my place and rode to the Faulkner home. As we rode on down Second South Street, we created quite a sensation because we were on horseback, ponyback, and muleback on Sunday morning riding in strange costume. There is a story that a spinster looked out of her parlor window and, when she saw us, fainted dead away. The gathering, however, wasn't broken up by the police, as some have said. The police didn't even know that there was a procession. We had a lot of fun! It was a memorable day!

As we approached the road to the Faulkner place, all the cats and other small animals, except the dogs, which Bill had collected, vanished; but the little dogs began to bark wildly.

We were met at the gate by old Uncle Ned, the retainer who had been with the Faulkners for many years. He was quite imposing in a sort of mortician's suit. The other colored boys who worked for Bill wore long underwear dyed black, and each had something that looked like a fez on his head.

Bill also met us at the gate with his yapping feists and his hunting horn, with which he piped us aboard. He then gave each of us a straight drink. No chasers. None of us could ride very well, but Bill made us ride around the grounds and do some jumping. And I was on a white mule!

Then we went in to breakfast. Bill had made a table in the shape of a horseshoe and had painted by hand on the table scenes from a fox hunt, with the horses going over the hurdles after the fox—

instead of the deer. But we enjoyed looking at the fox hunt as we ate the deer which had been killed at Grand Gulf, and it was delicious. Estelle is a wonderful cook, and the whole meal was excellent.

In contrast to the jubilant venison breakfast was the evening, some years later, that Bill had word he was to receive the Nobel Prize. We just happened to be at the Faulkner home, but there was no gathering to celebrate. Then the Faulkners came to our place the night before Bill left for New York to fly to Sweden to receive the award, but that, too, was a quiet evening: we just played pool until two or three in the morning.

Ross knew Bill from way, way back. When he was only seventeen and leaving to study at Washington and Lee, he and Bill had a night together in Memphis. Then each went his merry way. And when they were both young, they went on hunting trips together. In the woods Bill told Ross some good tales.

We saw a good bit of the Faulkners aboard the *Minmagary*, the boat that several of us owned together in the late forties. She just disappeared from Sardis Lake. The strangest thing is that not a trace of her was left, even though there were aboard things like plants and life preservers. She must have sunk at the deepest part of the lake. That is quite a mystery: some people think that they have seen her in various places. I kept hoping that Bill might write a story about what happened to her.

Our children were very fond of Bill and Estelle's daughter Jill. Billy Ross, who is close to Jill's age, often went to see the Faulkners. They were always having a party there and invited our daughter, Patricia, and Billy Ross. Bill was the cutest thing in the county when he took a group of children on hayrides. They liked to get him to tell them ghost stories. They loved him to death!

Bill was sort of unhappy after Jill's wedding; she was his only child, you know. The day after the wedding, he took one of his editors out to Patricia's home. "Just riding," he said. Probably he wanted to see one of Jill's friends, but he gave another reason for the visit. I had given Patricia an enormous four-poster bed, the one in which my great-grandmother was killed by a Union soldier outside Vicksburg during the Civil War. "Patricia," Bill said, "I want you to show my guest the bed back in your bedroom." They went back to the bedroom and stood there for the longest kind of time. Bill pointed to the bullet hole in the headboard of the bed and turned to the editor and said, "This is why the war will never die for these people in the South. This happened to this girl's family."

CECIL HULL

He Nodded or Spoke

By the late thirties William Faulkner, whom some called shy and others arrogant, had built his wall of privacy. He had his small circle of friends, of course. But he was sometimes as remote to the people of Oxford, even his own neighbors, as he was to outsiders.

A sensitive glimpse of Faulkner watching the road from the tip of his nose—which he always did—"He Nodded or Spoke" was written by Miss Cecil Hull. Miss Hull, the only daughter of a distinguished zoologist, spent her early life on or near the Ole Miss campus. As a "wispy fourth-grader," she moved across from Mr. Faulkner on the Old Taylor Road, an unromantic name for a romantic country lane.

❧ One hundred and fifty feet of woods and the depth of our front yards lay between our houses. Wisteria and kudzu screened us, while he, or they, were effectively moated by the taciturn cedars so that one would have seemed to emerge from night itself.

We went to live there in the late thirties, when I was a wispy fourth-grader. It did not surprise me that, passing back and forth along the road, he nodded or spoke to me frequently though irregularly. In general, he seemed more inclined to speak from his horse than from his car, as he seemed to observe the road from the tip of his nose.

At times I watched the horse and its rider: to that childish mind the horse was as valiant as any man. Then, too, scarcely anyone in the town rode, and it seemed a mark of singularity.

I was the only member of my family so selected, and when he spoke, he did so morosely enough. Why did he speak at all? Likely from some dim awareness that we were, factually speaking, neighbors. Some abhorrence of people asking a writer gruesome questions about his toil, and a resultant feeling that children were worthy, or at least safe? A tolerance, a kindness toward childhood?

Had I sought to talk to him—perhaps about his horse—I have no doubt that, at times, he would have talked with me. Unfortunately for this reminiscence, I was almost as retiring as he.

CLIFTON BONDURANT WEBB

Swing Low for Sweet Callie

It is significant that one of Faulkner's most memorable characters is Dilsey, the Negro servant in The Sound and the Fury, *and that she* was one of his own favorite characters. Dilsey is not a literal rendering of the Falkner nurse-mammy Callie Barr, but out of William's affection for one, certainly, came the other.

In "Swing Low for Sweet Callie" Clifton Bondurant Webb recalls the occasion when he and other members of his race gathered in the Faulkner living room for the funeral of Mammy Callie.

Bondy Webb worked in the cafeteria department at the University of Mississippi for almost fifty years, until his retirement in 1960. One of his duties in the early years was to pick up the mail, which gave him an opportunity to become acquainted with the young Postmaster Faulkner.

❧ I began working at Ole Miss when I was a very young man, in 1908, in the cafeteria department, which was then in Gordon Hall. I was in this department until I retired in December, 1960.

I first knew Mr. Faulkner when he was in high school. I became better acquainted with him after he was appointed postmaster on the campus. It was one of my duties to pick up the mail daily. A short conversation always followed my trip to the post office.

Not like most young men, playful and telling jokes, Mr. Faulkner was more the serious conversationalist. A nature lover, he liked to talk about what he liked most, horses and dogs. He was reluctant to start a conversation until he found you were interested in whatever subject you started to talk about.

I had a horse and buggy, and he had seen me pass through the campus many times. He would wave at me and stop me and start asking questions about the horse. I learned many things from him about how to groom a horse, what type of harness to use, and how to train a horse to give a beautiful performance in drawing a buggy. I also learned that a horse is sensitive and that, if treated in a kindly manner, it will give good service and obey.

At that time I often wondered why Mr. Faulkner walked alone most of the time. Often he would stop and for quite a while watch a squirrel or a bird. Trees also seemed to fascinate him. Although he had passed the same trees every day, he would stop and look as though studying each leaf.

When he became scoutmaster, he displayed leadership. His group of boys seemed to be as serious as he was. For a young man, he possessed unusual patience.

There is always one event in a person's life that seems stamped indelibly in his memory. In connection with Mr. Faulkner, I shall always remember the time that W. C. Handy played for a dance at Ole Miss and Mr. Faulkner led the grand march. At that time young men wore white shirts with fancy fronts, stovepipe derbies and cutaway coats with tails. Men looked very handsome then. When Mr. Faulkner came on the ballroom floor, he created a picture of the storybook type. A wonderful dancer, he created another splendid scene when the band played a waltz.

To me one of the greatest humanitarian acts of devotion was shown by Mr. Faulkner when "Mammy," whose real name was Callie Barr Clark, passed. She had been in the Faulkner household since the Faulkner children were born. Her home was on the Faulkner lot near the big white-columned mansion of Mr. Faulkner. Although she had grown too old to do any kind of work, she wore her stiff-starched long aprons and ruffled white bonnets. As Mr. Faulkner said, "She bossed the household."

The first funeral service was held in the Faulkners' living room, with the Faulkner relatives and close friends present. A choral group from all three colored churches circled around the casket and sang, at Mr. Faulkner's request, "Swing Low, Sweet Chariot," and two other numbers, after which Mr. Faulkner, with one arm leaning on the mantel over the huge fireplace, delivered the eulogy as tears rolled down the cheeks of all the family. He told of her devotion and intelligence, although she had not attended school very much. He placed special emphasis on "Mammy taught me virtues not found in colleges or books." * Mammy was born during slavery in 1840 and died in 1940, at more than a hundred.

* Faulkner dedicated his next book, Go Down, Moses (1942), to Mammy Caroline Barr, "who was born in slavery and who gave to my family a fidelity without stint or calculation of recompense and to my childhood an immeasurable devotion and love."

The special family service was held at ten o'clock in the morning, after which the body was carried to the colored Baptist church for the regular funeral service. Mr. and Mrs. Faulkner attended. Burial was in St. Peter's Cemetery, Oxford. A marble monument erected by Mr. Faulkner marks the grave:

"MAMMY"
1840   1940
Her White Children Bless Her
Callie Barr Clark

I consider it a great honor to have known personally Mr. William Faulkner.

A. WIGFALL GREEN

First Lectures at a University
From Notes of Richard M. Allen

*P*rofessor A. Wigfall Green, for thirty-five years a member of the University of Mississippi faculty and for the same period a friend of the Faulkner family, in 1947 made preliminary arrangements with Mr. Faulkner to appear before students at the University in a series of informal "lectures." This was the forerunner of later appearances by the writer, most notably as writer-in-residence at the University of Virginia.

"First Lectures at a University" is an account of negotiations with Mr. Faulkner and of what he said to the students, the latter based upon notes taken by Richard M. Allen, then an undergraduate, now an Indianola, Mississippi, attorney.

By the early 1940's Faulkner's earlier popularity had declined. But after the appearance of Malcolm Cowley's The Portable Faulkner in 1946, critical interest was revived. When Faulkner lectured at Ole Miss, he had not published a book in five years.

ξ̃ With the Second World War over and the happy return of many of our faculty from soldierly to scholarly pursuits, our neighbor William Faulkner, poet, fly-boy, and novelist, seemed closer than ever to us—so close that we hoped we could transform him temporarily into a fellow zombie and get him to talk to our advanced students in English at the University of Mississippi. Two members of the English staff individually and courageously urged him to help us. But they attempted to seduce by remote control: by letter and telephone. The result made it seem that both U.S. mail and Southern Bell had broken down; an imperious "Nay!" would have been preferable to the impenetrable silence.

It was my turn. Because I, too, was chicken-hearted, I resorted to proselyting by remote control, the telephone. Mrs. Estelle Faulkner, ever gracious, played intercessor with her husband. But he reacted typically: "I have never lectured; I can't lecture"; and the novelist shrilled further, "and I won't lecture!" To myself I said, "I must stall for time; I must use force." Mr. Faulkner agreed to talk with me and he was gracious, though surprised, at my instantaneous appearance at his house. "Mr. Faulkner," the plea began, "our students need to hear you. Talk about anything: your flying during the Great War; your South; the evolution of your characters; why you are a novelist; or anything else that you wish to talk about. No faculty people will be in the room; and, if you wish, no notes will be taken." He brightened, but he was still timid. With bravado he rationalized, "I shouldn't think of doing such a thing except for—MONEY!" Knowing that he was bluffing because he was then almost rich, it seemed that his bluff should be called with a grin. "All right, Mr. Faulkner," and I grinned, "we'll pay you a hundred dollars for meeting a couple of advanced English classes," a daring offer because the department, as always, was broke. He laughed, shook my hand heartily, and agreed. Somewhat later arrangements were made by the chairman of the department, Professor W. Alton Bryant, for him to give six lectures beginning on Monday, April 21, 1947, for $250.

Mr. Faulkner's original wish was that no verbatim record be made of his answers to questions, but later he said that he had no objection to anyone's discussing or repeating anything that he had said, for "it was true yesterday, is true today, and will be true tomorrow." The following answers to questions are the purport of what Mr. Faulkner said.

Asked how he happened to become a novelist, Faulkner replied that it was in New Orleans that he became really interested in writing prose. During the prohibition era he worked for a bootlegger there. After the seamen on schooners from the Bahamas had transported whiskey bottles with Scotch labels and had buried the bottles in sandbars, it was his job to dig them out of the sand and transport them to New Orleans. He had previously met in New York through Stark Young a Miss Prall, who later married Sherwood Anderson, and through her he met her husband, then living in New Orleans. He envied Anderson his easy life: writing at home during the morning and walking around, talking, and drinking in the afternoon. Not satisfied with his poetry, Faulkner decided that he would attempt a novel. Mrs. Anderson relayed this information to her husband. "You're writing a book?" Anderson said to Faulkner. "Well, if I don't have to read it, I'll send it to Liveright." * Liveright accepted the novel for publication. In the meantime, Faulkner had sailed for Europe on a freighter. He received the $200 publisher's advance for *Soldiers' Pay* while in Paris, but no one would cash it.

The question, "What is your purpose in writing?" was a good

* Horace Liveright, of Boni & Liveright, was Anderson's publisher. The firm published Faulkner's first two novels, then rejected his third, *Sartoris*.

one, Faulkner said, but one that he really couldn't answer. It was probably because of the hope that someone somewhere might say, "Yes, that's true!"

He said that for him writing was hard work and that he followed no rigid schedule, but that he found he had less trouble writing in the morning than at other times. The writer, he added, must set aside a part of his time to be an introvert. But he must not await a certain environment or a mood that would be conducive to writing; he must find time to write. Anyone who says that he hasn't the time is lying to himself. To this extent depend on inspiration: when inspiration comes, jot it down. Don't wait. The sooner you put it down, the stronger the picture will be. Don't wait until later to try to recapture the mood and color.

As for subjects, he said, there are only three: love, money, death. Titles of novels, he added, sometimes generate themselves. The title can be important; it can establish the whole tone of the book. Sometimes an author finds such a good title that he writes a book around it.

A novel begins in various ways. There is no rule. Sometimes the basic idea is an anecdote or an incident; sometimes a character is created first and then the story. *The Sound and the Fury*, Faulkner said, began with a mental picture of four children: first Caddy, the girl; and then, almost immediately, her brother Benjy, the idiot boy. Another character being necessary for the story, Quentin, another brother, was created. Then a devil was needed and Jason, the youngest brother, was put in to represent the devil, even in the earliest scene when the four children are playing in the stream. *Absalom, Absalom!* began with the character of Colonel Sutpen, and the story worked itself out around him. A vision of a pregnant woman walking down a road from Alabama to Mississippi in search of the father of her child was the initial idea for *Light in August*. The woman wasn't tired and probably didn't feel that she was undergoing any great hardship as a woman of a different class would have felt. Hers was the natural strength of the earth—a strength different from that of Dilsey in *The Sound and the Fury* because Dilsey's derived from oppression.

Asked whether the character Popeye in *Sanctuary* was modeled upon an actual person, Faulkner said that he was simply the protagonist of evil: he had given Popeye two eyes, a nose, a mouth, arms and legs, and a black suit so that he would be recognizable. "Popeye is a contemporary Satan manufactured in carload lots for, let us say, Sears Roebuck." The whole thing was allegorical, but the portrayal was probably bad because it was impossible to use anything like a scientific approach. Anything, like Popeye, that brings misery is bad, but there was no attempt to ascribe to Popeye qualities of evil like that in Milton's Satan because, to do so, is to assume that a trait is good or evil in its own right. Temple Drake, of *Sanctuary*, he said, proves that women are tougher than evil and can stand almost anything. *Sanctuary* was written to make money, two or three earlier books not having sold. The publisher said, "Good God! We can't print this. We'd both be put into jail!" Then the blood-and-guts period came in and the earlier books began to sell and the publisher wanted *Sanctuary* back; but Faulkner rewrote the entire book and had to pay for new galleys: for these reasons, the author never liked the book. Darl, of *As I Lay Dying*, he said, really did go insane; he was schizophrenic. The structure of *The Wild Palms* was deliberately made mechanical to bring out the contrast between two types of love: one man gave up his freedom for a woman; another to escape from a woman.

Sometimes, Faulkner said, he revised a good deal; sometimes not. *As I Lay Dying*, a successful tour de force, was written without changing a word. He said that he always felt a letdown when he completed a book and that he could do a better job if he could begin it all over the next morning.

It was difficult for him to answer in straightforward fashion the question, "What is your favorite character in your own books?" Dilsey, the Negro woman, he said, was the stabilizing influence in *The Sound and the Fury*; she was also one of his proudest creations. "Dilsey's a fine woman. I'm proud of her."

"How long does it take you to write a book?" Only a hack, Faulkner replied, can answer that question. The time varies. He wrote *As I Lay Dying* in six weeks because he knew exactly the direction in which he was going; *The Sound and the Fury* took six months; *Absalom, Absalom!* three years.

To ask an author of many novels to name his favorite, he said, is like asking the father of many sons to name his favorite. *Go Down, Moses* was a favorite because it started as a collection of short stories, but as he revised it he derived pleasure in creating of it seven different facets of one idea. In a different way, *As I Lay Dying* was a favorite in that it was the easiest and most pleasant for him to write and in that it continued to move him.

The South, Faulkner said, was what he knew best, and he wrote about it because it was what he knew best. But his point of view would have been essentially the same had he lived in any other section. He had to use the material he had without considering the reaction of people of other sections to his pictures of the South; but even had he foreseen their reaction he would have written as he had done and let the chips fall where they might. His purpose was to tell a story as best he could, to tell the truth about man, the truth inside the heart. The setting was incidental. He used exaggeration only when he had to, and cruelty only as a last resort. A poet, he said, has to overemphasize. He admitted that his pictures of the South were misleading, distorted, and he regretted that they were; but he tried to show not fact but truth.

The South, Faulkner said, is too closely tied to the other states for it to have a fate of its own; the fate of the South is the fate of the nation. He would not predict what was going to happen in the United States but he was certain about what was going to happen in his make-believe county, Yoknapatawpha: the Snopeses would drive out the aristocracy.

Faulkner said that he did not use living people as characters even though one may today see a lot of Shakespeare and Balzac characters on the street. Every writer, he said, is vain enough to believe that he can invent characters a little better than Nature can, though he probably cannot. A good creation is a real, three-dimensional character who stands up of his own accord and can "cast a shadow."

His characters, Faulkner said, do not express his opinions but speak only according to their own natures. When he began to write about his characters, he did not know how they were going to develop, but he knew that if they came alive he might have no more control over them than one would have over an incorrigible child.

There is, he said, only one way in which to learn to write dialogue: listen when other people talk. In the heat of writing, words must be put down rapidly. Later some of them may seem a little off and may need alteration. If, however, when the writer goes back over his work to redo it, the words still ring true, they must be left in. Sometimes the meaning of a word in its context transcends the dictionary definition.

It is not good to copy the style of another writer, Faulkner said. If an author has something to say, the story will evolve its own type of telling, its own style. An author wastes time in trying to invent a style. Style changes, so much, indeed, that sometimes even the author, much later, will not recognize it. Faulkner then cited an example. A magazine once rejected one of his stories, but kept the manuscript. Ten years later the editor sent him a check and a copy of the story. Faulkner did not recognize the story, the characters, the style, or anything about it; but it turned out later that it was his own work. The author will never get anywhere writing style for the sake of style; he must still have something to tell.

Faulkner added that he wrote as he did because he had to; he wished to God sometimes that he had a different style.

In reply to questions about the relationship between poetry and prose and the poetic element in prose writing, Faulkner said that primarily he was a poet and not a prose writer; that he began writing verse when he was seventeen; and that he quit writing poetry at twenty-three because he could not write so well as Shakespeare and Shelley had written and because he found his best medium to be fiction; but because he still thought of his stories as a poet would, his characters often do things that don't happen in Oxford but which are true to man. Poetry is like a skyrocket: all the fire is condensed in one rocket. Outstanding poetry is written by young men, he said; but he was interrupted by the question, "How about Shakespeare?" Conceding that there are exceptions, he noted that Shakespeare wrote much in both youth and later years.

Asked about Allen Tate, Faulkner said that Tate is an able poet. He replied to another question concerning women poets: he liked them when they were good, and he named as good Emily Dickinson, Sara Teasdale, Elinor Wylie, and Edna St. Vincent Millay; but he concluded that nobody was writing good poetry any more and that, as a symptom of the times, women had started writing detective stories.

A student, picking up earlier mention of Shakespeare, asked Mr. Faulkner to name his favorite plays by Shakespeare. *Hamlet*, he thought, is probably technically the best play, but his favorites were the Henry plays and *A Midsummer Night's Dream*. His favorite characters were Prince Hal and Falstaff. Shakespeare, it seemed to Faulkner, probably would have liked to be a prince and take part in tragic love, but, since he never got to, he wrote about it. Shakespeare also probably wanted to make money. The value in Shakespeare is that his work is a case book on mankind: if a man has a great deal of talent he can use Shakespeare as a yardstick.

Faulkner did not hesitate in replying to the question, "What makes the stories of other writers good?" Because, he answered frankly, of the truth that comes out of them—not fact, but truth. Fact and truth have very little to do with each other. Truth is the sum of things that make man bid for immortality, that make him generous in spite of himself, or brave when it is to his advantage to be cowardly—the something that makes him better than his environment and his instincts.

Huckleberry Finn, Faulkner said, approaches the "great American novel" and Twain the "great American novelist," but Twain never really wrote a novel, assuming that a novel has set rules. His work is too loose, a series of events, "a mass of stuff." *

* Twenty-five years earlier, in an essay in the Ole Miss student newspaper, Faulkner called Twain "a hack writer who would not have been considered fourth rate in Europe, who tricked out a few of the old proven 'sure fire' literary skeletons with sufficient local color to intrigue the superficial and the lazy."

The father of modern literature, Faulkner thought, is probably James Joyce, but the father of modern American literature is Sherwood Anderson. Anderson, he said, was an unassuming man, a fine, kind, sweet man who talked much better than he wrote. Before Sherwood Anderson, writers had written in the European tradition, used European phraseology and diction, looked at their work through the eyes of Europeans; they had looked east, but then they looked back west. He was the forerunner not only of Faulkner but also of Hemingway (whose style was strongly influenced by Anderson and Gertrude Stein), Dos Passos, Tom Wolfe, Caldwell, Steinbeck—of this entire group. Anderson's style was not derived from Europeans but was completely his own; it made it seem that Anderson had never read anything because it consists of short, jerky sentences: "I see a dog. The dog can run."

Faulkner answered candidly another question on his evaluation of his American contemporaries. In his opinion, he and all the others whose names had been coupled since they had begun to write had failed: Hemingway, Wolfe, Cather, Dos Passos, and Steinbeck. Wolfe made the grandest failure because he had a vast courage—courage in that he attempted what he knew he probably couldn't do; he banged around "like an elephant in a swimming pool"; he wrote as though he didn't have long to live—and Faulkner showed humility at the mention of Wolfe's name. Hemingway had always been careful and had never attempted anything he could not do; he had been like a poker player who plays close to his vest; he had never made mistakes of diction, style, taste, or fact; he had never used a word the meaning of which couldn't be checked in the dictionary. Faulkner once had great hopes for Caldwell, but now he didn't know. He would rank the group: Wolfe first; then Dos Passos, Hemingway, Cather, and Steinbeck. When a student called the writer's attention to his failure to rate himself, a faculty infiltrator said, "I'm afraid you're taxing Mr. Faulkner's modesty." But he rearranged his list: Wolfe, Faulkner, Dos Passos, Hemingway, and Steinbeck. (With modesty and only upon the insistence of the class Faulkner ranked—and perhaps underrated—himself.)

Native Son, he said in answer to a question about Richard Wright, is a very good book, but *Black Boy* is propaganda; a writer cannot be both an artist and a propagandist. He praised the work of Frank Norris, Theodore Dreiser, and Elinor Wylie; and he paid tribute a number of times to the stories of Willa Cather. Faulkner lost his usual reserve and smiled as he volunteered information about Eudora Welty, whose *The Robber Bridegroom* he had recently read and had found to be a "charming and fantastic story."

Some people can survive anything and some get good out of it, he said in responding to a question on the value of war experience to the potential writer. But war, he continued, is a dreadful price to pay for experience, and experience alone is not enough to make a story. He still liked to believe that he was sufficiently tough that the RFC/RAF did not hurt him much; it did not help much either; he hoped to live down the harm. The only good that can come from any war, he said, is that it allows men to be free of their womenfolk without being blacklisted for it.

With pretended ingenuousness he answered another question: the experience of having lived in a boardinghouse is neither good nor bad except in that the writer might want at some time to write about a boardinghouse.

One's perspective doesn't change after travel in Europe, and travel is not necessary preparation for writing. "Homer did okay without it." Just talk to people!

The best training for writing—and Faulkner ignored "courses in writing" and "experience" included in the question—is reading. "Read, read, read! Read everything—trash, the classics, good and bad, and see how they do it, just as an apprentice studies the master. Read! You'll absorb it! Then write. If it's good, you'll find out. If it's not, throw it out of the window. Observation also furnishes material. He did not, Faulkner said, have much confidence in the present system of education. Preparation for writing must be in the library. Just as one studies law from books and not from life, likewise the young author can learn more about human life from books than from life. Read everything! Talent and hard work are both important, but one never gets anywhere without hard work. Don't merely talk about writing. "If you want to write, do it now," whether it is poetry or prose; and remember that the poet burns out much sooner than the prose writer. Don't put off writing either poetry or prose. If it doesn't sound right to you, put it away and write something else; come back later to what you have written.

The best period for writing verse, Faulkner said, is from seventeen to twenty-five. The writing of prose is slower and the fire within the writer lasts longer; the best age for writing novels is from thirty-five to forty-five, when the author knows more than at any other age.

Returning to the subject of books, a student asked the speaker about his own reading. Faulkner replied that for many years he read anything and everything but that—deliberately understating —he had not read any new fiction for fifteen years. Nowadays he read only a few favorites, but he did read again, probably once every twelve months, the Old Testament, *Don Quixote*, the Henry plays of Shakespeare, some of Balzac, *Madame Bovary*, *Moby Dick*, *Pickwick Papers*, *Vanity Fair*, *Henry Esmond*, and *The Nigger of the Narcissus*. The Russian novels were the greatest novels of the nineteenth century, and they influenced his writing, as did the Old Testament, Melville, and the verse of Swinburne. Both Balzac and Conrad had a strong influence on his writing, but it was one of which he was more or less unconscious.

"Is humanity decaying?" seriously asked the youth who, like many others, believes that the creative artist is part prophet. Faulkner said that it is going through a phase of change; he had faith in human beings as individuals but not as a race. Americans hear the radio program of Fred Allen which ridicules American life but they are too blind to see that what he has to say is true; they laugh at characters like Senator Claghorn but haven't sense enough to realize that life is in a pathetic mess.

People prefer *Sanctuary* to *As I Lay Dying*, he said in answering another question, because the former has more commercial color. "That's another phase of our American nature."

After a discussion of current writing, detective stories, and cheap

stuff full of blood and thunder without soul, Faulkner said that
the condition of the human spirit is now poor and that what one
writes must uplift the heart, or otherwise it is not great writing.
Reading is, "like a clean collar and heaven, necessary but not important." We want culture, but we don't want to go to any trouble
to get it. When someone in the class remarked that his statement
seemed to be a slam on "our way of life," Faulkner replied that it
needed slamming. Everyone aims to help people, to turn them to
heaven, he said. The author also writes to help people.

At ten each morning Mr. Faulkner was free. His was not much
of a hand for clutching coffee and sharing professional conviviality,
but, sportsman that he was, he tagged along with several members
of the English staff and gave to the chatter what originality it had.
At ten fifteen each morning he rose formally from the table and
said, "I wish you gentlemen would excuse me. I must go home
and let the cow out." At ten fifty-five each day he got back, after
having let the cow out, and met his class. Free again at noon, he
offered to remain to answer any other questions. In the classroom
Mr. Faulkner was always gracious but retiring to the point of shyness.

On the last day after his last meeting, he looked a little sheepish
but more victorious. Had he known in advance how pleasant it
would be, he would have given five hundred—a thousand—dollars
to talk with interested, even adoring, students. He seemed a little
tired but also quite refreshed.

All had gone well. Each had come to have respect for the others:
Mr. Faulkner for the faculty and the cow, and the faculty for the
cow and Mr. Faulkner. But a Big Bertha was fired when Mr. Faulkner learned that the Ole Miss public relations office was planning
an article for the *Saturday Review of Literature* based on his answers. "I just hate like hell to be jumbled head over heels into the
high-pressure ballyhoo which even universities now believe they
must employ," he wrote in reply to a letter of explanation and
apology which the chairman of the department of English had
written to him. "The damned eternal American BUY! BUY! BUY!

'Try us first, our campus covers ONE WHOLE SQUARE MILE, you can see our water tank from twelve miles away, our football team almost beat A.&M., we have WM FAULKNER at 6 (count them: 6) English classes!' That sort of thing I will resist with my last breath." Then he resumed his mild manner and said, "But if the English department, not the publicity dept., uses the material, I shall have no qualms and fears." In the next to last paragraph he said, "If you decide on a 'repeat,' let me know." The last paragraph contains five words: "Thank you for the check."

MARY BETSY WADDLE

A Late Dinner with the Faulkners

*M*ary Betsy Waddle was such a close friend of the Faulkners that when she was a house guest they acted as though only members of the family were present. Thus, as Mrs. Waddle tells us in "A Late Dinner with the Faulkners," William did an almost unprecedented thing and discussed his writing with her; and he engaged in amusing social artifice in order that he might free himself of the formality of a large dinner party and later eat quietly with his favorite girl friend Estelle and her girl friend Betsy.

Mrs. Waddle (she was then Miss Maltby) served as private secretary to J. N. Powers during his two administrations as chancellor of the University of Mississippi. She taught for several years in Mississippi and later became curator of the Municipal Art Gallery in Jackson. She now lives in Boulder, Colorado, where the following interview was taped.

❦ My first association with Bill Faulkner was in the early twenties, during my employment at the University of Mississippi as private secretary to Chancellor J. N. Powers. During that time Bill was postmaster at the University. Every day we took care of the large number of requests for University catalogs because we wanted them to go out promptly. They were sent down to the post office, and we took it for granted that they were going out daily. Pretty soon we began to receive complaints from people to whom we thought we were sending catalogs. Chancellor Powers went down to the post office to see about it. He told Bill that people were complaining about not receiving the catalogs. "Well," Bill said, "I . . . the way I do: I put the requests in the cart that we take down the hill to the railroad station and when it gets full we take it down, and then I start on a new batch."

"Bill," Chancellor Powers replied, "we want the catalogs to go out every day." Bill was as nice and polite and kind as could be about it. He was a very quiet and unassuming man. Many people thought him distant, but he wasn't; he was a little timid. So that was settled and everything went along nicely. Things like that came up, but never anything disagreeable. The Chancellor thought a great deal of him. Whenever Bill wrote a book he always autographed one—a thing he did very seldom—and sent it right away to Chancellor Powers.

The first one that I remember was called *Sanctuary*. Some people thought it was terrible. Chancellor Powers said I must read it. I didn't want to, because it dealt with lots of things I didn't care so much about. He said, "Yes, you've got to read it because he wrote it and he expects you to read it. You must read it." And so I read it. I read it with the help of Chancellor Powers' wife, because it had so many things about life in it that I did not know what the characters were talking about. Mrs. Powers would explain them to me. Some of it was pretty raw—at least, I thought it was. But I knew Bill Faulkner and I knew he was a fine man, just as fine as could be, but very quiet. As I told somebody else, "He just did not know how to put his best foot forward."

Bill Faulkner, as a very young man, wanted to go to the University of Mississippi. He had attended the Oxford High School, which had a good reputation, but he refused to take English grammar, although he had earned many more credits than he needed toward his graduation from high school. Chancellor Powers was a sympathetic, kind man, and the students admired and liked him very much although he was bashful and timid and did not get well acquainted. He felt sorry for Bill Faulkner because he knew what a fine person Bill was and that he had to have a college education if he was going to succeed. So he helped Bill enter the University as a special student. Of course, Bill was grateful to the Chancellor for being so kind to him.

I remember the last visit I had with Bill Faulkner, sometime in the late forties. The Faulkners had invited me to their home to spend the weekend. I had left the University and was then working at the Municipal Art Gallery in Jackson. So I went to Oxford to spend the weekend with Bill and Estelle. The last day I was there Estelle and I were down in the drawing room visiting and Bill was sick in bed upstairs. The butler went by taking some hot soup to him upstairs. Estelle asked him how Mr. Faulkner was. He said he was very much better now—that he was lots better. Therefore I said, "Estelle, we've had such a grand visit that I think you ought to go up now and stay with Bill a while." "Well," she replied, "he's getting along all right now." "Anyhow," I said, "go and give him my regards." "Maybe that's a good idea," she replied as she started upstairs. She had been up there only a little while when she came to the top of the stairs and called, "Mary Betsy, please come on upstairs. Bill wants to visit with you; he wants to tell you about his last book, *Intruder in the Dust*."

I was delighted, of course. Bill Faulkner did not talk to people about his books. He did not want anyone to ask anything about them. If he wanted to talk, that was different.

So I went on upstairs to visit him and he was nice, and for him very cordial, for he was a very bashful person. "I consider this book," he said, "the best I have ever written. You are always interested, and I wanted to tell you about it." * I don't remember anything he told me about writing the book. He talked about it and was very interesting. After I read the book, I could see many good things in it. Later he gave me a copy and autographed it—as I've said, something which he seldom did. When he autographed a book, he charged a dollar. It was really strange, you know. He didn't care about the dollar; he didn't need it.

One thing that I remember was the lovely dinner party Bill and Estelle once gave for me. Bill was going to be at the party and many guests were coming. There was a big tableful, with two or three to wait on the table.

I was a little bit early because I was the guest of honor. When I went in, Bill came up to me and said, "Wait a minute. I want to talk with you a minute."

"All right," I answered.

"I'm not going to be at that dinner party," he said. "When you go to the table to dinner, don't eat very much—just enough to be polite—and when they all go, you let me know and you and Estelle and I will have dinner together." So that's what we did. "Why don't you eat some more?" people said to me, and I replied, "I guess I'm excited at seeing many old friends and having such a good time."

As soon as they left, I called Estelle and said, "Go tell him that now they have all gone and there is not a soul left in here." He came out. Then they brought out the dinner and we three had dinner and had the nicest time! He was at ease, you see, and we had such a good time. It was grand!

* Like many other authors, Faulkner may have considered the novel he had just finished the best. In 1956 he told Jean Stein: "Since none of my work has met my own standards, I must judge it on the basis of that one which caused me the most grief and anguish, as the mother loves the child who became the thief or murderer more than the one who became the priest." What work is that? Miss Stein asked. And Faulkner replied, "The Sound and the Fury."

MRS. GUY B. TAYLOR, SR.

William Stocks His Farm

To the consternation or delight of inqiuring reporters, William
Faulkner sometimes indulged in the charming fiction that he was in
fact a farmer, not a writer. As one of his neighbors recalls in the sketch
which follows, Faulkner did own a farm out in the country from Oxford. There he spent many happy hours. But it was the income from
Faulkner's writing that enabled him to buy the farm—and that gave
him the leisure time between books to play, alternately, country boy
and country squire.

Mrs. Taylor is the widow of Guy B. Taylor, Sr., an Oxford land-
owner. She is the mother of distinguished ministers, attorneys, and
businessmen.

Although I was never an intimate friend of the Falkners, I
have always liked all of them and have taken great pride in the
distinction achieved by William. When *Intruder in the Dust* was
filmed here—in 1949, I believe it was—I felt that Oxford had
been honored by William. During that hot summer I watched all
the filming, and I was pleased to see the attentiveness shown by
the four sons to their mother. Murry, or Jack as he is called, had
come home. Every evening when he took his mother out to dinner

in his car, he put his coat on even though it was sweltering. Those boys were brought up well.

At one time William and John had a farm out in the country, and John and his wife Lucille lived out there. I was raising Buff Orpingtons then. Often Estelle (William's wife) would walk over to my house to buy eggs to take to the farm. I wondered why they didn't raise their own chickens. At that time everyone in Oxford was raising his own chickens. Sometimes William and Estelle would drive by in their car to get eggs (they always rode in an old, battered car when they could have afforded the best one manufactured) and we had a pleasant chat. And often William drove by my place to get the granddaughter of a Negro minister who lived on the edge of town. He would take her to his big old home near mine to play with his little girl Jill. She had plenty of white children her own age to play with, but I suppose William wanted her also to know little colored girls.

A few years ago my granddaughter returned from Southern Rhodesia because of the fighting there. She visited me with her three children—a girl of seven, a boy of five, and Beth, the baby of two, who looked like a doll, pretty and babylike. At about that time I decided to go out of the chicken business. I placed an ad in the Oxford *Eagle* and offered my fine Buff Orpingtons for sale. A short while after the paper came out, William Faulkner drove over in a truck to buy the chickens. He had on old clothes; he never did dress up much when he was out working. He had a Negro boy with him, and he had brought a coop, but he did most of the work, and in a short time he had shooed the chickens into the coop and driven off.

But he had taken the time to admire and talk to Baby Beth. "Grandmother," my elder granddaughter said, "you could become famous by selling your chickens to Mr. Faulkner!"

MARYBEC MILLER SHAW
From Playmate to Maid

*M*any in Oxford knew William Faulkner not as the writer but as the father of their good friend Jill. One of those was Marybec Miller Shaw. Mrs. Shaw is the wife of Maynard Shaw, an engineer of Greeneville, Tennessee, whose father was for many years dean of the School of Education at the University of Mississippi. Her maternal relatives were neighbors of the Faulkners.

Through the years Jill was quite close to her father. She accompanied him on his trip to Stockholm to receive the Nobel Prize. And it was to be near her that Faulkner in the last years of his life bought a home at Charlottesville, Virginia, where she was living after her marriage to Paul Summers.

❦ Mr. Bill Faulkner was just another parent to us as we were growing up. I was three years older than his daughter Jill, but I spent a lot of time during my vacations with Jill and others of our crowd at the Faulkner home. We had so many good times together. An occasion that I remember pleasantly was one of Jill's birthday parties. It was a dinner party. I have no idea how old Jill was, but I do recall that there were no dates and there was no

pairing off that night. I remember that I arrived after several of
the other guests had already arrived and were laughing and talking
in the Faulkner living room before going into the dining room to
eat. Sitting just inside the living-room door on a small love seat
reading a book was Mr. Bill. He was dressed in short pants, as I
remember, with his feet propped up on a footstool. We went into
the dining room and then out on the side porch for watermelon,
and then back into the living room to play the piano and to hear
Miss Estelle sing some Hawaiian songs. As we got ready to leave,
Mr. Bill was still sitting there reading. One thing that none of us
ever did was to speak to Mr. Bill if he was busy.

After Jill and I had married and left Oxford, whenever we returned we got together with our sons. Little Paul Summers and
my son DeVotie are about the same age. Once when I went back
I went around to the back door as usual and found Jill and Miss
Estelle in the kitchen. Paul and DeVotie must have been about
eighteen months old. Suddenly we missed DeVotie. Mr. Bill had
both of them in the middle of the floor in his new den, and he
was on all fours playing with them. He was in seventh heaven
when he had Little Paul to play with. He was wonderful with
boys.

Jill and I were at home again when the boys were about three
years old. It was late in the afternoon when I reached Rowan
Oak. Since it was a winter day, it was getting dark early. Several
of the horses were in the paddock and DeVotie was having a fit
to go for a ride. Mr. Bill felt sorry for him and had Broadus catch
one of the horses long enough for him to sit on his back a minute.
That, of course, didn't satisfy DeVotie. He really wanted to ride.
Mr. Bill told Broadus, "Now any time this young man comes over
here and wants to ride, you fix up a horse for him and let him
ride." I'm certain he would have, too, although we never took him
up on his offer.

Mr. Bill was a wonderful person. Since Jill lived sort of out of
town and had no girls in the immediate neighborhood to play with
all the time, he brought a little colored girl to the house as a play-
mate for Jill. I'm not certain, but I believe that he moved her

family up from the farm. Anyway, her name was Estelle; so, to save confusion with Miss Estelle, we called her Lil' Estelle. Jill must have been about nine or so when she came to town. Mr. Bill bought Lil' Estelle a new tricycle—and later a bicycle—so she and Jill could cycle on the sidewalk on that side of the street as far around as the Coxes' corner. Then when Jill got a new saddle to start riding, Lil' Estelle got one too. The last time I remember seeing Lil' Estelle was on my thirteenth birthday, August 20, 1943. My aunt was giving me a formal birthday dance at her home on the Old Taylor Road. Of course, Jill and Lil' Estelle were invited. I have no idea what Jill wore that night, but I will never forget Lil' Estelle. She had gotten her first uniform for that night. It was black and she had on a stiff white organdy apron with the white cap and all the trimmings. She insisted on staying in the bedroom and helping the girls with their coats. Then she sat a while, while we danced. Aunt Sally had her usual maid there to help serve, but Lil' Estelle would have no part of that. She served each one of us a plate of refreshments and punch. Lil' Estelle, like the rest of the group, brought me a gift. I have long since forgotten what I received from the rest of them, but I still have the adorable gold umbrella pin that was her gift. I have often wondered what happened to Lil' Estelle.

DOROTHY ROANE WILLIAMS

Food for Friends

*W*illiam Faulkner had to pass the home of the Roanes every time he went to town, by car or on foot. He was attracted to the five Roane children because of the delightful and individual personality of each.

In "Food for Friends" Dorothy Roane Williams recalls the custom of taking food to a home in which there has been a death. That Mr. Faulkner recognized the custom is not noteworthy, but two things are: that in person he presented his offering at the back door, and that his offering should have been so palatable.

Mrs. Williams now lives in Jackson, Mississippi.

❦ Mr. Faulkner was not the overly friendly type of neighbor but was most pleasant and courteous and had his own special way of letting you know that he was your friend. One cold day he was walking to town and looked very cold. I drove up beside him and said, "Mr. Faulkner, would you like to ride?" "No thank you," he replied, "if I wanted to, I would have driven my own car." I didn't think a thing about a retort like that from him.

There was an all-out celebration in Oxford when *Intruder in the Dust* was being shown: people came from miles and miles; a band had been imported; parades filled the town square; and one could hear the noise for two miles. The movie was to be shown at seven thirty at the Lyric Theater and the producers and movie stars were to be there. At seven twenty Bill strolled in a leisurely fashion past my house and my father asked, "Bill, isn't this hulla-baloo for you? Are you going to make it?" Bill kept his slow pace and nonchalantly replied, "Yes, Mr. Roane. Think I'll amble up that way and see what's taking place."

Mr. Faulkner and my father were good friends. When my father was in the last days of his life, Bill Faulkner stopped by often to ask about him and to sympathize with us. Then after the death and burial of my father, as Mother and her five children sat in grief around the dining table, a knock came at the back door. There stood Bill Faulkner with a large broiler full of chicken breasts cooked in sherry. All of us thanked him heartily. "But that's not all," he said, and he reached behind him and handed one of my brothers a fifth of Old Crow. That was Bill's way of saying, "I've lost a friend."

When Bill died and the town was filled with curiosity seekers, press people, and celebrities, the word got around that everything was private. But several members of the family urged the neighbors to drop in, and particularly neighbors like the Roanes. It had been announced that the funeral would be private only because that was the way Bill would want it, but certainly he would want his friends to be there. Policemen at the gate greeted me pleasantly; and at the door Bill's brothers, Jack and John, seemed glad to see their neighbor and friend. I carried a platter of food, but it could not equal Bill's offering.

BRAMLETT ROBERTS

A Soft Touch, A Great Heart

*B*ramlett Roberts, whose law office looks out over Oxford's court-house square, is a man with great warmth and a great sense of humor. It was he who in 1950 helped John Cullen (author of Old Times in the Faulkner Country) write his hilarious letter inviting the King of Sweden to partake of Mississippi hospitality: a coon and collards dinner, as a reward for presenting the Nobel Prize for Literature to William Faulkner.

Mr. Roberts has practiced in Oxford since his graduation from the University of Mississippi Law School. He served in the Navy during World War II; for several terms he was the attorney for Lafayette County, and for eighteen years he was a part-time member of the Ole Miss law faculty.

The interview from which "A Soft Touch, A Great Heart" was drawn was recorded September 11, 1964.

As Bramlett Roberts notes, his father, Ike Roberts, one-time sheriff of Lafayette County, was a close friend and hunting companion of William Faulkner.

₹ My father and William's father were fast friends. William visited with his father in our home when we lived out here in the country about ten miles from Oxford. William was a youngster then, not yet in his teens. His father used to like to fox hunt, and so did my dad. I was five or six years younger than Bill, but as a child I remember that Mr. Falkner's son was there. William would follow his father and my father on the fox chases. That's how it started, the friendship of my father with William's father, and then my father and William, and that friendship ripened over the years.

I knew Bill back in the twenties. It's a shameful thing but the kids used to run around here about the time Bill published *The Marble Faun,* and they called him Count and that sort of thing, somewhat in derision. They were just kids. I think they meant no offense. It was just like shooting a firecracker and running from the officers.

Later William married Estelle. They had gone together some years earlier. It seems that Mr. Lim Oldham, Estelle's father, objected. Perhaps it was because any father dislikes the thought of giving up his daughter. She was going with Cornell Franklin, too. Son Barton, the Negro houseboy at the Oldhams, would tell me about William and Estelle. Son said that Cornell would have a date with Estelle and that after Cornell left, he (Son) would show William into the study for a late date with Estelle. Major Oldham was a brilliant conversationalist and a rather fine looking man. Yes, he was one of the most brilliant men I have ever talked with. He would have enjoyed a greater law practice if he had not been a Republican; in those days a Republican was not quite so popular in Mississippi as Goldwater is now.

But my father knew William much better than I did. He was sick for approximately a year before his death, and when Bill came in to see him, particularly at nighttime, he'd come around to the back door, and if there was no one in the kitchen he'd get a cup. The coffee pot was always going. He knew that. And if there was no one there, he'd just sit until someone came in to talk with him; if my father was able, Bill would go on up and talk to him some more. They were great friends.

Bill had a lot of stories. Oftentimes I've heard him, in his remi-

niscing, tell my father about himself and a man by the name of
Westmoreland going hunting. He called Mr. Westmoreland
"Wes." He—Westmoreland—had a single barrel, rickety shotgun.
It was pieced together with baling wire. Bill heard some shooting
over in a clearing and when he got in sight he saw a large oak
tree with no other trees around it and the squirrels were playing
all over the tree. Wes had shot his gun. When it fired the barrel
came off: the stock went one way, the barrel another, and the
forearm another. Bill went up and was going to kill some of the
squirrels; it was full of squirrels. And Wes said, "Oh no, don't
bother 'em; don't bother 'em! They're mine!"

I never went hunting with my father and Bill, but I did go on
hunting trips with my father before Bill started going with him.
That was a good many years ago. Bill and my father were of
kindred nature. Bill liked the big woods, and, of course, my father
did too. I think my father lived in the most enjoyable time for
him. The big woods are now gone. He was a man closer to the
earth than I think Bill was.

Bill and my father shared ownership in a horse. A short time
after my father's death I was in the City Barbershop. While I was
sitting there I heard someone knock on the glass front. I looked
and saw Bill Faulkner motioning for me to come out. He asked
if the horse was still out on the place. When I told him that it was,
he said that he would like to have it. I said sure he could have it.
"Saddle and bridle, too?" he asked. I said yes. He went out and
got the horse, saddle, and bridle. About six weeks later I met Bill
on the street. He drew from his trench coat pocket a slightly
rumpled, slightly soiled check dated several weeks before—a
check for $300 that he had been carrying in his pocket. "Mr. Ike
and I each had $300 invested in that horse," he said. "I figured
this amount would pay what he had in it." I took the check somewhat reluctantly. Bill would have had it no other way.

Jimmy Faulkner told a story about William. He's William's
nephew and he called him Brother Will.* William's agent came

* Jimmy Faulkner is the elder son of William's brother John.

down from New York three or four years before his death, and Estelle asked Jimmy to locate William. He knew William was out sailing on Sardis Lake, and he went out to get him. The agent stayed at William's home until William and Jimmy got back. "I owe this man the courtesy of seeing him," William said, "but I'm not going to write another damn word this year. What's the use—the government will get it all. I've made all the money I expect to make this year. I've made enough." Then he did go in to see the agent. And he did not write any more that year.

Incidentally, I have advised with the attorneys from Charlottesville who helped settle Bill's estate. They were not conversant with Mississippi practice; so they asked me to help them some, and I have done it gladly with the understanding from the first that there would be no charge. And I have learned a good deal about William that I didn't know—about his being such a soft touch. I wonder sometimes if that wasn't the reason—one of the reasons—for his withdrawal from society, because he knew his weakness. Anybody with a sad story, whether it was true or not, could get money from Bill Faulkner, and in large amounts. I know of cases that were uncovered after his death, and of course I realize, too, that, in addition to that, the life of an author is a lonely life anyway.

Bill Faulkner was a man with a great heart. Of course, we all knew about Bill here: he was well respected here, especially among the intelligentsia, but you didn't have to belong to the intelligentsia to appreciate Bill. If you knew him, he was a very communicative fellow; but, he tended to Bill's business, and he had nothing to say about what anybody else did. If ever a man was identified with freedom of thought and action and ascribed that to everybody, I think Bill did. He was one of the most charitable fellows in his thinking that I ever saw.

JERROLD BRITE

A True-Blue Hunter

The following account of William Faulkner on hunting trips was taken from the tape recording of a conversation with Jerrold (Red) Brite made on January 16, 1965. It was given spontaneously on a cold morning in the back room of a filling station in Oxford.

Red Brite is a mountain of a man—good natured, relaxed, and friendly. With his slightly graying red hair, two hundred and seventy-odd pounds, and big, strong hands, he could hardly have fear of man or beast. During World War II he was a military policeman. He talks easily. Had we been sitting in total darkness, we could have discerned that the voice, though not loud, was from the chest of a huge and friendly man. At the present time Red works on the Mississippi River. He comes home to Oxford on weekends.

Red went on a number of hunting trips with William Faulkner. These hunting parties were composed of men from various walks of life bound by a love for hunting game and sitting around the fireside at night in the big woods.

❧ Bill Faulkner was the best hunter there was. I'd say he was as good as they come. He was a good shot and true—what you'd call a true-blue hunter, I'll tell you that.

I knew Mr. Faulkner quite a number of years. I don't know just how many—quite a few. And I hunted with him several years. We hunted down in Issaquena County—down there on Big Sunflower at a little old place called Boyle. Let's see if I can remember some of the fellows who went along. I know Mr. Ike Roberts was one of them. And there was Bud Miller, Mack Wardlaw, Sherman Wardlaw, Hub Wardlaw, William Hudson, Son Hudson, Willie Lewis, Albert Lewis, Bob Harkins, Jimmy Harkins, Paul Harkins, Bill Evans, Ole Man Bob Evans, and a fellow up there in Memphis—he went with us a lot. And John Cullen went with us several times. He's another good hunter. We'd sit around John. At night he always sat around and told big yarns. He always tried to tell the biggest ones.

We never played poker in our crowd when I was there. We do now, but we didn't then. We'd play setback, tell yarns, and sit around the fire until eight or nine o'clock, and then we'd all go to bed. If we decided to drink a little we'd have a few drinks. Everybody in camp took a few—I mean, everybody who ever went to camp had a few drinks. That's a part of it. But we never did too much drinking. We kept the drinking down because hunting and guns and whiskey don't mix.

Mr. Faulkner wrote a story about a bear once, but I never went bear hunting. That was in the old, old days. I guess I was too young. Deer is the only thing we ever hunted together much. We fox hunted together a few times. Sometimes he'd coon hunt. When he wanted to go coon hunting, if nobody wanted to go with him, he'd go by himself. He was a great sportsman, if there ever was one.

Bill was a good—oh, yes, an awfully good—rider. He took his own horse down there. I rode his horse about as much as he did. As far as him being a good honest hunter, he was. He'd stay right there until the drive came in and the driver was out with the dogs (everyone was supposed to stay out in the woods) before he came in. He would, regardless of whether the rest of them did or not.

I saw Mr. Faulkner shoot a deer one afternoon. I rode by when I was checking the stands of the hunters, and I said, "Mr. Faulk-

ner, did you get him?" And he said, "Yeah, I hit him but he didn't
fall." We got to looking on the ground and found the blood and
saw part of his heart laying out there on the ground where the shot
had come all the way through it. We got the deer. The dogs ran
him, and about four hundred yards down from there he fell.

On these camps, we'd stay about seven days most of the time.
I always drove the dogs and he always was a standard. I liked to
run the deer over because I knew he'd kill it. The deer that we got
we cooked right down there. We had deer meat on the table at
camp twice a day, or three times a day if we wanted it. I'd say we
had a good time, but a man who's never been down there might
not say it was a good time. I don't know.

Mr. Faulkner did his share of the chores. He'd take the front
end of the log the same as I would, or anyone else. And the weather
didn't get too rough for him. He'd get out there in it; he was the
same as you or me or anybody else in the woods. He didn't back
up on anything. I've seen him lay down on the river bank. One
afternoon we all had moved into camp on Sunflower River. That
afternoon the water was up and we couldn't get the truck in there
like we generally did. It had rained and was muddy. We hauled
all our stuff down the river, about two miles down the Sunflower,
and put it on the bank—with a motorboat. He laid out there on
the river bank that night like the rest of us did. We were all trying to get to camp, and part of us up the river and part down, trying to get there.

Out on the camp he wasn't very talkative. Most of the time he
sat around and read. But if you asked him a question he'd answer
it. He'd stop his reading and answer the question, and if you
wanted to talk to him, he'd talk to you. Sometimes at night he'd
tell stories. He'd tell some tall tales like the rest of us would around
there—yarns and things. I don't remember too many of them.
There were so many tales told I didn't try to keep up with them.
He could tell some big ones all right. Some of them he kind of
made up as he went along. Most of them were pretty true, though.
He'd tell about some hunt he'd been on, or something he'd seen
in the woods, or where he was and how he was standing when he

shot the deer, or something about the hunt that day. He'd tell everything that happened on the hunt.

But talk about him shooting: I've seen him take that .30-.30 rifle and shoot turtles off of logs while he was going down the Sunflower River in the motorboat. We'd go up and down in the motorboat lots of times. The sweetest motor I ever heard in my life was the time he was sick and we had to bring him out of camp there. A man we hunted with down there had a boat and we didn't have one. Clarence Bernard. It was his boat and his motor. But he was up the river fishing and laying some nets. Mr. Faulkner got very sick and we were worried about him. We had an old cook, Ed Means, at the camp that morning. I rode into camp tired, and as I rode into camp Ed met me. He ran out of the tent, the kitchen tent, and met me and said, "Mr. Red, get off quick and go look at Mr. Faulkner." I jumped off my horse and ran in the tent. He was laying on the ground in his sleeping bag. I saw that he was a sick man, real sick. I got on my horse and went to some of the other standards and told them to go to camp —told them what the story was. Uncle Bud Miller, Mr. Ike Roberts, and Ed and Bill Evans, I believe it was. Several of the boys went to camp and they got Mr. Faulkner up and got him out of the sleeping bag and got him up on his feet. He had just been laying there and hadn't got up because he was sick. We hadn't noticed because he stayed by himself a lot. The sound of that motorboat was the best sound I ever heard in my life. When he got him to Oxford, Dr. Culley told us that if we hadn't got him there he would've been a dead man.* That was, I would say, in the late thirties or early forties. It was before the war, probably in the early forties. He was an awfully sick man.

On another hunt down on Sunflower River, down there out from Anguilla, Clarence Bernard and a fellow named Bill Blue Sanger went with us. They had several dogs apiece, and we had dogs. We

* Dr. John C. Culley, a prominent North Mississippi physician and surgeon, now retired, was for many years director of the Oxford Hospital. He and William Faulkner often went bird hunting together.

always tried to turn three packs loose every morning, and then
we'd get out at night and look for them. Mr. Faulkner had a jeep,
and he'd take the jeep and we'd look for dogs all over the country
—go from camp to camp looking for dogs.

Dr. Felix Linder missed a big deer down there one afternoon.
We had had bad hunting that morning—didn't have too much
luck. That was the morning the dogs went the wrong way. They
went to Flat Lake and not back to the river where we thought
they'd be. Dr. Linder was sitting there and he thought—well, he
hadn't had any luck that morning; he hadn't seen anything—he'd
kill some black squirrels. He'd seen some of them hanging around
there. So he unloaded the buckshot from out of his shotgun and
put in ball shot for squirrels and killed one or two and then slipped
up on some more. He heard something and looked around. And
there was a deer right there at him—running by. Course, he shot
at the deer with the small shot. He was too far to hurt it too bad.
The dogs came on through and went in the river and I was following the dogs. On Bill Faulkner's horse. I didn't have any better
sense than to fall off in there with them. We went out on the
other side and killed the deer. I told Dr. Linder, "Well, this deer's
been shot on the righthand side," and he said, "Well, I shot him
on the left side." We skinned the deer and, of course, I got half
the deer and brought it back to camp. The squirrel shot had gone
just under the hide good and made him bleed a little bit. We
laughed at Dr. Linder a lot about that. We laughed and told him
we'd all go squirrel hunting if we could have luck like that.

I remember going down to Big Steele in Issaquena County on
my last hunt with Bill Faulkner. It was somewhere between 1950
and 1952, maybe 1952. We were down there and camping
in tents and hadn't had much luck. The second day we hadn't had
a bit of luck at all. We decided to go hunting in the afternoon.
John Cullen found a thicket over there where the deer were going
in and not coming out. You could see where they went in there,
but you couldn't tell whether they'd come out or not. John told
us, "You all go down there and get around that thicket and get the

dogs and run in there; there's a buck in there." Everybody got ready to go and we went over to the thicket and we ran in there and they ran a big buck out, and John killed it. He hollered, "Let's go, boys. We got all the meat we want." It was a six-point buck. So we loaded it on the pickup and went on back to camp.

That night everybody was so glad John had killed a buck that everybody got to giving everybody else a drink from his bottle. One of the fellows got a little high and went in there to go to bed. After a while he got up and fell all over the wood in the tent—stacked up there—and skinned his hand; it was hurt pretty bad. Some of them asked him what in the world was happening there. He couldn't stand up or nothing else. Bill Evans told him, "Your head got drunk, and your knees got drunk the same time your head did." Somebody else asked him what happened. He said, "I'll tell you: it was raining, and lightning struck me."

"Yeah," I said, "white lightning."

He said he needed some air. He couldn't walk; so I was going to help him out of the tent to the yard. It was dark and we couldn't see too good, and we didn't have a flashlight with us. I said, "O.K., get started!" He got started. Bill Faulkner was laying over there on the ground pretty close to the tent. He hardly ever slept in the tent. He'd always sleep on the outside in a sleeping bag—never would sleep in the tent with us. The only time I ever saw him move in the tent was when it was raining; then he'd move in the tent. He said he liked to sleep out in the open air. Well, we got outside the tent and we heard a voice at our feet—Bill Faulkner's voice: "Hey, I'm laying over here!" And I said to the fellow I clung to, "Don't you fall over Mr. Faulkner like you fell over that stack of wood!"

I remember a hunt we went on down on Sunflower one year. It was Thanksgiving, and it was the year he got the Nobel Prize. Thanksgiving Day we were all running around in our shirt sleeves, and when we got up the next morning there was snow and ice all over the tent, and that was the year we had such an awful time getting in there and out. We had a pair of mules and one wagon and we like to have never got all the stuff in there with a pair of mules, the roads were so bad with mud. Anyhow, it had just been announced in the papers that he was going to get the Nobel Prize.* So we all got to talking about it. Bill didn't say much. He was a man you couldn't tell much about something like that. One of the fellows in the Air Force got to drinking a little, and he said he was a major and he'd fly Bill across there to get the Nobel Prize. Of all the tales you never heard until three o'clock in the morning! I went to sleep. Later one of the fellows shook me and asked if I wanted a drink and I said, "No thank you," and went back to sleep. He was toting whiskey to people outside and everywhere else. Yes, we all celebrated the Nobel Prize just a little bit there.

I never will forget one time we ran short of groceries in there and so we decided to go to the store and get some, Mr. Faulkner and myself. We came across the river and got in the car and went on to the grocery and came back. But in there Mr. Faulkner asked the man if he would take a check. The man asked him who the check was on, and he said, "William Faulkner," and the man acted like he was surprised it was William Faulkner down there at the grocery store buying groceries. He finally took the check, but he was so surprised that he made a mistake on the check, and the next time we went back he told us, "Mr. Faulkner, I was so surprised the other day I charged you too much," and he gave him some money back. Course, we had to have a few drinks along there, and then the man gave us a drink or two.

That was the last time I went hunting with Bill Faulkner. I talked to him more, I reckon, than anybody else. On the hunt, I mean. We talked about high water on the river a little, but most of his stories were about horses. He loved horses. He told me about going out to Texas and buying a jumping horse—and he told me about going all the way to California and bringing back a horse. He got six of them out there. We were always out together somewhere, going to town or going to get groceries or going out looking for stands or looking for deer or more where they had laid or

* News of the award had reached Faulkner some days earlier. He and his daughter Jill traveled to Stockholm the following month for the presentation itself.

bedded down or something or looking for dogs. We always had a pretty good hunt every year.

The last time I saw him, about two weeks before he died, I talked to him up here on the street in Oxford. Just like you and I'd walk up and shake hands, we shook hands and we asked how each other was getting along, with comment about the weather. We talked a little while and he said he had to go. He was in kind of a hurry and he went on back over toward the courthouse. The last time I saw him he was going in the courthouse door. For what, I didn't ask him. He was a man who might speak to you and he might not, but I never have seen him fail to speak to me. I thought he looked all right when I saw him. I was surprised when they told me.

There were three hunters! Ole Lucky Pettis. I forgot to name him a while ago. He was in there. Lucky Pettis, he died, I think it was March. Bill Faulkner died in June, I believe it was—no, July. And Uncle Bud Miller died in October. They were all three true-blue hunters. They'd stay right there with you; through thick and thin they'd be with you. Bill would stay through thick and thin; if it was muddy he was there, or if it was dry he was there. That's what we—everybody—called a true-blue hunter down there!

PHILLIP E. MULLEN

The Fame and the Publicity

*P*hillip E. Mullen was for almost twenty years (from 1933 to 1951) associate editor of the Oxford Eagle, William Faulkner's hometown newspaper. During that time he had the opportunity to see a good deal of the author and to follow the popular and critical reaction to his work: the curiosity of the thirties, the indifference of the early forties, the acceptance and acclaim of the fifties.

Phil Mullen worked on the staffs of newspapers in Paris, Tennessee, and Canton, Mississippi, after leaving Oxford. He is presently editor and publisher of the Osceola (Arkansas) Times.

Mr. Mullen gives Faulkner the ultimate tribute of the newspaperman: "Everything Bill Faulkner said was quotable."

Bill Faulkner and I were not what you would call intimate friends. I doubt if he had any. But he liked the way I wrote about him, which was respectful without going overboard. Of course, Bill liked favorable publicity as much as anyone else.

Through the early years of his work, recognition came slow and hard. Critics were unfriendly; some of his homefolks made fun of him. So when fame did come, he rebuffed all efforts to lionize him, with withering iconoclastic humor and with cool refusal to be interviewed or photographed. When they made a movie of *Intruder in the Dust* and wanted a picture of him for promotion purposes, he said, "Take a picture of the book."

When it was announced that he had won the Nobel Prize, I called him and said, "There is one damn newspaperman you are going to see this morning." He said, "Who?" I said, "Me!"

"Well, come on," he said.

So I went on down to the Faulkner home. After we had talked for an hour, Bill said, "Phil, would it be unethical if I read your copy before you send it to the AP?" I said, "No, but they are yelling for it."

He said, "Call me and I'll come right down to your office."

That was a long story—the one the AP used all over the country. Bill came down and read it, protested mildly about my mentioning that his mother was an artist, and then he made just one correction. Where I had written that he "served with the RCAF in World War I," he said, "Change that to 'I was a member of the RCAF'—I didn't see any service."

A little earlier that year, when rumors were rife that he would get the Nobel Award, I saw him downtown one day and told him, "Bill, now that we have sold the *Eagle* (which we had, and I stayed on to work for the new owner), I'm not making as much money as I used to. I may not have any Christmas whiskey this year unless you help me out." (He could understand being without whiskey.)

"How can I help?" he asked.

I said, "By letting me come out and make some pictures of you and your wife and Jill. When you get the Nobel Prize, they will be worth something."

He gave me that half-grin and said, "Wait until I get the damn thing first."

When the prize was announced, and when newspaper photographers came to Oxford to find him, he sent them all to me.

In 1952 he allowed the Ford Foundation to make a short film about him and about his life in Oxford for the television program

WILLIAM FAULKNER

"Omnibus." I was working on the Paris (Tennessee) *Parisian* then, but Bill asked me to assist the producers in preparing the script and staging the show. I'm in one scene with him restaging the time, in 1950, when I went out to his home to get the AP story about the award. My acting sounded "too worshipful," he said. "We're old friends," Bill said. "You should have told me that morning, 'You sap, you've got the fame and you got to take the publicity.' "

The last time we met was on the streets of Oxford and we compared notes on our grandchildren. His daughter Jill and my daughter Phyllis were about the same age and high school classmates. He was happy over a new grandbaby.

Bill Faulkner was one of the kindest, most courteous men I ever met. His love for his mother, for his family, for Negroes, marked him as a great gentleman. He was one of the greatest friends of the Negro people because he wrote of them as people he not only loved but, more importantly, respected.

He was a character, a pure genius who believed in doing exactly as he pleased. His best friends were the plain people. He was egotistical without being vain. He was always confident of the greatness of his work but always in anguish over its accomplishment.

Once I remarked to him that Hemingway must have felt very bad over *Across the River and Into the Trees*, to work as hard as he did and to "come up with little or nothing." Bill said, "Hemingway tries too hard. He should be a farmer like me and just write on the side."

Bill's books are famous world-wide but his world was Oxford, Lafayette County, Mississippi. The humanity of that North Mississippi section, which is the locale for most of his books, he proved true to the humanity of all the world.

Bill Faulkner did care about what his fellow Mississippians thought of him. In one note he wrote to me:

"I fear some of my fellow Mississippians will never forgive that $30,000 that durn foreign country gave me for just sitting on my —— and writing stuff that makes my own state ashamed to own me."

Another time he wrote: "Sweden gave me the Nobel Prize. France gave me the Légion d'Honneur. All my native land did for me was to invade my privacy over my protest and my plea. This seems to be a pretty sorry return for a man who has only tried to be an artist and bring what honor that implies to the land of his birth."

Well, if Bill saw the tributes that were paid upon his death—and I believe he did—then that sentiment has been changed for him.

There is no point in my laboring the greatness of his writing, or arguing about it with those Mississippians—most of whom never read anything he wrote—who resented his stories of violence and degradation. World opinion has established his greatness.

It is true that he has written some of the most violent, brutal, and shocking passages in literature. At the same time, he has written some of the most beautiful.

EARL WORTHAM

So I Could Ride Along with Him

High on a hill east of Oxford is the blacksmith shop of Earl Wortham, who spoke spontaneously on September 10, 1964, of his relationship to the Fa(u)lkners, four generations of whom he has known. For William he made minor repairs to farm equipment; he shod the horses; and he cared for them while Mr. Faulkner was away. His little shop

*keeps him, his wife, and some fifteen children. Even though he does
not know how old he is—he thinks he is past seventy—and has had no
formal education, he is mentally alert.*

*The transfer from tape to type loses Earl Wortham's easy, rich, and
wholesome laughter and his soft intonation. To retain some of the
flavor of his pronunciation, spelling is occasionally made phonetic.
Through the unlettered but venerable style one can glimpse a flash
of humor and, even more, a restrained devotion.*

*On the gable of the blacksmith shop is a horse of the size found on
the merry-go-round for small children. Perched precariously on the
horse's back is a weathered doll. Horse and rider were placed in position
soon after the death of Mr. Faulkner. They are poised, it seems, to take
off on the last ride into the heavens.*

Ï I really liked Mr. Faulkner myself, and I don't know anybody
else of any color that didn't. They all liked Mr. Faulkner and
them (that's the way they were about his daddy and granddaddy).
I've known 'um ever since they come from over here about New
Albany. That's where they come from, over there to here. And so
I learnt 'um then. They had a livery stable in town. Mr. Murry
Falkner, that was Mr. Bill's daddy, and Old Colonel, he was a
lawyer and . . . I remember when he drove that old car Mr. John
Buffaloe made.* They didn't have cars then. The first one that
come into town, why, people didn't know what it was, and they
followed it. It come in on North Street and they followed it clean
out here on top of the hill right up there, and they stopped him
. . . stopped the man. They had to take a good look over it, you
know, to see what it was and all like that. That really was a fact
now.

* One of the characters in Faulkner's last novel, *The Reivers*, is a Mr. Buffaloe.
The automobile which he made frightened Colonel Sartoris' carriage horses into
bolting. When Earl Wortham speaks of the "Old Colonel," he is referring to William's grandfather, John Wesley Thompson Falkner. J. W. T. Falkner was usually
spoken of as the "Young Colonel," to distinguish him from his father. Faulkner's
uncle and one of his brothers perpetuated the grandfather's name.

Anyhow, the first car we had here was one Mr. John Buffaloe made. He took a buggy and got him a motor and put in there, you know, and it was a rubber-tired buggy, and so he drove it up and down the streets and round about, and Old Colonel (that was Mr. Bill's granddaddy) got kind of stuck on it and he bought it. So then, after so long a time, he carried it to Memphis and got him a T-Model and brought that back here. He drove that for ever so long. It'd make an awful racket. And Chester Carruthers (he was a colored fellow) drove for the Old Colonel all the time, you see. He was a kind of mechanic and so he drove the Colonel. The Colonel got him a nice car after that, and Chester got burnt to death under it.

Mr. Bill and them, they had an old lady they brought here with 'um called Callie Barr, and she was their nurse.* That was in the time that we didn't have any concrete—nothing but just plank walks, you know, by certain ones' houses. And then you'd walk on the dirt. Didn't have any gravel. And she'd walk 'um up town— Mr. Bill and them. But she couldn't keep him on those plank walks and out of the road. He'd just walk out in the road, and she'd try to get him to come back up there where they were, where she was leading the others along, and he'd say, "Naw." He called her Mammy. He said, "Naw, Mammy." Said, "I'm gonna walk right out here. Do me just as well." So he'd walk to town and all around the streets over the ground, just like that.

Up until Mammy Callie died (I think they counted her at right around a hundred and something years old) they always wanted her to be with them, and I think picked out a place in the cemetery in their lot for her to be buried. She had helped to raise 'um—from start to finish, you might say. She had come here with 'um. She was with 'um from the time, I reckon, the first one was born up until the last. She'd come out here and stay with us in her off time. We had a farm, raised watermelons. We didn't call her Callie Barr . . . called her Callie Watermelon. She'd eat so many watermelons. She never did get enough, I don't believe.

* Earl Wortham mistakenly assumes that Mammy Callie came to Oxford with the Falkners. She joined the family after they had made the move.

I've known Mr. Faulkner from before I worked for his daddy, from when we were boys. I was older than Mr. Bill, but I don't know how much older. I never kept no records, and my daddy never did tell me. I was born way back yonder on an old plantation, you know, and we didn't get any schooling and so we just never could tell our age. Later I worked at the livery stable. Mr. Bill was a mighty good fellow. Mighty good. I worked for him— shoed his horses most of the time he was living, after he got grown, you know, and wanted horses. Shod 'um a few times here, and after I learnt their feet it was more convenient to go to his house, to put shoes on 'um.

Mr. Faulkner was just as friendly as you want to see somebody— when he'd talk. He wasn't a talking man, you know, just to get out and enjoy himself with other boys or men, but if you called his attention he'd stop and spend a few minutes with you and then go right on, with his head up, just like he wasn't studying nobody, walking around the streets to the post office, and on back to his home, and into his office to start to writing, you know. Mr. Faulkner's temper was just as quiet from, you might say, the time I knowed him up till the last. A horse get out there and act a little contrary or something, he'd talk to him just as nice, you know, and go right on. Any of 'um round the place he told to do something, like Andrew, if they didn't do it, or if they did it wrong, he'd come out and say, "Andrew, I did not tell you to do like that; you know that is not right," and turn right around and go on back to the house. He'd turn just as quick. If he was mad, nobody couldn't tell it.

Sometimes he'd tell of something about himself way back. Just like when me and him would be setting round talking or standing round somewhere talking and he'd tell of some little something or other that he had seen or heard of way back, you know. One day he told me that he was writing books, and he says, "Well, I tell you, you all is good people and all, and I'm going to try to prepare a way for it to be easier on you than what it *is* been." So far as what that meant, I don't know.

Mr. Faulkner liked the colored people. And as far as I know, they

all thought mighty well of him. One fellow—a colored man—
come over here and asked me to recommend him to Mr. Faulkner
because he wanted to borrow ten thousand dollars. He wanted
him to go on a note, or either loan him that much. He was a kind
of young fellow. He's got a little old farm outside of town here yet.
His daddy's place was in debt, and his daddy died and he wanted
to redeem that. So he sold some of it—a bunch of houses his
daddy had out there, and he's got a part of it yet. I told him,
though, I says, "Now, the thing you ought to do is if Mr. William
is good enough to help you out—you ought to be sure to try to
pay so much ever year (whatever you promise to pay) and don't
give him no trouble about it." So I just talked to Mr. William a
little bit about it. I told him he should use his own judgment
about trusting this colored fellow that way. Later on this colored
fellow went to him and in a few days he come back to me and
told me that Mr. William went right on and let him have some
money. I don't know how much or how it was arranged. I didn't
never ask him.

When Mr. Faulkner went off, he'd leave his horses over at the
house. He'd turn 'um over to me just like they was mine, because
he knowed I'd take care of 'um. He paid me just for the work I
done for him. He'd pay that the time he'd drive up here, or
either before he left home. He'd give me what I charged him for
my work for shoeing the horses.

Mr. Faulkner learnt his own horses. He broke 'um in jumping,
you know, and riding. He was mighty good at that. I never saw
him fall off his horse, but he fell off a mare that he raised, called
Tempy. Went to make a jump, and she jumped out from under
him. And then he went over to California and got an old gray
horse and a race horse and brought 'um back. He never did get to
drive the race horse. The old gray, he was a jumper, you know. Mr.
William enjoyed that, enjoyed that better than I reckon he did
anything else. So he throwed him once—didn't throw him, jumped
out from under him. That horse was awfully contrary. I didn't
want to hurt his feelings in no way, but I noticed the horse, and
I know the nature of horses. I've handled lots of 'um—broke 'um,

raised some, and on the plantation there could be a hundred and fifty, a hundred and seventy-five, you know, at a time. And my daddy being a horseman, I learnt the nature of 'um. I wanted to tell Mr. William I wouldn't fool with that horse, 'cause he just really didn't have good sense. One day over there he jumped out from under him, and I think broke two or three ribs or something or another like that. I was with him a while in jumping his horses around through Bailey's Woods, all back through in there; and he wanted me to go back out on Thacker's Mountain and put up some jumps over there.

When he died he had four horses here and one away from here. Last time I heard, Mrs. Faulkner had a truck come here and get 'um. I shod his horses during the last month of his life, and I seen him about a week before he died. He hadn't changed, don't seem like, very much; he just never would shave up like nobody else. I went to the funeral for Mr. Faulkner. I was right there: went to the house and from the house to the cemetery.

I put that horse and rider up there on the roof for me to think of Mr. Faulkner. I really did. Right on after his death, two or three weeks after his death, I put that horse up there to represent his riding. I've had many a one that wanted it, the white children, the grown men and women, and I tell 'um, "No, I set that up there to think of Mr. Faulkner." I was always particular with him, you see. He wanted me to go along on rides through the woods and hills and ditches and things. He believed I'd take care of him. I was always watching him ride and thinking that at the particular time he might get hurt or something like that. I used to tell him he was getting a little old to ride those fiery horses like he did, but he didn't think so. He used to say he was going to get me a horse so I could ride along with him.

FELIX LINDER
A Gentleman of the First Order

*D*r. *Felix Linder was William Faulkner's doctor and good friend.
The two men had known each other since boyhood. They hunted
together. And it was past the Linder home that Faulkner frequently
rode on horseback out Old Taylor Road.*

*A graduate of Ole Miss and the University of Virginia School of
Medicine, Dr. Linder interned in New Orleans and practiced in Memphis before returning to Oxford, where his father had practiced medicine. Though ill health has forced his retirement from active practice,
he maintains an office in Oxford and occasionally sees former patients,
particularly those who are financially distressed.*

*Dr. Linder's recollections of his friend and neighbor William
Faulkner were recorded on September 11, 1964.*

❧ My association with William . . . I called him William . . .
goes way back. He used to stay all night with us. He was that close.
We lived right here until we tore the house down and built another one. He'd come down here and stay with us. He was just
a very good friend of ours. There were three of us boys and the
three older Falkner boys, and we were all about the same age.

Bill! It's hard to tell all you know about old Bill because he did all sorts of things. I've been around him every which way you can imagine. I've known him in my practice. I've been hunting with him. I've been fishing with him. I've been on the place with him: he's got a farm out here on Highway 30 East.

William was a gentleman of the first order, and if somebody started telling dirty stories, he was gone, whether ladies were there or I was there or who was there. It didn't make any difference. He would leave and he wouldn't come back until you got through with the story. Then you'd have to beg him to listen to one of your stories. Oh, he was a gentleman; that's all there was to it. I never heard him say a dirty word in my life. I'm sure of that. I know I'm right about it.

I used to go on hunting trips with William. He was a good hunter. Very good indeed. A good shot. We'd go down in those Delta bottoms, down in the Sunflower River bottoms, and we'd hunt deer. One time, I remember, we were running short of meat and so William says to me, "You go down there." It was windy, cold. You could hear the dogs running. He says, "Go out there, get us some squirrels." Says, "We're getting short of meat." And I says, "Well, I'll be glad to do it." So I went down across the Sunflower River, on the other side, and I went down there, and it was the prettiest day you ever saw in your life. I remember I had an old 12-gauge shotgun, and I got me a whole lot of squirrels, but didn't get any deer. I ran into one deer and I shot him six times. It wasn't enough, though.

It used to be a custom that if you came down there to get a deer and then missed one they'd cut your shirttail off, sure as shooting. And I had a brand new red wool shirttail and they were about to cut that off. And William says, "Gentlemen," says, "the rest of us just been sitting around here taking a drink and Felix's been out shooting us something to eat," and says, "I don't think we ought to do that." He was that sort of fellow. We had some good times down there.

William never did talk about his writing. Never even spoke to me about it. Never said a word about it to me. I didn't want to ask him. I remember I went out there to his house one time and he was reading . . . I believe it was *A Gentleman of the Confederacy*. He was sitting there reading, and I stood there, and after a while he looked up and closed the book, and I said something about what he was reading, but he didn't tell me anything about it. He was that way about his writing—never talked about it. It takes a good reader to read his books . . . to read any of his books. I think some of his books weren't fit to read.

William was crazy about jumping horses. There are a lot of fences down there in the woods that he built for his jumping horses. I guess he was the sorriest horseman in the world. He took some bad falls. That was what killed him: helped to. Of that I'm positive. He fell off every time he got on. He rode very spirited horses. First it was a red horse, tall—I don't know how many hands high. And nimble, very nimble. He fell off of him right out there about the mail box. And that like to have killed him. And then another horse, a gray horse, threw him. William was black and blue all over. That old gray horse really threw him.

But the one that got him was the other one—the old red horse. I don't know whether he was trying to jump or not. I think he was trying to protect that shoulder: that was about the same time he had the fracture. And that hurt him bad. It came out in the papers that he wasn't hurt much, but he was. He cried. Old Bill would have to be hurt bad to cry. He says, "That's hurting me." And I says, "I can stop that." He didn't want help. He was as tough as you ever saw.

He walked a half mile . . . a good half mile down here two or three times and told me he didn't want to die. I'd be sitting on the porch there. "Felix . . ." he'd say. He called me Felix. "I don't want to die." That's what he told me. He didn't come to me in a professional way, but he came to me, it looked like, just to talk. I says, "I could give you something to keep you from suffering. I could do that. I'll be glad to." William says, "That ain't what I want." It's hard to tell what he wanted. Peculiar fellow.

He's gone now and I miss him. We were very good friends. Old Bill was the best fellow I believe I ever had anything to do with.

HOWARD DUVALL, JR.

Captain Ahab and the Sloop

A few miles to the north and west of Oxford flows the Yalobusha River. There, in the late 1930's the federal government constructed one of the largest earthen dams in the world, creating a man-made lake which covers thousands of acres and serves to prevent flooding in the Mississippi Delta.

In the forties William Faulkner and three of his friends, Ross Brown, Colonel Hugh Evans, and Dr. Ashford Little, built a houseboat in Colonel Evans' backyard in order to take advantage of any pleasures the lake had to offer. They christened the craft Minmagary, held a launching party, and elected Faulkner skipper.

In addition to his interest in the Minmagary, Faulkner owned a small sailboat. Through some circumstance the boat sank and he called on his young friends to give him a hand in raising it. One of them was Howard Duvall, Jr., who recalls the incident in the sketch which follows.

Mr. Duvall and his father own a men's shop in Oxford. And he and his wife now own the old home on University Avenue in which William and Estelle Faulkner had an apartment after their marriage in 1929.

❦ If memory serves me correctly, the expedition to locate and raise Mr. Faulkner's sailboat took place in the spring of 1953. For some reason Mr. Bill had left the boat at anchor at Cole's Camp on the Sardis Reservoir during the winter months; and in the early spring, it was discovered to have drifted out into the cove and sunk in about eighteen feet of water. The recovery of the boat would not have presented any great problem had Mr. Faulkner called Memphis for a professional diver and rig; however, this would have been too conventional and commercial for his adventuresome mind. Therefore, he chose to make use of local talent, which I'm sure he felt would provide for a much more interesting day on Sardis Lake.

On the appointed morning Billy Ross Brown, a neighbor and close friend of the Faulkners, and I reported for salvage duty at Mr. Bill's home. Also along was the Browns' houseboy, Isom Gillum, who would act as all-round handyman for the project, as we were sure that we were in for some heavy work ahead. Upon arriving, we were surprised to find that a new member had been added to the party. His name was V. P. Ferguson; he was a student at Ole Miss, and I think it would be safe to say the "Veep," as he was locally known, was something of a character. Billy Ross and I were quite familiar with the kimono-wearing, Koran-reading orchestra leader from the University, but we were admittedly quite surprised to see him here primed for the occasion. We were later to learn that V. P., upon hearing of the sinking of the sailboat, had called Mr. Faulkner and offered his services in recovering it. He explained to Mr. Bill that he was preparing for a summer excursion to the Caribbean to dive for black pearls, and that the Sardis outing would be good experience. I'm sure Mr. Bill discounted much of this story, but I'm also sure that he saw possibilities for an interesting day on the lake, and so invited him along. (Whoever says Faulkner had no sense of humor should have been along that day.)

The chief preparation for the outing seemed to have been the securing of enough food to satisfy the appetites of the would-be salvage crew. Miss Estelle was in charge of this department and she had already sent Norfleet, the Faulkners' Negro houseboy, out into the side yard with a large picnic basket of food. With the picnic basket safely secured in the Faulkner family station wagon, the five of us set forth to the Sardis Dam to begin salvage operations. To look over the crew—a Nobel Prize-winning author, two young college friends, a would-be pearl diver, and the faithful Negro houseboy—one could wonder about the prospects for the success of the mission. The route carried us through the University campus out Highway 6 West some eighteen miles, and then about seven miles up a gravel road to Sardis Dam. Our plan was to board the houseboat anchored at the dam and then to travel up the reservoir about five miles to Cole's Camp, where the sailboat, as has been previously mentioned, lay some eighteen feet below the surface.

I think it would be well to pause here to say a few words about the houseboat which would be our base of operations for the day. Contrary to the general principle of shipbuilding (or in this case, boatbuilding), this vessel was built in the side yard of Colonel Hugh Evans of Oxford, many miles from any body of water. Being a neighbor and friend of Colonel Evans, Mr. Bill became interested in the boat and soon was a full-time partner in its construction. Two other families were involved in this venture, namely the Ross Browns and the Ashford Littles. After the completion of the boat came the problem of getting the rather large craft through the narrow streets of Oxford and out the main highway to Sardis Lake without tying up traffic for hours. It was decided to hire a a professional mover from Memphis to undertake the task, and at the appointed time the boat was transferred by night to the lake. That morning the owners, their families and interested friends gathered at Sardis to watch her slide down the ways, and down she went, only to bob like a cork on a fishing line. It was quite evident that the boat was riding much too high in the water. The propeller screw did not reach the proper depth. Mr. Bill and his friends put their heads together and the solution was soon reached: put concrete in the bottom of the boat. Concrete was then placed

in the hold, and the *Minmagary* set forth on her maiden voyage to
reign as queen of the Sardis Reservoir for many years.*

Mr. Bill was indeed master of his ship as we pulled out of the
inlet onto the main body of water. After estimating the time of
arrival at about an hour, and with Mr. Bill at the wheel, Billy Ross
and I settled back in the deck chairs to enjoy the spring morning.
I think we were doubly enjoying it because we were cutting classes
at the University in order to make the trip. I know, too, that Mr.
Bill was relaxed in his khaki pants and military-style khaki shirt,
sitting at the wheel and smoking his favorite briar. In sailing and
boating on Sardis, he seemed to find the peace and privacy that
was more and more of a struggle to obtain after receiving the
Nobel Prize.

V. P., always the nervous type, soon tired of watching the shore
line go by and asked Mr. Bill if he could take over the wheel. Offering no objection, Mr. Bill let him have it and then joined us on
the back deck to relax and discuss the problems of getting to the
sailboat. Presently we were interrupted by the clanging of the deck
bell and sharp commands being issued by the "Veep" sitting hard
by the wheel.

"Full steam ahead; we are approaching the salvage area. We
must have more steam," he shouted into an imaginary tube that
led to an equally imaginary engine room. The only person available
to heed his commands was Isom, our houseboy turned cabin boy
for the occasion, and he was thoroughly mystified by the whole
proceeding. I'm quite certain that Isom thought Mr. Ferguson
was "tetched in the head," for he came back to me and said, "Mr.
Howard, you know we don't have no engine room down there,
only that 75 marine engine and there sho ain't nobody down there
to hear him."

It seems that V. P. had just finished some popular novel of the
day concerning the rescue of a British submarine down in the

* The *Minmagary*, started in August, 1947, was launched in June of the following
year. Faulkner, by virtue of whatever authority he may have inherited from his
great-grandfather, appointed her a "Ship of the Line in the Provisional Navy of
the Confederate States of America." See Appendix.

South China Sea with all hands aboard, and through his imagination we were the crew pushing full steam ahead to make the rescue. I believe Mr. Bill thoroughly enjoyed the fantasies of the "Veep" and he was soon resting again in his deck chair, probably assuring himself that he had made the right decision in bringing along Mr. Ferguson.

As we approached the entrance to the cove that led to Cole's Camp, Mr. Bill took over the wheel again and steered us into position near the sunken boat. There was no real problem in finding the boat because of a safety line that was still attached from the sunken hull to a tree on shore. The plan of action was for us to take down a steel cable attached to a winch on the bow of the houseboat and hook it through an iron ring in the bow of the sailboat. After securing the hook, the idea was to crank the winch, thus pulling the boat to the surface. When this was accomplished, Mr. Bill planned to move the houseboat with the sailboat in tow to a nearby boat ramp, where we could wade in to maneuver the sailboat onto a boat trailer which would be backed into the water. The station wagon would be used to pull boat and trailer out and to Mr. Bill's backyard drydock for repairs and overhaul.

All of this seemed relatively simple except for the fact that V. P. began complicating things from the start. For example, after his first dive he came up on deck, bowed in true Arabian Night style before Mr. Bill and exclaimed, "Oh, Captain Ahab, there is an octopus down below guarding the boat. Do you happen to have a machete aboard that might afford me some protection?"

Much to our surprise, Mr. Bill, with his usual composure, disappeared below deck, came up with a machete and gave it to Ferguson, who immediately dived over the side with the weapon and disappeared below the surface while Isom stood by in wide-eyed wonder.

Just before noon, the hook was finally secured to the sailboat, but "Captain Ahab" decided to wait until after lunch to bring it to the surface. Isom broke out the picnic basket and began serving the food, keeping one eye, I'm sure, over the side for any sign of the octopus. Snakes were no problem for Isom, but an octopus was something else!

About halfway through lunch we heard the sound of someone on the other side of the lake trying to get our attention, and before any of us could answer, V. P. jumped upon the top deck and began wigwagging signals with a couple of towels. Before anyone knew what was going on, we observed an appreciable number of slightly disreputable looking fellows approaching, and within a short time the houseboat was boarded by what turned out to be the entire membership of V. P.'s dance band. It seems that V. P. had made slight mention of the expedition to his colleagues, and had in fact invited them to join him for lunch. They made short work of the contents of the picnic basket, and then they spread out all over the boat for an afternoon of sunbathing. I must say, at this point, that for a man who enjoyed his privacy, Mr. Bill seemed to take the whole affair in a very calm and understanding manner. The taciturn Nobel Prize-winner, in quiet and sly fashion, maintained his aplomb while V. P. all but took command of the situation.

The rest of the afternoon went by somewhat uneventfully with only the routine of securing the sailboat to the side of the house-boat and loading it on the trailer as described earlier. At dusk the sailboat was placed on the trailer and towed to its drydock in Faulkner's backyard.

Some several days later Mr. Faulkner invited the group down to his house for a lawn supper, and I remember that the highlight of the evening was Mr. Bill's dancing the soft shoe with Paul Pitt-man, one of the Ole Miss students.

William Faulkner spent many hours of sheer pleasure in the little sailboat that went to the bottom off Cole's Landing and that was raised to sail again by Faulkner and a group of college students on that happy and carefree day. He usually referred to it as "the sloop."

One afternoon while he, Miss Estelle, Hunter Little, and I were cruising, dark clouds appeared in the northwest and it was soon obvious that a squall was imminent. Fishermen, we observed, were scurrying shoreward. Faulkner calmly dismissed the idea of a squall and was maneuvering the sloop down the lake when a gust hit the craft and almost upset it. Life preservers were passed around. Faulkner declined his. Another gust took his hat, and Hunter went overboard to retrieve it and was almost drowned. After he was pulled aboard and matters were as much in hand as circumstances allowed, Faulkner called to me, "Howard, hand me a preserver. I am getting a bit chilly."

In looking back over the years to the event just related, it becomes more apparent that the people who knew Faulkner best, outside of his own family, were the young people who grew up around the Faulkner home, as children playing with Jill, his daughter, later dancing and eating at her parties, and sharing many carefree moments with the man we all knew as Mr. Bill.

W. MCNEILL REED

Four Decades of Friendship

The William Faulkner of the 1950's was in some ways a different man from the one glimpsed earlier. He was older, of course. Fame had come, and the distinction of the Nobel Prize; whereas once he went abroad because that was what young artists did, he went now as the emissary of his country. He gave more interviews. He allowed himself to be recorded at Charlottesville and West Point and Nagano.

Among those who had an opportunity to observe both Faulkners was his good friend Mac Reed. In the sketch which follows, the Oxford druggist tells much about Mr. Faulkner and much about himself. The modesty and shyness of the two men created between the two an immediate rapport which, through the years, matured into a close friendship.

Mac Reed was one of those named by Faulkner to administer the education fund set up from Nobel Prize monies. When the author died, Mr. Reed was one of the two pallbearers who were not members of the family (Phil Stone was the other).

This interview was taped at the Gathright-Reed Drug Store on September 9, 1964.

❦ For nearly forty years Bill Faulkner visited our drugstore, and fairly frequently. I wish I could remember exactly when I met Bill, who introduced us, or what we talked about, but it is utterly impossible for me to recall that time except that it was in 1923. I came to live in Oxford on July 1 to join the drugstore which had been started in February of that year. The store was at that time on the other side of the square, the north side. I should say that in twenty-three Bill was in and out of the store from time to time. That was when he was postmaster at Ole Miss. It's quite possible that Phil Stone, with whom I had gone to school at Ole Miss, made the introduction. It could be that Phil's brother, Jim Stone, or Dr. J. M. Gathright, or his son, pharmacist O. Holder Gathright, introduced us, or Coach Sullivan of the University—any one of several who might have been in the drugstore from time to time. And so I came to see Bill Faulkner throughout that year. I can't recall whether he was there all the rest of the year. I just do not remember exactly.

But my one long day's visit with him, I should say, was a year or two later when his uncle ran for district attorney of the circuit court district. That was J. W. T. Falkner. He was called Judge Falkner because, I believe, he had been appointed judge to serve a time or two or to fill out an unexpired term until an election could be held. But the lawyer, the uncle of William Faulkner, asked

that I go to Chickasaw County with William—or asked if it would
be all right if William went with me to drive the car and to meet
people over there and for me to talk with people that I knew,
letting them know that I knew the candidate, Mr. Falkner. I had
a delightful visit with Bill that day. We talked, among other
things, of my brother Rad, who was said to be a promising writer
but whose life was shortened by an injury sustained in the collapse
of a grandstand at an Ole Miss football game. I was impressed, as
always, by Bill's utter interest in anything which was said, any
story that was told, any answer to any question, his deep concentration and his quiet comment from time to time on any subject
that was brought up.

There was no similarity between Judge J. W. T. Falkner and
William. William was not at all interested in politics, even on
behalf of his uncle. On that particular day he would go with me
to a place of business where I had known people for many years.
And after the introductions, why, pretty soon he would be out on
the street, looking over the town, looking at the traffic, watching
the movements of the people, not talking with anybody. He was on
a corner or leaning against a store building. But he had nothing
whatever to say about the candidacy of his uncle. He said that he
didn't know anything about politics.

Most of my visits with Bill were at the drugstore. From time to
time he would, maybe after having taken a long walk in the woods,
come by the store and look at the old *American Mercury*, or the
old *Scribner's* or *Atlantic* or *Harper's*. I think that he didn't mean
to stay for any length of time probably. But his looking at a magazine or some periodical there would be something in which he
would soon be absorbed, and so he would lean against the counter
or the magazine stand and, in all probability, would just, not thinking, sit down on the floor. In later years, when we had a rental
library and when pocket books came along, he was quite interested
in mysteries, and so would search for them.

When *Intruder in the Dust* was made here in 1949, Lydel Sims,
the columnist for the Memphis *Commercial Appeal*, asked if it
were true that Bill came to the drugstore and sat and read for a

great length of time, and that he did that because he didn't have the money to purchase the magazines. I told him I wanted that cleared up right then, because if Bill didn't have the money he had the credit. And he also said that he understood Bill came to the drugstore barefooted. And so I told him that I remembered one time . . . probably a few times . . . that Bill did that. Probably he had been walking out to the west of the University (you know, through the woods, and particularly did he like to do that during the rainy weather,—walk in the wet leaves) and he would find himself coming out on the street somewhere and, knowing that he hadn't been by the post office to get the mail, would come on up here and stay in here for a while and go by and get the mail and walk on home. It was true that he did sit on the floor from time to time, but those were very terrible days for us back there. We hardly could afford chairs, and therefore, naturally, if he was going to sit at all he would sit down on the floor. Bill was usually unconscious of anybody's presence at all. But he enjoyed people very, very much. If he thought that they were endeavoring to seek him out and to ask him some questions, why, he just would go the other way.

There were very few long conversations I ever had with Bill. Very few. His real bit of visiting was done in front of our store. I've seen him lean back against the glass and talk with some old friend, maybe for an hour. And a number of people could come, knowing his habits, early in the morning and would probably stop to talk with him ten or fifteen minutes. Cold weather seemed to bother none of them. Of his old friends, Ike Roberts would be one. And John Cullen. And there were many farmers from time to time who would be in town early anyway, and they'd see Bill there and they'd stop by and talk with him. That was something that all of them seemed to enjoy very much. They'd laugh heartily and I could imagine that they were talking about some deer hunt they'd been on, or some story some farmer wanted to tell him about. But he would never tell or listen to off-color jokes. I remember that he told a story to me in the store one morning I thought was tremendously funny, and it was not an off-color story, but somebody

WILLIAM FAULKNER

could interpret it that way. I never knew of his telling a really off-color story.

During the years of struggle for acceptance of manuscripts by publishers of magazines and books, I noted in our visits—always brief—the tremendous drive and effort of Bill Faulkner. When his first story, "Thrift," appeared in the *Saturday Evening Post* in September of 1930 I felt that he could reach pleasing heights.* "Turn About" came later in the *Post*, as did "The Bear" and others. When *Harper's*, the *Atlantic Monthly*, *Scribner's*, the *American Mercury*, and others carried stories, many of us were delighted at the accomplishment. In our visits I talked with him briefly many times about his short stories. I shall always feel they are the best of him. Of course, Bill's style of writing presented problems to the reader who had been drilled in punctuation and short sentences. Had I been a teacher of English, I think I should have endeavored to study fully the Faulkner writing technique as so many thousands have done.

It is granted that he brought out many a word that so many of us had never used and had never heard. On two different visits he asked about a word for something in the military and a word for something else. I cannot recall what either was, or with what it had to do. But I was amazed that he did not find the words himself to provide apt description: he never seemed at a loss in his writings. It is a fact that William Faulkner had no dictionary for quite some time except an English-French dictionary. That period, I believe, was prior to his Nobel Prize award. Every dictionary publisher in the U.S.A. must have presented him with one of his best at some time or other, but they were passed on to libraries and individuals, evidently. Why, then, did William Faulkner who, of late years, referred to himself as the "oldest living sixth grader," ferret out so many unusual words? Someone may answer that question for me some day.

Thousands of visitors to Oxford from every part of the world

* "Thrift" was the first of many Faulkner stories to be published in the *Post*. Earlier that year "A Rose for Emily" had appeared in *Forum*, followed by "Honor" in the *American Mercury*.

want to know about the Snopeses and other characters that people Faulkner's books. They want to know in what generations such types existed. I am pleased to know, I tell them, that they don't think we are that way now! I also tell the people from elsewhere that doubtless all of us have seen characters worse than some of the people in Bill's books, but that it would be difficult for us to describe them so effectively.

The year Bill received the Nobel Prize, the Ford Foundation made a television film, "Faulkner's Life Story," showing Faulkner at home, on his farm, on the streets of Oxford, and in the chapel at the University at the time that his daughter Jill was being graduated from high school, when he delivered the commencement address. In Phil Stone's law office, Bill and Phil talked of the early struggles as he worked toward acceptance and publication, and Bill thanked "Stone," as he often called Phil, for his interest, helpfulness, and encouragement. A bit of the film showed Bill and me "visiting" across the counter at Gathright-Reed's. Sometime later, Bill received a copy of the film. "Hard as I worked," he commented, "looks like they ought to send me a hay-baler or something." The great problem was to get Bill to see it. Months later he finally viewed it and told several of us he thought it was "done up" all right. My daughter Kitty in Illinois asked, "Would Mr. Bill let me have it for a week?" I told Bill it would be insured heavily in the event shipment was made. "You tell Kitty," Bill said, "if it gets burned up or lost, it's all right because I don't ever aim to see it no mo."

Bill said nothing about his trip to Stockholm. The one thing that I recall is what he said before he went. I went down about 10:30 on the morning the news came, and he was in his pasture with a beat-up jeep and mechanized equipment used for the distribution of slag. He looked awfully dirty and ragged that morning. Bill Fielden, Mrs. Faulkner's son-in-law, was there, and he and I went over to the gate and watched Bill as he circled his machine. As far as I knew he had never looked up in our direction at all, but when he came up abreast of us he stopped and looked up and turned off his motor and came on over. I just shook hands with him, didn't say a word. He said, "Mac, I still can't believe it." That's the only comment that he ever made to me about that before going or coming back or anything.

I have a little correspondence from Bill—just a small amount. He wrote me a letter from Japan. He had gone over, you know, for the State Department and he was interested in helping a young Japanese lady whose people were lost at Hiroshima.* She was to have some education in the United States with some of his Nobel Prize money. It was his desire that this be known in order that if anything happened to him, the aid would go on. As you may know, there was in the beginning his statement to the effect that the Nobel Prize money would be used as far as possible for the education of worthy people from his home county.

He at first named three people (I was one of them) to administer the fund in the event that something should happen to him. Then, in later years, the Faulkner Foundation was set up at Charlottesville. He notified the three who were on the committee that this change had been made and that any duties they may have been asked to perform had come to an end with the placing of this money in the Foundation. Therefore, we were released, so to speak. The work is being carried on through the Faulkner Foundation and has had some assistance from friends here in this country and in other countries. The thought was that there would probably be a committee to select worthy students.

Bill never told me anything about this or consulted me about it. I don't mean that he would ask my advice about it, but he didn't say anything to me about my being a member of the Faulkner Foundation. I had to find out about it through the New York Times! The story said that it was his desire to have this money used for the education of worthy young people, those who might become teachers or who might write, and he would like to emphasize the need for young colored boys who showed good possibilities for accomplishing things to get an education that would en-

---

* Faulkner visited Japan in 1955 at the invitation of the State Department and took part in the Nagano Seminar. In the 1950's he made similar trips to Europe and to South America.

able them to come back and teach their own people; there were words to that effect. And so that was planned and carried out as far as possible for a time, but I think that they ran into a little complication and it was decided grants for education should not necessarily be confined to the group mentioned: the Foundation would simply leave decision to the universities and colleges in which a scholarship fund might be placed.

The thought on the part of some in those days was that I would know something about the administration of the fund. I had long-distance calls because Bill was quoted in Rome—something about his plans for the education of people. Long distance was just calling, calling, calling Mrs. Faulkner, and this was even after Bill came back, about who was going to administer this fund. Estelle thought and said that they would have to consult me. I told them —the people who were calling me long distance—that any comment which was made with regard to the administration of the Nobel Prize money would have to come from Mr. Faulkner himself. They wanted to know if I were a member of the committee, and I said, "I have no comment. You must ask Mr. Faulkner any question you desire." I didn't think they could get Bill on the phone, for that matter. And he had nothing to say about it.

Bill was that way. Throughout all the years I never knew the proposed title or the suggested title of any story that he ever sent in. During the very early years, of course, Phil Stone handled his manuscripts. Later, Bill would just come in and say, "Mac, I . . . I didn't have anything down at the house to wrap this in. Do you have a box or something?" So we'd go ahead and wrap it and get it all sealed and ready to go, you know, and he'd have an address label there, and so that would be all there was to it.

I look back to the mailing of the manuscript for what proved to be his last book, The Reivers. As we finished packaging and labeling it, he leaned over the counter and said, "I been aimin' to quit this foolishness."

The only time I ever talked with him about anything that had not yet been released was about that book, and I simply mentioned one morning that I understood it had a number of good laughs in it and I could hardly wait. And he smiled and said, "You know, I think some of it *is* funny."

I do remember, too, what he said when I wrapped a copy of *The Reivers* for him which he was mailing to a friend in Sweden. I don't know whether she translated his works into Swedish or not. But, anyway, he said, "I come off and forgot my glasses this morning. Would you address this for me?" I was wrapping it in the meantime, and I said, "I'll get the necessary foreign postal forms and get that all set." And he said, "I already got 'em." You know, he would drop down in the vernacular. He was able to ride a bit, but still wore his back brace since being thrown from his horse some weeks before. "I . . . my back was hurting me so I just couldn't think of anything much this morning."

That was on the morning of July 3, 1962. He had picked up the daily paper he reserved and bought his favorite tobacco. It was my last visit with Bill.

J. AUBREY SEAY

A Day at the Lake

Fisherman, hunter, and restaurateur J. Aubrey Seay is usually in the woods or on the lake when he is not greeting guests—students, faculty members, statesmen, and authors—in his white-columned restaurant off Oxford's town square. When William Faulkner dined out during the last years of his life, it was usually at The Mansion.

In "A Day at the Lake" Mr. Seay recalls what may have been Faulk-

ner's last outing—a trip the two men made together on July 2, 1962, four days before the author's death. In this account, drawn from an interview tape recorded September 11, 1964, we get a glimpse of the oral tradition out of which Faulkner's writing sprang.

Aubrey Seay came to Oxford from Memphis in 1934 and for several years before opening his restaurant was director of food services at the University of Mississippi. He has given a good deal of his time to the Mississippi Game and Fish Commission.

❧ Bill and Estelle Faulkner didn't eat out too often, but I think nearly every time they did they ate in here, and for several reasons: no one bothered them and we disconnected the music. People who were passing through would ask, "Is that William Faulkner?" When I answered, "Yes," they'd say, "Could I ask for his autograph?" and I'd reply, "He came here to enjoy his dinner. I wouldn't bother him; he might embarrass you." So we protected him.

As to the music, I remember once when Dr. and Mrs. Ashford Little were having a big wedding party on their lawn down there and Martha and I slipped off to go down, and while we were gone the Faulkners arrived at The Mansion. We had a juke box then, and we always disconnected it when Bill and Estelle came in. It was my idea because I hated the thing myself! We would put an "Out of Order" sign on it, and if someone complained we would refund his money. The employees knew that we did that, but we were gone that particular evening and some students asked why the juke box had been disconnected. One of the coeds said, "Because the great Mr. Faulkner is in here." Some of the students resented that and they went up and turned it back on, connected it up and turned the volume up as loud as it would go—and the Faulkners left. As soon as we got back to The Mansion, I found out why William was offended. The students had turned it on as loud as the devil. He didn't know that we weren't here, I suppose. He hadn't asked me to keep the music down, but somehow I found out that he didn't like a juke box. When we got the background music, I thought he would like that, but he didn't. I think Paul Flowers, who has a column on literature and literary people in the Memphis *Commercial Appeal*, explained that better than anyone else: William resented being a captive audience for canned music. That's what Paul said, and I guess that's about the way he was.

The Faulkners usually sat in the third booth on the right side going toward the back. We should probably put that booth back because everybody always wants to know where he sat. Bill always faced the front. They would come in after the rush—he and Estelle. Sometimes Mrs. Faulkner's son, Malcolm Franklin, would be with them, and sometimes Dorothy Oldham, Mrs. Faulkner's sister. By the way, once when Estelle was out of town William came to The Mansion alone. My wife Martha urged him to eat well and to take care of himself during Estelle's absence. "I'll be all right," he said, and smiled. "Dorothy's my den mother." Bill was always very quiet. I never bothered him. If he didn't say anything to me, I didn't say anything to him.

One evening former Governor J. P. Coleman and his wife stopped here—on her birthday, I remember. We were sitting over in the corner booth when the Faulkners came in. Governor Coleman said, "Isn't that William Faulkner?" "Yes," I replied, but I made no effort to get them together because, you know, Faulkner was usually in a shell. So it was a coincidence that they left at the same time, the Faulkners going this way and the Colemans going that way. They met at the cash register and I introduced them. I had not read at that time about what Faulkner said when President Kennedy invited all the living Nobel Prize-winners to dinner at the White House and Faulkner was the only one who declined to go, but Governor Coleman had read about it. When he met Faulkner he said how much he had enjoyed Faulkner's remark about going a hundred miles just to eat.* Faulkner seemed pleased

* The White House banquet honoring Nobel Prize-winners was held April 29, 1962, less than three months before Faulkner's death. The author, then at his home in Charlottesville, was quoted as saying, "Why, that's a hundred miles away. That's a long way to go just to eat."

and smiled. I was amazed. When the Colemans left, he stayed on and bragged on Coleman and what a great man he was. That was unusual for Faulkner, too.

The Faulkners also came here because they liked my children and the waitresses. We had a waitress who giggled all the time. Every time she said anything she would giggle. If you said anything to her she would giggle. It worried me to death. She waited on Faulkner every time he came in. I was watching in the mirror and I finally decided that he wanted her to stay and talk. All the time they were eating, she would stand there and say things and giggle, but he would send for her when he came back.

He didn't like to talk about his writing or to be talked to about his success. About the time of the Nobel Prize award, I saw him coming down the street and a lady meeting him. I opened the door and watched so I could hear what they were saying, and I heard her saying, "How proud we are! How proud we are!" If he said anything, I didn't hear it. He just kept walking.

One time I was down there in his yard when he was working on his sailboat. He had it bottom side up and was sanding it. He was out there in old raggedy shorts: he looked terrible. A big automobile came in the driveway, full of ladies. I paid no attention because I thought it was some relatives or something like that. There was a sign at the gate that said, "Private Property—Do Not Enter." But the lady who had driven in got out of the car. She walked up to me and said, "Are you Mr. Faulkner?" "No," I replied. "That is Mr. Faulkner." She went up to him and said, "Mr. Faulkner, we are probably intruding, but I am Miss So-and-So from Tupelo High. I have some of my students, and I would like for you to give them your autograph if you would." "I'm busy," he said, and turned his back. I didn't blame him; she was intruding! She turned red and left. He purposely left his driveway bad so it was hard to travel. That driveway was always full of holes.

A friend, Bill Minor of the New Orleans *Times-Picayune*, called me once and said, "I've been trying to get William Faulkner, but he won't talk to me. *Newsweek* wants me to do a story on his play, *Requiem for a Nun*, opening on Broadway. Can you help me?" I told him I couldn't help him. "But I know where he is," I said. "He's hunting quail." William usually went hunting by himself. He was a very good shot; his favorite was the bobwhite quail. And Bill Minor repeated, "He's in his jeep out in the country hunting quail." So we rode all over the country trying to find him, but we couldn't. You know Jim Silver? He has more nerve than a burglar. I called Jim and asked him if he would help.* So Jim Silver took Bill Minor down to Faulkner's house and saw Faulkner in there and walked in—Silver did. He asked him if he would see Bill Minor. Faulkner agreed to see him provided he would not discuss his writing. So he was the perfect host and served them a drink. Bill Minor, when he got ready to leave, turned around and asked what he had come to ask. Silver said, "Why, you so-and-so." He was mad about it. But Faulkner said, "Why should I go to Broadway to see my play? After all, I wrote it. I'd rather be in the sagebrush of Mississippi hunting bobwhite quail."

Bill was a sailboat enthusiast. One time he had his sailboat out on Sardis Lake. I had my fishing boat next to his sailboat anchored out there from the bank. We would go for weeks at a time without saying anything to each other. I wanted him to put his boat on Enid Lake, the place I am interested in. I have money in it. I had been talking to him about it and he wanted to go over there and see it. We made several dates, but every time something happened to keep us from going. One day Estelle called and said that William wanted to go; so I made an appointment to pick him up at two o'clock on July 2.

To show you how agreeable he was, I have an air-conditioned car. It was hot on July 2. I asked him if he would like to go by Water Valley and come back by Batesville, and he was agreeable to whatever I wanted to do. I asked if he would like the air-conditioning on or the windows open, and he said, "Whatever you like." So I cut the air-conditioning down low. Neither of us said very much going over. One thing I have is a buzzer to warn me of speeding. You know how it works. I had it set at seventy, and it didn't occur

* James W. Silver, professor of history at the University of Mississippi, is the author of *Mississippi: The Closed Society.*

to me to explain it to him. Every once in a while the buzzer would go off and he was startled momentarily. Finally I told him what it was, and, as a matter of fact, I turned it up a little.

We got over there and he studied the lake and the layout and where he might put the boat: maybe here, or maybe over there: finally he elected to anchor it out from the bank so that it could ride the waves. Incidentally, I had called the manager over there and told him, "I'm bringing William Faulkner." And I told him, too, "Don't you say anything about his being famous; don't talk about his work; treat him like he is just anybody and he will like it all right." Rex played his part beautifully.

I saw a school of bass out there feeding on shad. I pointed them out to Faulkner and said, "Look at those bass. I have two rods and reels in the car. Would you like to catch some of them?" "No," he replied, "but I'd like to watch you." So I thought that, with an audience like that, I couldn't lose. I got out my paraphernalia and got it rigged up and put it on the deck. Rex McRaney had a swank boat from the Bank of Jackson. We used it as a sort of houseboat. Rex jumped over and got his trouser cuff caught in my line. I called, "Wait, wait!" but he didn't hear me. In the confusion the boat drifted over the fish; so we decided just to cruise around. I had my binoculars and I had my movie camera. It was loaded and in my right hand, but I decided to wait until another time to use it. Rex and I ignored him, and William had a great time looking through the binoculars. I could see him from the corner of my eye. He didn't talk much. I had told Rex not to talk to him. He just looked around.

After a while I said, "Well, Meredith is supposed to come on the thirteenth. Do you suppose we'll have any trouble?" * "If we do," William replied, "it will be because of the people out in Beat Two who never went to the University or never intended to send their children to the University." I don't know why he said "Beat

---

* Mr. Seay was referring to James Meredith, the first Negro to be admitted to the University of Mississippi. There was indeed trouble when he was escorted onto the campus by federal marshals the following September 30.

Two": he owned a farm in Beat Two but lived in Beat One, but he did say "Beat Two." Coming in on the boat we got to talking about Governor Ross Barnett, and I said, "Rex, how was Barnett elected governor?" Faulkner took the binoculars down and said, "Eighty-two Beat Two's." Now wasn't that great? There are eighty-two counties and that would be 410 beats in the state, one out of five of which would be like Beat Two in Lafayette County, and all of them got together.

We had a couple of bourbons apiece and, of course, both of us talked more on the way back home. I told him a couple of things he laughed about coming back from over there that night.

I polished up—exaggerated—a little bit one of them I told him about, but he seemed to like it. It was about the first birthday party I ever went to. Back many years ago, Mary Garden chocolates were quite the thing. They came in red boxes; we didn't have cellophane, but a big red ribbon was on each box. The party was for a little girl named Edith Van. Girls didn't wear silk stockings in those days, but Edith's mother let her wear her discarded silk stockings. I thought she was the prettiest thing in the world. So she asked me to this birthday party. We lived out in the country. I had thirty cents; that's what that box of candy cost me. It must have been a quarter of a pound, but it looked big. I had one pair of shoes and they were terrible looking. They were dry and hard and didn't have any holes in the eyes. I didn't have any polish; so I got some tallow and rubbed them, and the more I rubbed the better they looked. I got my box of candy and started over there. As I walked down the dusty road, the dust would stick to my shoes and the tallow, so I got out in the pasture. I got there late and presented my box of candy. We had ice cream, lemonade, cake, and stuff. I took my seat along with the other boys and started looking at their shoes—and then looking at mine. I was beginning to feel better about mine: they looked pretty good! All of a sudden someone opened the door and about six cats came in —and started licking my shoes! Such a licking of cats you never saw. Faulkner just cackled when I told him that!

Another thing that I told him about was taking a shortcut

through the pasture on a frosty morning barefooted. My children don't believe this. It had to be mighty cold for me to put on shoes. One time I stepped on some hot coals in a charcoal furnace, but didn't know it until I got down deep and the coals got on top. I'd find an old cow down in the pasture that had been there all night chewing the cud and make her get up so I could warm my feet on the ground where she had rested. My children don't believe that either, but Faulkner did. He believed it!

I told him, too, about my Uncle Jim who carried the mail on a bicycle in Jackson, in a place called Doodeville. When he got through in that neighborhood, he knew a shortcut to another neighborhood where he wouldn't have to ride all the way through town. He would go through a pasture on his bicycle. One day I was on the other side of the pasture when I saw Uncle Jim dismount and pull the bicycle under the fence, put his mail pouch on, and start across the pasture to the place where I was standing. A bull took out after him. The faster he'd peddle, the faster the bull would run after him. He didn't put on the brakes. When he got to where I was, he just hit the fence and came through it. Mail was all over the ground. The bull was snortin' and pawin'. I was helping him pick up the mail while he was dragging the bicycle under the fence. "Uncle Jim," I said, "that bull almost got you, didn't he?" "Yup," he replied, "he almost gets me every day." Faulkner cackled again.

To go on the trip to Enid Lake I picked him up at two, and we got back a little after six. As we approached Oxford and passed the Ole Miss Drive Inn, he remarked that progress was destroying his wonderful riding path up there near the new highway, where he often used to ride his horse. He complained some about his back hurting a little bit; he had fallen from his horse before that time. But he seemed healthy and in good spirits on that trip. That was on July 2, 1962.

About 8:30 he and Estelle came in to eat dinner at the usual time. If he had had another drink, it didn't show, and I don't think he had. On July 3 they came back at the same time. He looked well and strong and fine on the last evening that I saw him.

On July 4 we were closed. Very early on the morning of July 6 my wife Martha woke me and said that she didn't know whether, or how, to tell me: William had left us.

MURRAY LLOYD GOLDSBOROUGH

Sitting for a Portrait

The Goldsborough portrait of William Faulkner which now hangs in the University of Mississippi Library was painted only weeks before the author's death. The painter did his studies while observing Faulkner at small social gatherings; these he supplemented with photographic poses for which Faulkner agreed to sit.

An alumnus of the University of Virginia, Murray Lloyd Goldsborough studied military science in Germany before World War I. He has engaged in legal work; he has been in the service of the federal government; he has been a large-scale real estate operator; and he has painted portraits of a number of distinguished people. He now makes his home in Florida.

Mr. Goldsborough's stepson, William Strickland, is chairman of the Department of Modern Languages at the University of Mississippi.

I had never met William Faulkner until I went to Oxford to paint his portrait for the University of Mississippi in March of 1962. The evening of my arrival he and Mrs. Faulkner came to my stepson's house for a preliminary get-together. He appeared in ragged cotton trousers, an old sport jacket, bowler hat, gloves and stick, and a three-day beard! He was very quiet and obviously on the defensive.

I assured him at once that he need not fear a boring discussion of his work as I had never read a word he had ever written and probably never would. At this he laughed heartily and thawed out immediately. We discovered quickly that we had about forty good friends in common and spent a delightful evening together with no lack of conversation on his part.

He asked how I wanted to paint him. I told him that I wanted him as he thought of himself, as I wanted the portrait to be relaxed and characteristic. He thought this was admirable, and, taking me at my word, came for my studies in the same clothes (only with an added eight-inch tear in the trousers) but without the bowler, gloves, stick, and beard. I did mend his trousers in the painting, but otherwise handled him exactly as he was. He seemed delighted with the results.

I found William Faulkner and his wife to be most charming and gracious hosts and we made plans to see each other during the coming summer when my wife and I expected to be in Oxford.

He was very fond of horses and had a young hunter of which he expected great things. Knowing that I, when young, had some reputation as a horseman, he asked me if I would help him school this horse; he thought that during the two months that I expected to be there we could polish him up in fine shape. I was looking forward enthusiastically to this when his death put an end to our plans.

JAMES W. WEBB

William Faulkner Comes Home

*J*n the piece which follows, James W. Webb tells of an aging, almost mellow Faulkner who came home to Oxford early in 1962—the year in which he died. As chairman of the Ole Miss Department of English, Professor Webb hoped to persuade the University's most distinguished alumnus to sit for a portrait. Here he recalls the chain of events which culminated in the Goldsborough painting.

Webb, a native Mississippian who holds degrees from Mississippi State University and the University of North Carolina, served as a major in the army during World War II and left the service as a lieutenant colonel. He joined the Ole Miss faculty in 1947.

Since then Faulkner has been one of his prime interests. It was through his efforts that the University, after Faulkner's death, was able to enter into a lease agreement whereby Rowan Oak is opened to scholars interested in the author's life and work.

❧ Early in 1962 William Faulkner came home to Oxford from Charlottesville, where he had been serving as writer-in-residence at the University of Virginia. He had just completed his last book, *The Reivers*, a picaresque tale of the adventures of young Lucius Priest and his friend Ned McCaslin, the old Negro retainer, written, one could almost say, for fun. And he seemed to have mellowed a good deal.

By 1962 Mr. Faulkner was beginning to show age, but he appeared to be in excellent physical condition. His hair was bushy and almost white. There was no evidence of baldness. He had allowed his mustache to grow full and to droop Mark Twain style. The lines in his face had deepened, but the piercing brown eyes were as bright as ever. Not only could he look you in the face, he could look through you. His face still crinkled with amusement at hearing a good story, or froze with scorn at something that met with his contempt.

During the late winter and early spring of that year he resumed his habitual stroll from his home each morning, walking along Old Taylor Road east to South Lamar and on to the Gathright-Reed Drug Store to call on Mr. Mac Reed, a close friend for many years. After a brief visit there he usually crossed the street and took a shortcut up the alley to the studio of Mr. J. R. Cofield, the local photographer. From there he made his way around courthouse square. On these rounds he rarely spoke to anyone, even when greeted by a close friend. Sometimes he would pass on, then stop and turn and say, "Why, good mornin'. Didn't see you." On other occasions he lifted his hat and formally returned a greeting, especially if it was an elderly lady whom he recognized. This was not interpreted by Oxford people as being particularly indifferent. It was just Bill Faulkner. Faulkner had many friends in Oxford, although he sometimes complained about people slipping into the woods below his house to shoot his "pet" squirrels, or about citizens who would rather see local bootleggers patronized than have legalized liquor laws passed.

And so that spring Faulkner turned to his farm, to riding his favorite horse Tempy, to repairing fences around the paddock at Rowan Oak, and to seeing local friends. Now he could wear his soiled khaki trousers and his old ragged jacket. In short, he had come home.

One morning that spring I met Professor William Strickland, who is chairman of the Modern Language Department, in the hallway of the Graduate Building on the Ole Miss campus. In the course of the conversation Bill commented that Ginette, his wife, had seen Mr. and Mrs. Faulkner in Kroger's the previous morning buying groceries. While Ginette and Mrs. Faulkner exchanged greetings and indulged in small talk, Faulkner indulged his pipe and watched customers as they bustled about the store. The conversation then turned to Bill Strickland's step-father, Mr. Murray Goldsborough, who resided in Lakeland, Florida, but who was then in Oxford, and who had only recently recovered from an eye operation. Mr. Goldsborough was so elated with the success of the operation that he wished to try his renewed sight by doing a portrait of a really worthy subject. Before World War I he had attended a German military school, and while in Germany had had an opportunity to paint a portrait of Kaiser Wilhelm. The conversation turned back to Faulkner. Naturally, here was a subject made to order if it could be arranged.

It occurred to several of us that we might arrange for Mr. Goldsborough to do a portrait of Faulkner for the University of Mississippi. I discussed the matter with Professor A. Wigfall Green and found him enthusiastic. We wanted the portrait for the Faulkner Collection in the University of Mississippi Library, but there was the problem of where to begin. Being academically oriented, we decided to begin by setting up a committee composed of Mrs. Strickland, Professor Green, and myself. I then consulted Mr. Hugh Clegg, assistant to the chancellor and director of development. We found him most encouraging and helpful.

In the meantime, the Stricklands talked to Mr. Goldsborough and to Mr. Faulkner. Faulkner stated that he would think it over and would talk to us later about the proposal. Shortly after lunch two days later Bill Strickland informed me that he and Ginette had seen the Faulkners that morning while shopping, that they had invited the Faulkners to their house, and that my wife Anne and I were invited. Mr. and Mrs. Goldsborough would be there, and it was understood that we could discuss the matter of the portrait.

At four o'clock on the afternoon of March 19, 1962, Anne and I called on the Stricklands. They told us that Mrs. Faulkner had phoned to say she and her husband would be about fifteen minutes late. Faulkner was out in the back paddock with his stable-keeper spreading manure, and he wanted to see the job finished before leaving. Bill Strickland was afraid that this meant they might not come at all. Within a few minutes, however, we saw their new red Rambler coming around the curve.

Greetings were exchanged, introductions made, and we were seated in the living room—all in short order. "Would you care for a cigarette?" asked Mr. Goldsborough.

"No. Smoke a pipe," replied Faulkner, and reaching for it and his special-order blend of tobacco he began the silent ritual of filling and lighting his pipe.

Before long, Mr. Goldsborough had begun to engage him in conversation about mutual acquaintances in and around Charlottesville. When they got around to horses, I joined in. I knew that Faulkner had used the topic of horses and his farm over and over as a sort of defense against those who would pry into his writing practices, an area which he regarded as his own private world. I took no chances and therefore kept matters going on horses, farming, and people. I knew that he was fond of mules also, and I recalled the little essay he had written on a mule in *Sartoris*. Mr. Cofield had copied it on the back of a photograph of a long-eared mule taken several years ago, and Faulkner had autographed it.

In the meantime, Mr. Goldsborough scrutinized Faulkner's face, his eyes, and his mannerisms—the way he held his head at an angle when he referred to someone else in the room, the way he lighted his pipe and reflected over a question before answering. Then he leaned forward and, in a most forthright manner, said, "Mr. Faulkner, I wish to do a portrait of you."

Faulkner said nothing, and there was a short period of silence. I was genuinely worried and could say nothing.

"I'd like to do a portrait of you in an academic cap and gown—

in your Oxford cap and gown," Mr. Goldsborough suggested. There was another brief pause. "Don't you have an honorary doctorate from Oxford?"

"No. Don't accept honorary degrees. I think they should be earned," Faulkner replied, rather quietly and deliberately.

At this point I was very uncomfortable and wondered what I could say. I thought of this man before me, a writer whose prose had not been equalled in the twentieth century—the man who had written such magnificent words in his Nobel Prize acceptance speech. I looked at him here in the room and took note of the manner of his dress—the tweed coat, the brown trousers, even the handkerchief tucked in the cuff of his left sleeve. "I'd like to see Mr. Faulkner done informally in his tweed jacket," I said, "dressed as we see him around Oxford. It would be an easy and natural pose."

There was a pause. Faulkner struck a match, held it deliberately to his pipe, took several short puffs, and then, inclining his head in my direction while directing his words to Mr. Goldsborough, said in his soft, southern voice, "This whole thing ain't my idea. It's the University's idea. In fact, I'd like to have it done as Mr. Webb has suggested."

Mr. Goldsborough said that he would be pleased to paint him in casual attire. "I'd like to paint you sitting in your favorite chair. I know you have one. You could sqush down in it in an informal manner."

"Yes, I do have one. It's squshy, but I don't believe too squshy," replied Faulkner with a smile.

"It's pink, though," spoke up Mrs. Faulkner. "But Mr. Goldsborough could paint it some other color in the portrait."

With this comment from Mrs. Faulkner, I felt that the battle was half won. We still had a long way to go, however. Then, with a bold stroke of assurance, Bill Strickland suggested that he might call at the Faulkner home about three the next afternoon, get the chair, and take it to Cofield's studio. "Will this be all right?" he asked.

"Yes," answered Mr. and Mrs. Faulkner, each in turn.

It should be stated at this point that arrangements had been made by Mr. Clegg to have Jack Cofield of the University public information office use his father's studio to take as many shots from as many angles as Mr. Goldsborough and Mr. Faulkner thought necessary. Now Faulkner was agreeing to subject himself to the whole business. I could hardly believe it, but there he was agreeing.

The conversation turned back to Faulkner's life in and around Charlottesville and on the campus of the University of Virginia. I suggested that we wanted him to visit the Ole Miss English Department again. Mrs. Faulkner commented that her husband found it somewhat painful to lecture formally but rather enjoyed seminars and question-and-answer sessions. This was just the manner in which we wished to have him, I said. In fact, this was the method he had employed at Ole Miss in 1947. Both Mr. and Mrs. Faulkner implied that such an arrangement might be possible during the following fall or winter.

Faulkner drew his watch from his pocket. He opened the hunting case, checked the time, snapped it closed, and suggested to his wife that they be going. It was now shortly after five o'clock. Then followed the chatter and bustle in preparation for parting— Ginette, with her attractive French accent, in the middle of it. Before leaving, Mrs. Faulkner invited all of us to the Faulkner home the following Thursday afternoon shortly after five. This occasion, as we all knew, would give Mr. Goldsborough another opportunity to study Faulkner and perhaps to see him with his favorite horses. We went out to see them off. Bill Strickland gave directions for backing and turning the car and they were off, Faulkner at the wheel.

On the afternoon of the following day, plans for making the photographs at the Cofield studio were carried out. Jack Cofield made the pictures, two dozen of them. Before Faulkner left, Jack took one final shot of him sitting in a studio for a picture. Faulkner later inscribed one of the mounted copies to me and signed it.

Jack and his assistant, Edwin (Budgie) Meek, also called on Faulkner at his home and were allowed to take pictures of him as he rode his horse and worked about the stables. When Budgie produced the finished pictures for inspection and approval, Faulkner told him yes outright.

"I'd like to have you take a look at them," Budgie suggested.

"Do I have to?" Faulkner asked. "I've seen this face enough already—every time I shave."

He politely refused to look at the pictures, which were later used in *The Mississippi Magazine*, a student publication. I recount this incident, trivial though it may seem, as an indication of a relatively little noted aspect of the man's character—his fondness for young people, especially students, and his basic desire not to displease. In contrast, a few days later a professional photographer from New York called on Faulkner and asked permission to take a picture of him with his home in the background. "I'd rather not," he laconically and emphatically replied.

It was a beautiful spring afternoon—Thursday, the twenty-third of March, to be exact—when Anne and I turned off Old Taylor Road to call on the Faulkners. We parked at some distance from the house, not far from the end of the long, tree-lined brick walk that leads up to the front steps. The Faulkners greeted us at the door. Faulkner was dressed in riding boots, khaki breeches, and, alas, the frayed English tweed jacket. Obviously he had been out at the barn working with his horses. He took Anne's coat as we were shown into the library to the left, where we met Vicky Fielden, Mrs. Faulkner's granddaughter. Vicky was one of my students in American literature. Following the usual pleasantries, Mrs. Faulkner observed that it was a bit cool and that perhaps a little fire would remove the chill from the room. Faulkner quietly disappeared and within a few minutes returned with two logs and a wad of newspapers. I removed the screen and he stepped over the rail around the hearth and started the fire. Again, I noted the frayed jacket.

After the fire began to blaze, I glanced about the room. There was a library table in the center loaded with books. On the table was an exotic wood carving, a gift from admirers in South America. In one corner of the room was a mahogany carving of the head of Don Quixote. The north and east sides of the room were lined with shelves of books. On top of the bookcase in the corner to the right of the fireplace was a huge stuffed horned owl staring down rather balefully on the assembled group. The owl had been mounted by Malcolm Franklin when he was interested in taxidermy. Paintings graced the walls, one of them of Faulkner as a youth done by his mother, Miss Maud. There was one of Colonel Falkner, author of The White Rose of Memphis. Another was of the Falkners' old Negro nurse, Callie Barr Clark, also by Miss Maud.

We had hardly settled when the other guests arrived—Bill and Ginette Strickland, Mr. and Mrs. Goldsborough, Miss Dorothy Oldham (Mrs. Faulkner's sister), and others. The formalities were hardly over when Mr. Goldsborough asked about the horses, and off we went to the stables with Faulkner leading the way, leaving the ladies to chat and to bring in refreshments. Faulkner seemed pleased to take us out to the stables down in the paddock. On the way we were greeted by two spotted dogs. "A bit skittish of strangers," commented Faulkner as he stamped his foot and shooed them off to the nearby barn. Almost immediately they came slinking back to sniff cautiously at our trousers and feet, trying to make acquaintances. We went on down some seventy-five yards to the lot gate, which was fastened with a piece of trace chain. Two Negro men were in the lot; upon instructions from Faulkner they saddled the bay mare, a beautiful animal with a coat the sheen of satin.

"What's her name?" Mr. Goldsborough asked.

"Temptress," Faulkner replied in his soft voice. "She has a long, fancy name on her registration papers, but we've shortened it. We call her Tempy. Bred and foaled right heah. She's spent all of her life right heah—all of her eight yeahs."

With a bit of assistance from one of the Negroes, Faulkner mounted Tempy. He rode a short distance and then suddenly pulled up the reins. "I want you to meet my help. Mr. Goldsborough, this is Andrew Price," and on around he went until he had completed introductions. Then he cantered around the paddock several times, leaning over now and then to pat Tempy on the withers and to speak to her in a low conversational tone. He

encouraged her to pick up speed, and soon they were racing around
the paddock. He then pulled her in the direction of the hurdles
and over they went one after the other. It was an impressive sight.
After several rounds Faulkner pulled her up for dismounting. Andrew approached to take her to the stable.

"Too fat. I keep tellin' 'em they're feedin' her too much. They
think so much of her that they keep slipping more feed to her
than I tell 'em to."

"A beautiful horse," Mr. Goldsborough commented.

Someone suggested that she appeared to be a very intelligent
animal.

"A horse ain't got much sense," countered Faulkner. "A mule's
got more sense. A mule will take care of himself and you too.
Actually, a rat has the most sense of nonhuman animals, then a
dog, then a cat, then a mule and then a horse. A horse does only
what he's trained to do for you and no more."

Later, after I had obtained a copy of The Reivers, I found that
Faulkner had included essentially the same statement in its pages.
It was obvious that he had thought out the relative intelligence of
these animals and was not merely tossing off ideas that had just
struck him.

We returned to the house, going in at the back door, through his
office where I glanced at the little homemade desk that he and his
stepson, Malcolm, had made and where he had done much of his
writing. I saw an unframed painting of a mule on the mantel over
the fireplace. There was the single bed where he rested after long
periods of writing. The room was very conveniently located, almost
hidden. Here he could seclude himself to write when he felt urged
or driven to write at any time, any season of the year when he was
at home. Here written on the east wall in bold letters was his outline of A Fable—under the headings of the seven days of the week
and "Tomorrow." We went on into the parlor where the fire was
now burning cheerfully. Mrs. Faulkner had the hors d'oeuvres
ready. Faulkner set about preparing the drinks. Most of us, including our host, took bourbon and water. Mrs. Faulkner and some of
the others took coffee. Faulkner moved quietly from one to the

other. He seemed quite relaxed. He spoke in a soft voice and responded to questions with good humor. After a few minutes, I became aware that he was no longer present, but shortly he reentered the room. He had changed his threadbare coat for a smart new English tweed jacket. Now I was certain that I knew why he was wearing the old jacket when we arrived. He had been out riding and doubtless he expected us to ask about his horses. In the old jacket while working or riding, he was comfortable. Wearing the old one was after all not to be explained away simply as an eccentricity.

As Faulkner moved about, I took note of a little bronze lapel pin. Someone with the same curiosity asked him what organization the pin represented and was told that it represented membership in the Quiet Birdmen, an exclusive organization of pilots of World War I days and the years immediately following. The members—usually without their wives—brought their bottles, met, talked old times, told tales, played poker, or did whatever struck their fancies and then went home. The brotherhood was simply an exclusive order of old pilots.

Eventually Faulkner made his way over to Ginette's chair and I overheard him trying out his command of French. "He reads French rather well," Mrs. Faulkner commented. "Years ago, he traveled all over France with scarcely any knowledge of French." She turned to Faulkner. "Bill, what phrase did you use?"

"*Je suis un poète,*" Faulkner replied. "I threw that statement around all over France, and got pretty good results, too. They respect a poet over there."

Bill Strickland had brought some twenty-four proofs of photographs that Jack Cofield had taken of Faulkner at the studio two days before. They had been taken from various angles, and here they were for us to look at and to select a basic pose. Each of us in turn went through the lot and privately made his choice. Interestingly enough, we all, including Faulkner, made the same selection. Mr. Goldsborough assured us that he would use it along with the others in bringing out significant features. Already he had had several opportunities to study Faulkner at close range, to talk to him, and to make notes and sketches. These photographs would be a great help.

Mrs. Faulkner particularly liked the pose in which her husband was looking at the floor with a pleased expression on his face. "I'd like to have a print of that one," she said. "He seems to be looking at his grandchildren playing on the floor."

At that, I assured her that we would see about getting one made up for her, and she seemed pleased. It never occurred to me then, even remotely, that it would not be until after Faulkner's death that I would pass the negative on to "Colonel" Cofield for a print to be made. In time the photograph, as a gift from Mr. Cofield, was prepared and with loving care, placed in a folder for her.

It was now almost six o'clock. Anne and I decided that we should take our leave. The Faulkners accompanied us to the door and saw us off.

I did not see Faulkner again for several weeks. In the interim he spent some time in Virginia. Mr. Goldsborough went back to Florida with his notes, sketches, and photographs; putting away all other projects, he set to work immediately on the portrait. Two weeks later I learned that the work was progressing well and that he was sure he would produce an excellent painting. His eyes were now almost normal and he was enthusiastic about his subject. I hoped that the painting would be completely acceptable to the Faulkner family, particularly to Faulkner himself and to Miss Estelle, and I sent word to Mr. Goldsborough to that effect.

It should be emphasized that William Faulkner had a remarkable face. Character was there—intelligence, pride, and keen insight. There were lines on his forehead and around his piercing dark-brown eyes. His acquiline nose, drooping mustache, thick gray hair, and those eyes were prominent features. How could a photographer or painter miss those features?

I found, however, that I had to get on to other matters—namely, paperwork and paying for the portrait. After consulting with the other members of the committee—Bill Green and Ginette Strickland—and with Hugh Clegg, we prepared and mailed hundreds of letters to the faculty of the University campus, administrative personnel, students, and to scholars and admirers of Faulkner's work over the United States. We had arranged to borrow money to assure payment to the painter. Before the money was raised the painting arrived. Professor and Mrs. Green, Professor and Mrs. Strickland, and Anne and I had a crate-opening one afternoon at the Stricklands and saw the portrait for the first time. Unanimously, we agreed that it was magnificent. A few days later Mr. and Mrs. Goldsborough came up to Oxford from Florida. Mrs. Faulkner came over, and at sight of the portrait she approved it completely. We now found that we had only to maneuver Faulkner into seeing it to see whether he approved, knowing at the same time he resented maneuvering. Bill Strickland managed to get him to come over after Vicky Fielden's graduation from the University.

About two weeks later—on Sunday afternoon, June 17—Anne and I went to a party at the home of Professor and Mrs. Green. Those in attendance were largely of the University community— the Stricklands, Goldsboroughs, Bunkleys, Hineses, Bickerstaffs, Quarleses, and others. Mr. and Mrs. Faulkner were there. Faulkner had been thrown from his horse that morning. Walking was painful even with the assistance of a cane. However, the cane, along with his gloves, added dignity to his bearing.

Bill Green ushered him to the den at the back of the house. Mrs. Faulkner remained with other guests in the front sitting room. After he was seated in an easy chair, we were soon engaged in conversation. There was even a bit of yarn spinning. Faulkner listened with amused interest and added his own comments.

At one point I found myself alone with him. This was my opportunity, it occurred to me, to ask about the portrait. I posed my question.

"I like it," he replied.

It was a brief comment, but he appeared genuinely pleased.

After a few minutes, Mrs. Faulkner felt concern for her husband and came back to see about him, knowing that he was sore from the fall from the horse that morning and that he might wish to go home. She returned saying that he was not ready. Later, I found Faulkner standing and conversing with a group of ladies. With the same bemused and happy twinkle in his eyes, he had asked Mrs. Strickland to tell the little story of her first sojourn in an American hospital. It seems that on the occasion referred to, Ginette was in the hospital in Durham, North Carolina, with her first child. One morning she was quite thirsty; not yet able to speak English, she motioned to the attending nurse, and with gestures said in French, "J'ai soif." She pointed to her mouth and patted her throat. The panic stricken nurse called the attending physician and he in turn, after trying to determine her difficulty, called another physician. After some consultation and looking around, they saw the Negro janitor near the door leaning on his mop. He appeared knowing and responded to their questioning glances by saying simply, "De lady wants a drink of water." It was learned later that the Negro had served in France with the army of occupation. Faulkner liked the story, but I rather suspect that he was entertained just as much by the attractive French flavor of Ginette's speech and gestures.

While I was in the sitting room I heard Mrs. Faulkner give an account of the accident that her husband had that morning while riding. It seems that he had gone out riding on the horse purchased the past fall in Oklahoma. She, not feeling well, had gone back to bed upstairs. After a time the cook looked out and saw the horse returning riderless to the stable. Quite obviously there had been a mishap. She called Mrs. Faulkner, who threw on a housecoat and came down. She sent Andrew out one way, the cook another, and she got into the Rambler to go up the street. She found her husband up the street a short distance on his way home—as mad as a hornet. The horse, according to Faulkner, had "roached" his back and thrown him. He landed on the ground in a sitting position—undignified but nevertheless sitting.

Professor Bickerstaff commented to Faulkner that he had always heard that for the best effect one addressed men in Italian, women in French, and horses in German. Someone else turned to Faulkner and asked what language he used that morning to his horse after he was thrown.

"I just used good old Anglo-Saxon, and I believe he understood," he replied. "I know now why I was able to get him so cheap."

It was getting late, seven o'clock by now, and Faulkner commented that it was about time to depart and asked for his coat. Then, laying the gloves across his wrist and hanging the cane on his left arm, he moved about the room shaking hands and said goodbye to each one. Bill Strickland reminded him that he was about to leave for France and asked him not to forget his promise to accompany him and his group of students to Aubigny the following summer. Faulkner assured him that he would not forget. He turned to me and held out his hand. I told him that I hoped I would see him often this summer. He replied that he would be pleased. Dapper and correct, he went on to the front door to join Mrs. Faulkner. After exchanging goodbyes with hostess and host, he and Mrs. Faulkner went down the path to the red Rambler station wagon and rode off. I never saw him again. He died in the early morning hours of Friday, July 6, 1962, and was buried in the cemetery not far from the graves of other members of the family and not far from the final resting places of Augustus Baldwin Longstreet and Lucius Quintus Cincinnatus Lamar.

JOHN FAULKNER

His People on the Square

𝒥ohn Faulkner was four years younger than his brother William. Like William, he aspired to write. He published a number of short stories while he was writing novels, the two best known of which are Men Working (1941) and Dollar Cotton (1942).

Johncy, as he was known to his friends, was awarded a degree in engineering by the University of Mississippi in 1929, and later, but only briefly, taught classes in creative writing at the University. He served in the Navy during World War II.

Not long after the death of William, John Faulkner wrote My Brother Bill: An Affectionate Reminiscence. He died in Oxford in 1963, while completing revision for the book.

The excerpt which closes this book is from My Brother Bill and is reproduced with the kind permission of the Trident Press.

❦ There is one somebody who goes into every piece of writing and that somebody is the man who writes it. I have never known anyone who identified himself with his writings more than Bill did. He seemed to be as much a part of the story he was telling as were the characters in it. To see him was to recreate all the stories he had ever told.

Sometimes it was hard to tell which was which, which one Bill was, himself or the one in the story. And yet you knew somehow that the two of them were the same, they were one and inseparable. When we would see Bill we would see him surrounded by his stories. And still he was the Bill Faulkner we knew, the someone who appeared among us on the Square in his khakis and old tweed coat, in T shirt and sun helmet, or even in one of the outlandish costumes we saw him in on occasion.

Little wonder it was as I sat on the steps of the funeral home that early morning, waiting for them to bring Bill there, that I saw his people on the Square just as surely as I saw him and Jack and me. Will Geer, the sheriff in *Intruder in the Dust*, was there. It was at about this same early-morning hour that he, with galluses drooping, was cooking breakfast for his visitors in the jail and, as he cracked eggs into the skillet, saying to them, "If anyone wants more than two eggs, say so."

From where I sat I could see the section of the Square across which Joe Christmas was led from the jail to the courthouse and where, manacled, he had broken away from his guard and run, chased by Percy Grimm on his commandeered bicycle. And on below the sheriff's house, facing the very road that ran under my feet, was the small frame building where Preacher Hightower lived and from the front window of which he watched at dusk each evening as the ghost cavalry swept past to the sound of falling trumpets.

Everywhere I looked there was Bill and his stories: Oxford, Jefferson, and Lafayette County, Yoknapatawpha.

Bill is dead now. He has stepped into an eternal tomorrow that has left him forever in Yoknapatawpha County; here forever. He can never leave us again.

APPENDIX

The following sketch was written by Louis Cochran following his visit to Oxford late in 1931. At that time Cochran, who had known Faulkner during their student days at Ole Miss, was a lawyer practicing in Jackson. This is an early draft of the article which appeared almost a year later (November 6, 1932) in the Memphis Commercial Appeal. Apparently it is the draft which Cochran sent to Faulkner's friend Phil Stone and which Stone commented on in the letter following.

These valuable documents are reproduced with the kind permission of Mr. Cochran and of Mrs. Phil Stone.

215

WILLIAM FAULKNER

A Personal Sketch by Louis Cochran

€ Before *Sanctuary* first exploded upon an otherwise fairly peaceful literary firmament the novels of William Faulkner had caused considerable uproar among the more or less intelligentsia. With *The Sound and the Fury* and *As I Lay Dying* the young Mississippi novelist had definitely established himself as a writer to be reckoned with, and his name as a synonym for horrors was slowly filtering through to that great unknown layer of readers which critics scorn and publishers strive so zealously to please. Arnold Bennett had already made his world resounding diagnosis that Faulkner "wrote like an angel," and lesser critics, eager to climb on the band wagon, agreed with the statement of R. E. Sherwood

in *Scribner's* magazine that if he did not write like an angel he
at least wrote like a fiend from Hell. And with *Sanctuary*, the last
of the captious, or the scornfully aloof, capitulated and there was
no critic, save a maiden lady columnist on a Southern newspaper,
who did not join in the acclaim. From the chaste pages of *Mc-
Call's* magazine and the venerable *Harper's* to the rowdy *Mercury*
of H. L. Mencken, the astonished and reserved young Southerner
found himself overwhelmed with a torrent of adulation which
could compare him of American writers only to James Joyce, while
critics who had ignored or scorned his earlier works made amends
by working themselves into a very froth of enthusiasm and hung
upon his few utterances with bated breath.

It was all very new and strange to Mr. Faulkner and totally dis-
similar to his previous experiences, or what he had expected. Like
most artists he had endured a period of neglect and near penury,
a slow working out from oblivion, and to have precipitated upon
him an unexpected deluge of acclamation was more than his genuine modesty could suffer in total silence. He was not acting out
of character when he declined to enter largely into the talk-fest of
Southern Writers gathered at the University of Virginia during the
fall of 1931. He was only himself. He was not a poseur when he
declined invitations to the multifarious teas and play-parties of
literary New York during his visit to the metropolis in the December following. He honestly dislikes literary people as a group,
and never enters into any purely literary gathering except reluctantly. For recreation, as well as for creative purposes, he prefers the
society of lesser mortals, and has no hesitancy in showing this
preference. He said to the writer after his return from his 1931
triumphal entry into New York (which he had intended to be
only a quiet business visit to his publishers) that he "had never
been so tired of literary people in his life." And this was no pretense with William Faulkner. He meant every word of it.

It should not be forgotten in studying the personality of this
writer that he is, in common parlance, a man with one idea. Since
his earliest childhood he had known he was to be a writer, or
nothing at all. And, consequently, he had been, in turn, a student,

loafer, dishwasher, carpenter, house painter, book store clerk, post-office employee, an aviator serving under the Union Jack, a poet, a writer of prose so difficult to read that two publishers thought him a bad bargain, and at last a novelist hailed on two continents as a genius. That is a long road for any man to travel who quit school in the fifth grade, and who is now only thirty-six years of age.* But the journey, filled as it has been with obstacles which at times may have seemed almost insurmountable, was marked by a grim perseverance and a tenacity of purpose which would admit of no defeat. And like most writers who succeed he has been given a friendly helping hand more than once by kindred spirits, as he is the very first to admit.

Faulkner's early ambition was to be a poet. From the time he left grammar school he had been an omnivorous reader, and much of his time was spent in writing verse which nobody read, and making idle sketches which drew no interest in his home town of Oxford, Mississippi. As a boy he was moody, and variant, given to solitary walks, and a disinclination to mingle with his fellows which set him strangely apart from the romping, frolicsome youth of the town. But he was writing, and reading a great deal, and subconsciously accumulating much of the material which he was later to foist into the mouth of a gaping world.

As a slender, coolly aloof lad of eighteen he entered the University of Mississippi, as a special student in English but had little to say in class, and never failed to absent himself from the examinations. During this period, as during his whole life, he walked in large part alone except for the companionship of his life long mentor and friend, Phil Stone. His fellow students thought him queer. He spoke to no one unless directly addressed. He mingled not at all with his class mates. He entered into no college activity. But he was not snobbish, as his fellows thought. He was merely indifferent; subconsciously and unconsciously indifferent to the thoughts, companionships, friendships or contacts of any sort, with the other students. He did not care for the student activities.

* At the time Cochran wrote this, Faulkner was thirty-four. Apparently he went beyond the fifth grade, but he never finished high school.

He did not care for the students. Why should he be put to a pother about them? Following his inclinations he bothered not at all. The other students misunderstood this attitude, snickered at him behind his back, called him "Count No-Count" and passed him off as one of the inexplicable freaks of nature. Now these same students, more mature and settled in their habits and reasoning, are aghast and dumfounded lest they had a Moses in their midst and knew him not.

It was during this period of late adolescence that the future novelist published his first work, a poem. The writer, at that time the editor of "Ole Miss," the college yearbook, by severely screwing up his courage managed to break the ice of the poet's indifference and requested him to write a poem for the publication. Like many abler critics of today the editor failed to understand the poet's poems; therefore, they must be good. Entitled simply "To A Co-ed," the verses sing the usual strain but may be of interest as an evidence of earlier efforts and ambitions, and of a hidden strata in the novelist's nature known only to a few of his admirers.

> The dawn herself could not more beauty wear
> Than you 'mid other women crowned in grace,
> Nor have the sages known a fairer face
> Than yours, gold-shadowed by your bright sweet hair.
> Than you does Venus seem less heavenly fair;
> The twilit hidden stillness of your eyes,
> And throat, a singing bridge of still replies,
> A slender bridge, yet all dreams hover there.
>
> I could have turned unmoved from Helen's brow,
> Who found no beauty in their Beatrice;
> Their Thais seemed less lovely then as now,
> Though some had bartered Athens for her kiss.
> For down Time's arras, faint and fair and far,
> Your face still beckons like a lonely star.

His college studies, such as they were, were broken for the time by the war, and reasoning that if he could enlist in the British forces he would see France much quicker than otherwise, the young poet journeyed to Montreal and enlisted as a private in the British Royal Flying Corps. He was never to see France as part of His Majesty's forces, but he did win his epaulets as a flyer, and managed to smash one flying ship for good King George with damage only to the Crown. The Armistice ended his ambitions as a warrior, and he returned to the friendly grey squirrels and oaks of the University of Mississippi campus, smart and dashing in his British uniform but seemingly more aloof and alone than ever.

Unfortunately, perhaps, his scholastic days were soon ended, and for a while he drifted. Once he washed dishes in a city restaurant for his meals. For a while he clerked in a New York book store. Then through the influence of his family he was appointed post master of the office at University, Mississippi, his compensation the munificent salary of fifteen hundred dollars per year. Dull and tedious work this was for an embryo novelist but it marked the publication of his first book, The Marble Faun, his first and only collection of verse.* The poetry does not compare with his later prose but it, at least, shows a side of the novelist about which his readers know little or nothing. Few of them would suspect that his poetry would be mild, and fresh, a pleasant, pantheistic appreciation of nature. It is a far cry from the pleasingly honest sensitivity of these verses, unremarkable as they may be, to the Popeye of Sanctuary or the well nigh incredible characters of As I Lay Dying. But perhaps there lies somewhere beneath the Freudian obsessions of William Faulkner a hidden love which will yet find expression such as his present day camp followers wot not of. Phil Stone, who contributes an introduction to this volume, says that "these are primarily the poems of youth and a simple heart," and that Faulkner has his roots in the soil "as surely and inevitably as a tree." This may be true, though many will be found who maintain that his characters have not the healthy, vigorous qualities usually spawned by honest earth, and that no simple heart could

* Two years after Cochran wrote this, Faulkner published a second collection of verse, A Green Bough.

concoct the tales which have filled with delectable horrors both
sinner and maiden lady alike.

After the dull plopping of *The Marble Faun*, Mr. Faulkner tired
of the monotony of his post office clerkship and with the half
finished manuscript of his first novel journeyed to New Orleans to
acquaint himself with the Southern literati. Establishing lodgings
in the more or less Bohemian Old French Quarter of the Crescent
City he made indifferent progress with the novel until by chance
he met an old friend with whom he once had worked in a book
shop in New York. As Aladdin had it, the friend was none
other than the wife of Sherwood Anderson who invited him to
meet her famous husband, and to tea. That two men so alike and
yet so bizarrely unlike should be friends was inevitable, and to
Sherwood Anderson, William Faulkner owes a debt which he
freely acknowledged in the dedication to his fifth novel. Anderson
introduced to a doubting world both Ernest Hemingway and William Faulkner, and that he is more than proud of his protégés the
Apostle of the Mill Towns evidenced in a recent article in the
American Mercury which he began by stating that in his opinion
the two most promising writers of this generation were the two
young men he had sponsored on the road to fame.

With the mighty Mr. Anderson interested, the road ahead was
clearly marked, though still not without its obstacles. An introduction to Horace Liveright, of Boni and Liveright, followed by
an enthusiastic endorsement of the embryonic novelist, and William Faulkner was launched. With *Soldiers' Pay* but half finished,
a contract was tendered him for three novels, and the publisher
wended his way back to the North to await the plaudits of the
multitudes for his find. This first novel was followed by *Mosquito*,
a six-weeks study in human futility after the manner of Aldous
Huxley. Then a summer in France, to await royalties never realized, and William Faulkner was back to Oxford to write *Sartoris*,
produced under the imprint of Harcourt Brace. But alack for men
of great talent as well as men of none! As far as the man in the
street was concerned *Sartoris* was a dud, but the novelist had
definitely found himself, and what is equally as important, he had

found his publisher. In the office of the publishers of *Sartoris* was Harrison Smith, a young man who dreamed someday of being himself a publisher, and when the firm of Harrison Smith & Jonathan Cape was formed, the unknown William Faulkner was given a prominent berth. If two publishers had thought he was, perhaps, a Pegasus who could not fly, the third found both fame and profit. In rapid succession followed *The Sound and the Fury*, *As I Lay Dying*, and *Sanctuary*. And with the arrest of a venturesome young man who dared to sell the story of Popeye and Temple Graves in chaste old Boston, despite the edicts of the Watch and Ward Society, William Faulkner had definitely and vociferously arrived!

The purpose of this sketch is not to discuss the merits of Mr. Faulkner's works. The critics acclaim him; the populace shudder at him and denounce him, and buy his books. He is successful. What William Faulkner reads, thinks, does; the tilt of his nose, the color of his eyes, the size of his incisors, is news. And his fellow Oxfordians who had regarded him as "that no-count Faulkner boy" are aghast with stricken wonder and a faint indignation that fame had to slap them on the nose before they would do more than acknowledge the bare existence of this native Daniel so suddenly come to judgment. And one cannot blame them. No prophet, or son of a prophet, however rash, would have dared prophesy that a lineal descendant of the author of *The White Rose of Memphis* would ever write novels such as the six which have erupted from the mind of William Faulkner.

In personal appearance the author is unobtrusive. Of slender height, not over five feet seven, he has the delicate step and waist line of a girl. His eyes are a soft, luminous brown; his hair, darkly of the same tint, is thick and more often tousled than otherwise. A thin face, wide forehead and high cheek bones complete a countenance that is at once remotely aloof and sensitive to every living thing. His voice is low and pleasing to hear; a drawling, soft voice which one could not imagine uttering the gusty epithets of the characters so blindly and ruthlessly tramping across the pages of the author's novels. And yet perhaps it could. For the personality of William Faulkner is curiously detached except in moments of rare enthusiasm. He observes and writes. He does not feel except in those rare moments when he touches upon some phase of earthly beauty which is the real love of his soul. William Faulkner is unsocial. He will tell you so frankly and unequivocally. He does not care for the society of his fellows. He disembowels them, cuts them into little squirming tentacles, and studies their futile struggles against the flails of fate with an Olympian detachment which is overwhelming. Indifferent as ever to human likes or dislikes, he goes his own way, alone, speaking to none he meets unless some rare humor strikes him, offending the porcupine sensitiveness of many by his very silences. He especially abhors literary people and wonders not at all that there is no great writing done in New York "where everybody talks about what they are going to write, and no one writes anything."

Contrary to the dreams of the maiden ladies who thrill to the "shocks" he so lugubriously provides, William Faulkner is a man of normal habits, and tastes, and aside from a personal preference for fresh pork, cares little for either meat, or drink. He lives a sane, well balanced life, writes every day "because he likes it," and works as regularly as though he were still a carpenter, a journeyman painter, or a postoffice employee. He does not believe in inspiration per se, and can write anywhere, though he prefers the somnambulant peacefulness of The Cedars, the ante-bellum home in Oxford which he recently purchased and which he painted and remodeled himself, and where he lives with his wife and two children.* He delights in solitary walks, reads little, and beyond mild semi-annual libation, enjoyed with some boyhood crony who never read a book in his life, looks but rarely upon the cup that cheers.

There are those who predict that Faulkner will change the tenor of his writings now that he has shocked the great mass mind into a greedy hunger for his works. He is now enjoying the Jack London relish of having editors, who once scorned his offerings, besiege him for them, and he is reaping the same sweet revenge. Stories

* Cochran is referring to Faulkner's two stepchildren. His daughter Jill was born later.

which once were fruitlessly peddled from editor to editor are now featured with avidity in magazines which formerly caressed them with rejection slips. Perhaps, after all, as his future Boswell, Phil Stone, says, William Faulkner may yet be the great American humorist. Unquestionably he has humor, of a retching, sardonic sort, which crops out in his writings more than once. His story "Spotted Horses" is a sample. "Thrift," originally appearing in that journalistic High Priest of Conservatism, *The Saturday Evening Post*, might perhaps be taken as another. The two lads with country dew fresh upon their faces who so unwittingly, in *Sanctuary*, took lodgings in a Memphis assignation house and at night prowled the streets to satisfy their amorous impulses may be accepted as classic examples. Or perhaps we may take an utterance of the novelist himself, as when once while on a hunt for *atmosphere* he was importuned by a hand maiden of the original "Miss Reba" and completely stunned his would-be charmer with the reply: "Please leave me alone. Can't you understand I'm on my vacation!" The combined wits of Bill Nye, Walt Mason and Will Rogers could not have done better, and perhaps the ironic shade of Mark Twain may have smiled with the foreknowledge that there yet cometh, mayhap, a spirit who can fill and broaden the Master's shoes!

December 28, 1931

Hon. Louis Cochran
Standard Life Bldg.
Jackson, Mississippi

Dear Louis:-

I received your letter of December 23rd. inclosing copy of your article regarding William Faulkner.

I think your article is allright though there are some inaccuracies. I have numbered the pages of the copy and will give them to you as follows:-

No. 1. For your information, "The Maiden Lady Critic," Miss Monte Cooper of Memphis, Tennessee, got peeved at Bill years ago. The trouble was that Miss Cooper was very proud of being the literary arbiter of Memphis. Before Bill had made his reputation he was in Memphis and Miss Cooper invited him to lunch, probably a literary one, and Bill accepted. When the time came for lunch Bill was getting drunk with his friend Reneau De Vaux, well-known Memphis Gambler and road-house proprietor and now proprietor of the Club Seville near Memphis. Bill simply did not go to the lunch and Miss Cooper has never forgiven him for it and never mentions his work in her column if she can help it. It is most amusing.

No. 2. With reference to your statement on Page 2 to the effect that Bill is indifferent to the present adulation of his work, this is true. However, it is not true that he and I never expected it. On the contrary we have seen so much of the effect of contemporary literary propaganda and have seen stupidity and poor work proclaimed so often that he and I have always been sure that the present furor would arrive in time.

No. 3. Your statement on page 2 that Bill does not like literary talk is true but the reason is a natural weariness after writing about 5,000 words every day. Lawyers don't like to talk law business while they are playing golf.

No. 4. With reference to the statement on Page 3 regarding Bill's tenacity of purpose, I rather doubt this. I think he kept on writing because he couldn't help it and not through any determination to succeed. I think he would have quit writing years ago if he could have done it.

No. 5. With reference to the statement on page 3 as to his being a poet, I doubt if it was his early ambition to be a poet as much as it was my ambition for him to be one.

No. 6. The statement on Page 3 as to him having no help nor sympathy is bunk. I lent him books, read every line he ever wrote, criticized it and revised some of it. This was an almost daily routine of his literary training for years and years. God only knows how many thousands of lines of his verse that I have read and some of it was pretty poor at that.

No. 7. The statement on Page 3 as to his solitary walks is hardly correct. Most of these walks through the country were not solitary but with me and on these occasions we discussed aesthetics, Bill's future literary plans, his work of the past few days and I often pointed out to him tricks of other writers which he could use to advantage.

No. 8. Bill did not go to Montreal to enlist in the Royal Air Force. He was not twenty-one and went first to New Haven where he worked in the plant of Winchester Arms Company two months and lived with me. He enlisted in New York and went to Toronto. He did not enlist as a private but as a Cadet candidate for a commission.

No. 9. Your statement on Page 6 that he got the job as Postmaster at the University of Mississippi, through the influence of his family is not correct at all. His family had nothing to do with it. Major L. E. Oldham, now his Father-in-law, got him the appointment and I forced Bill to take the job over his own declination and refusal. He made the damnedest Postmaster the World has ever seen.

No. 10. As to his having his roots in this soil, with reference to pages six and seven of your article, I am sure about this. My present discouragement about him is as to whether or not this part of him will ever be articulate in prose. Watch out for the book of verse which Harrison Smith is going to publish soon and you will see that my remarks along this line in the preface to "The Marble Faun" were true. I know Bill and I still stick to these remarks.

No. 11. You are right on Page 7 about the magnitude of Bill's debt to Sherwood Anderson but he owes Stark Young a big debt also and this you should mention and do not mention.

No. 12. With reference to Page 8 of your article, the title of the second novel is "Mosquitoes," not "Mosquito."

No. 13. On page 8 of your article you give the name of the girl in "Sanctuary" as "Temple Graves." Her name is "Temple Drake."

No. 14. You say on Page 9 that even Daniel would not have made the prophecy about the kind of books that the great grandson of the author of "The White Rose of Memphis" would write. I am no Daniel but I made the prophecy years ago. It was just due to the revolt in the air and was to be expected but my present discouragement is due to the fact that Bill has not yet come out of this adolescent groove.

No. 15. The statement on page 10 of your article "Earthly Beauty is the love of his soul" is true. I tell you that the Hills of North Mississippi are in his very blood. He would live nowhere else in the world.

No. 16. The statement on Page 10 of your article that Bill is unsocial is not entirely right. He is mainly non-social.

No. 17. Your statement on Page 10 about him personally is not, to my mind, strong enough. As I told you, he is the most normal, the sanest man I have ever known. He has less tendency to any sort of excess— either physical, mental or emotional—and has more practical common sense than any man I have ever known. He can make almost anything on Earth with his hands and is a good carpenter and a good housepainter. When he is not practical about the things other people are practical about it is not that he doesn't realize it but that he doesn't think it worth the trouble sometimes to be practical about such things. And this, I think, is the very apex of practical common sense. In other words, in such cases, he disagrees not with the conclusions of others but with their premises.

No. 18. Your statement on Page 11 that I am his "future Boswell" is not true. I am not his present one nor his future one. I never, never intend to let myself be infected with that horrible itch of messing up clean white paper with little crooked marks. It is too much fun living life in Lafayette County, Mississippi, to waste time writing about it. Besides, if I have to write what good is Bill to me?

No. 19. Your statement on Page 11 is not quite correct in that I did not say that he *would be* the greatest American humorist. I said that he *might be.* He has a kindly humor and a roaring humor as well as the retching kind, although the first two have not been very apparent in his published work.

No. 20. You have left out of your article all mention of "The Creative Will" by Willard Huntington Wright, the S.S. Van Dine of popular Detective fiction. I think this is a serious omission because the aesthetic theories set forth in that book, strained through my own mind, constitutes one of the most important influences in Bill's whole literary career. If people who read him would simply read Wright's book they would see what he is driving at from a literary standpoint.

No. 21. I think you should also mention the fact that some of the disagreeable things in Bill's published novels are due, at least to my idea, to that strange sensitive blindness which he has in spots and are really for this reason lapses of taste. I mean lapses of literary taste and not otherwise. This statement may be misunderstood by the stupid but I haven't time to elaborate it further.

No. 22. I think your article on Bill will be seriously defective if you do not mention that he shares with me the opinion that Balzac is the greatest novelist who ever lived and that Ernest Hemingway is so far the greatest American fictionist.

You can use this letter or any parts of it as you see fit and can let your magazine publish it as a supplement to your article if you so desire. If they want to publish it they will have to take it like it is. I will not take the time to elaborate it further.

Your friend,

Phil Stone

$\mathcal{T}$he two documents reproduced on the following pages show William Faulkner the writer-artist at his playful best. In the first, the original hand-lettered by Faulkner in colored ink, he recounts the conception, birth, and launching of the good ship Minmagary, the houseboat which he and three friends built in a backyard in Oxford. In the second document, also written in Faulkner's hand, the author appoints the Minmagary a Ship of the Line in the Provisional Navy of the Confederate States of America.

Both of these documents were reproduced from originals in the possession of Mr. and Mrs. William Ross Brown of Oxford.

231

M/S SUMMARY OXFORD

Port Watch
Maggie Brown

Starboard Watch
Winnie Ruth Little

Hugh Evans, Master
Ross Brown, Mate.
Ashford Little, M.A., Surgeon.
Mary Evans, Cabin Boy

Out of Confusion by Boundless Hope:

Conceived in a Canadian Club bottle She was born A.D. 15th August 1947 by uproarious Caesarean Section in prone position with her bottom upward in Evans's back yard eleven miles from the nearest water deeper than a half-inch kitchen tap & waxed & grew daily there beneath the whole town's expert cynosure:

Whereupon there stood already on the horizon of her tender infancy Six Impassable Milestones:

1. They can't turn her over.
2. They can't find a truck big enough to haul her to water.
3. They can't load her onto the truck
4. The truck can't turn the first corner outside the yard
5. They can't get her off the truck into the water.
6. She will capsize or sink the moment her bottom is wet.

Thus waxed & grew & on the 7th January 1948 rose up & stood on her own cleat and winch and hook & on the first day of June the truck arrived: & that was the Second Milestone:

And in the gloam of afternoon was raised tenderly in the myriad hands of her conceivers owners & architects & their children friends well-wishers & dogs & the neighbors & merely curious & their friends & well-wishers & dogs: onto the truck: and that was the Third Milestone:

And at dawn's crack next morning the truck turned the first Impassable Corner: which was the Fourth Milestone: & at Three Bells in the Sixth Watch floated free from the launching ramp into deep water & was warped into moorings: and that was the Fifth and the Sixth Milestone:

And the Captain came aboard: at which moment she went into Commission: of which it is hereby decreed and avowed that any and all Panola County nations bordering that Oxford Ocean contumelously maliciously & feloniously miscalled Sardis Harbor, and HENCEFORE shall take cognisance of these Letters of Marque, and

Given under my Hand & Seal
This May Anno Domini
2nd June 1948
William Faulkner

First Sea Lord
Lafayette County Mississippi

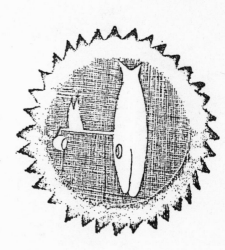

By virtue of whatever authority I may have inherited from my Great Grandfather, William C. Falkner, Colonel (PAROLED) Second Mississippi Infantry Provisional Army Confederate States of America, William C Falkner II reposing all trust & confidence in the staunchness & stability of M/S Minmagary & in the courage & fidelity of her officers & crew do by these presents constitute & appoint her to be a Ship of the Line in the Provisional Navy of the Confederate States of America & further direct that all seamen soldiers & civilians recognising the above authority recognise her as such & accord her all the priviledges respect & consideration of that state & condition.

Given under my Great Grandfather's sword this Twenty Fourth July 1948 at Oxford Mississippi

William C Falken II